# Scotland's Parliament

## Fundamentals for a New Scotland Act

# Contents

# Executive
# Summary

## Introduction

A change of Government at the coming election would usher in an administration committed to legislate for Scottish home rule on the basis of the proposals of the Scottish Constitutional Convention (SCC). The Constitution Unit has considered what that legislation might look like; what other changes would be needed in the UK political system to make devolution work; and how Scottish devolution might relate to other proposed constitutional change.

### Lessons from the 1970s

There are lessons to be drawn from the experience of preparing devolution legislation in the 1970s (the Scotland and Wales Bill of 1976 and the Scotland Bill of 1977) and taking it through Parliament. They include the following:

- in spite of a formidable commitment of Ministerial and official time between February 1974 and July 1978, the resulting Scotland Act was widely regarded as unsatisfactory. The Act was repealed following a change of Government and never brought into force.
- officials worked hard to meet Ministers' wishes, but the Cabinet was divided. The Bill was viewed as a political expedient to counter nationalist sentiment in Scotland (and in Wales) and Parliament reacted accordingly.
- the parliamentary debates were dominated by doubts about the feasibility of legislative devolution in principle within a unitary state. The 1977 Bill was a stronger package than the 1976 version and fared better as a result.

Success this time round will require leadership from the top, political commitment throughout the Government (and therefore in all Whitehall departments), a Minister in charge of preparing the legislation with a clear view of what is required rather than simply a brief to reach lowest common denominator consensus, and a coherent picture of how this reform fits into a package which will benefit the whole of the UK, not just Scotland and Wales.

### Allocation of Legislative Competences

The 1978 Act sought to define with great precision the legislative competences of the devolved Assembly by reference to statutes then in force in Scotland. This was a mistake. No allocation of powers is without its grey areas - but the Act failed adequately to acknowledge this. As a result it was impossible to understand without reference to other legislation, would have been difficult to use in practice, and would have required frequent amendment. Instead:

- the Act should list only powers retained at Westminster rather than those devolved.
- express provision should be made for Westminster to legislate outside its areas of retained competence in certain circumstances e.g. to comply with international obligations, or when the Scottish Parliament requests Westminster legislation; and for the Scottish Parliament likewise to be able to encroach on Westminster's retained powers when necessary - with their consent.
- these arrangements will apply mostly to European legislation: it will be necessary to reconcile UK membership of the Union (and liability for non-implementation of EC law) with an overlap of legislative competence between the EC and Scotland.

## Resolution of Disputes

However tightly the legislation is drawn, disputes about the precise scope of the Scottish Parliament's competence will arise. They might be resolved, or avoided, by:

- scrutiny of bills in advance of introduction by the Scottish Law Officers and the Speaker of the Parliament.
- provision for a direct challenge to Scottish Acts on *vires* grounds following Royal Assent but before entry into force (this period to be a maximum of one month except in cases of urgency).
- provision for indirect challenges - where devolution points occur in the course of other cases - to be referred to the final court of appeal for an opinion (by analogy with the Article 177 procedure for taking advice on points of EC law).
- provision for the direct challenge of executive acts of the Scottish Executive at any time.

The choice of the final court of appeal is finely balanced. The report favours the House of Lords.

## Entrenchment

The SCC's proposed Westminster Declaration will introduce a political hurdle to repeal or significant amendment of the devolution legislation. The same effect - a political one - might be achieved by including a declaratory clause, or a clause specifying special procedures for amendment, in the bill itself.

A **referendum** has also been canvassed as a possible entrenchment measure. There is no constitutional doctrine which requires a referendum: previous referendums in the UK have generally been held when the normal political process has broken down because of party splits, etc. The 1979 referendums were of this sort.

The choice whether to hold a referendum on the question of Scottish devolution will be a political one. Strong and explicit popular endorsement of the principle of establishing a Scottish Parliament might add to the political inhibitors in the way of repeal or emasculation of the devolution legislation. If obtained in advance, a positive referendum result might also smooth the passage of the legislation through Parliament. But in those circumstances the referendum itself would require a short bill. No referendum result could be binding on the Government; nor on the Scottish people, who would reserve the right to pass judgement on the Parliament in the light of experience once it had come into operation.

The Unit will publish findings of the Commission on the Conduct of Referendums later this year which will provide technical guidance should a referendum in Scotland be deemed appropriate.

## Financial Arrangements

The arrangements proposed by the SCC are a sensible basis on which to establish the Parliament, but do not promise stability in the longer term. The Barnett formula, which determines changes in the Scottish Office budget each year by reference to changes in equivalent English spending plans, is under pressure in any event and could not provide a basis for financing eventual English regional government. The bill should aim to promote greater stability (and longer term applicability throughout the UK) by specifying mechanisms for keeping the funding formula under review and making adjustments when necessary.

The key will be the establishment of an independent Commission to gather reliable data about spending levels and to relate them to relative need. The Commission might conduct a periodic UK needs assessment, say every five to ten years, to inform periodic review of the funding formula. The first such assessment might commence immediately following the establishment of the Parliament. The Commission would make recommendations to central government for approval by the Westminister Parliament. It would also provide an independent audit of the results of applying the formula in practice.

Autonomous revenue raising powers are essential to achieve a sense of fiscal responsibility and accountability to the Scottish electorate. The proposed power to vary the basic rate of income tax is intended to spread any tax change widely and visibly. Achieving those aims in practice might require tighter definition, since both the level of the basic rate and the income range to which it applies will be determined by Westminister. The proposed variation of three pence in the pound would have no significant macroeconomic effects for the UK as a whole.

The Parliament will need capacity to borrow for revenue smoothing purposes (an overdraft facility) in order to function effectively. Assigned revenues might find a place in a longer term settlement, but only once reliable data are available and familiar.

## The European Union

The overlap of legislative competence between the EU and the Scottish Parliament will make it imperative for Scotland to find ways of effective participation in the framing of EC legislation, in Brussels and in London:
- by direct representation in the European Parliament and the Committee of the Regions, and the establishment of a Government office in Brussels.
- through the negotiation of an intergovernmental agreement with the UK guaranteeing consultation over new legislative proposals, also covering levels of representation in the Community institutions, and attendance at all relevant Council and working group meetings, and at intergovernmental conferences to review the Treaties.
- by establishing sound procedures for legislative scrutiny and exchange of information within the Scottish Parliament, including with Scottish MEPs.

## Central Government

The Secretary of State for Scotland will have a key role to play in the early period, not least in interpreting the devolution settlement to his or her colleagues. But the role may diminish and - although it will still be open to the Prime Minister to fill it - will be difficult to justify once the Parliament becomes established.

The West Lothian question will still be asked so long as one Scottish MP remains at Westminster. The only two genuine answers - no representation at all, and 'in and out' (Scottish MPs taking no part in Commons business dealing only with the rest of the UK) - are unjust or unworkable.

A political response might lie in reducing Scotland's representation at Westminster. But there are practical difficulties involved in implementing **any** change with so many other relevant factors to consider - Wales, Northern Ireland, conflicting Boundary Commission rules, the speed of development of English regional government. The question might be remitted to a Speaker's Conference, perhaps to set political guidelines for subsequent review by a UK Electoral Commission. It might prove impracticable to reach a conclusion with a referendum on change in the Westminster electoral system in prospect.

There will be numerous channels for communication and negotiation between the two administrations. A Joint Council of the two Governments might nevertheless prove a useful forum in the early years. Scottish - and other - MPs at Westminster might join a Scottish Affairs Select Committee to monitor the devolution settlement. In time its terms of reference would expand to cover other devolved territories and regions i.e. 'Devolution Affairs'.

## Local Government

The bill should contain a commitment to the Scottish Parliament maintaining a strong and effective system of local government. But there would be little value and some risk in including a specific reference to "subsidiarity" - which could at most be taken only as a guide for the court in construing any piece of legislation - or any attempt to specify a division of responsibilities. The Parliament might instead negotiate a Concordat with local government establishing criteria against which to judge any proposed change in local government's powers, and embodying rights of negotiation, information, consultation, etc. on matters such as the allocation of finance.

To encourage cooperative working, the Parliament should be able to second local councillors on to relevant committees - without voting rights - and councillors should be allowed to stand for the Parliament.

## Economics and Industrial Policy

The scope for Scotland to pursue an independent economic or industrial policy within the context of UK policy - which will become increasingly shaped by the European Union - is limited. There will be advantages in the ability to review the institutions of economic development (Scottish Enterprise, Highlands and Islands Enterprise, the Local Enterprise Companies, etc.), in an enhanced capacity for strategic planning, in giving incentives and support for small and medium-sized enterprises, and in fostering a closer relationship between business people and decision makers : geographically - the presence of the decision makers in Edinburgh, and psychologically - potentially the presence of local business people among them.

But control of macroeconomic policy will remain at Westminster, and the risk of competitive bidding between UK nations and regions argues for the framework for incentives to inward investment and domestic regional investment to be set by central government too. The EU dimension is significant, especially given the rules on matching EU grant funding (additionality) and the gap between the level of state aid permitted under EU rules and the lower (cost per job) limits set by the UK Government. Tolerance and mutual accommodation will be required to preserve the benefits for Scotland of the present UK regional assistance regime.

## The Transition

As much preparation as possible should be carried out in advance of Royal Assent. But even then it might be up to nine months before elections could take place. The first meeting of the Parliament could be held shortly thereafter, with a further three months of running in operations - settling standing orders, committee structure, dry-running operations with the Scottish Office - before full powers are transferred.

## Concluding Observations

Devolution to Scotland takes its place in a package of proposed reforms to the UK political system. It will in any event itself promote further change. It will open up to scrutiny parts of the political system which have remained relatively hidden to date: distribution of resources, of inward investment, of gains from European policies, and the attitude of Whitehall Ministers and departments to Scottish issues. This new visibility will require a greater political trust and tolerance at the centre - and in the regions - and a new appreciation of the nature of the British state as a *union* rather than a *unitary* state. Devolution is a loosening of control, which carries risks. But breaking the central monopoly on the design of public policy could bring overall benefits through the encouragement of competition, diversity, and wider participation in the political process all round.

# Chapter 1

# Scottish Devolution: Context and Policy

*"In the ideally-sized [administrative] unit a dissatisfied farmer
anywhere within its boundaries ought to be able to travel by public
transport to the administrative capital, horse-whip the responsible official,
and get home again by public transport, all in the same day."*

Report of the Royal Commission on the Constitution 1969-1973, Cmnd 5460, October 1973

*"Nations are not primarily ruled by laws; less by violence...
Nations are governed...by a knowledge of their temper."*

Edmund Burke, 'Thoughts on the Causes of the Present Discontents', 1770

## Introduction

1    If there is a change of Government at the coming election, it will usher in an administration, either Labour or a Lib/Lab coalition, committed to legislate for Scottish home rule on the basis of the proposals of the Scottish Constitutional Convention (SCC). The bill will take its place in a legislative programme which, over the course of a parliament, might include Freedom of Information legislation, reform of the House of Lords, incorporation of the ECHR, devolution to Wales and to the English regions, and a referendum on proportional representation. In addition, there is likely to be legislation to incorporate any Treaty changes agreed at the 1996 European Union Intergovernmental Conference and to implement any Northern Irish settlement.

2    This is a heavy legislative agenda. If Labour honours its pledge to legislate in the first year of Government, Scotland - and Wales - will lead the way. That gives rise to two potential challenges which the Constitution Unit was established to tackle:
- the devolution legislation might prove more difficult to enact than expected and might be fudged and amended to such an extent in order to get it through that it satisfies neither supporters of devolution nor of wider constitutional reform. That charge has been levelled against the 1970s devolution legislation.
- the legislation could fail to take account of links with other constitutional measures- e.g. House of Lords reform, extension of devolution to the English regions - and effectively close off options which in the long run make the entire package less satisfactory.

3    The Unit's work in Scotland has considered proposals for Scottish home rule from this perspective. Our aim has been to consider how to draft a devolution bill which is sound and workable; what other changes in the UK system of government will be needed to make the devolution settlement work, beyond those included in the legislation ; and how Scottish devolution relates to other proposed changes in the British political system. The Unit has chosen to examine in depth only legislative devolution from among current proposals for change in the government of Scotland. That is not to suggest that other options, including independence, are constitutionally unsound.[1] It rather represents a judgement about the likelihood of a policy of independence being implemented in the near future, and an appreciation that it is devolution which will have the greater effect on the constitution of the UK as a whole.

4    The focus of the Unit's work on devolution has been less on the internal workings of the settlement in Scotland - how a Scottish Parliament might operate, what policies it might pursue - than on the relationship between the Parliament and the rest of the political system. If the Scottish Parliament is to succeed then it will be necessary, through the devolution legislation and other instruments and agreements associated with it, to carve out a secure constitutional space within the British state in which it can freely operate.

5    This report is offered as a further contribution to the debate on how that space can be secured. The following chapters consider the relations of the Scottish Parliament with other levels of government and Europe, financial and economic  policies, and a range of issues about how the devolution legislation should be drafted and subsequent disputes arising from it resolved.

6    This chapter provides an introduction to the political and constitutional context in which proposals for Scottish home rule are presented. It examines the responses of the political parties determined to address the problems of Scottish government within a continuing Union:  the

Conservatives, and Scottish Labour and Liberal Democrats participating in the SCC. It concludes with a statement of the Unit's approach in the light of these proposals.

## The Scottish Context

7  This report on Scotland is published in parallel with two other reports by the Constitution Unit, *An Assembly for Wales* and *Regional Government in England*. There are clearly links between these three subjects, particularly if devolution is seen as a rolling programme - geographically, chronologically, and in terms of the powers and functions devolved. The Unit has endeavoured to make the recommendations in the three reports compatible and complementary in recognition of that fact, although each report makes a free-standing case of its own.

8  The differences between the three reports partly stem from the different contexts in which the devolution issue is raised in Scotland, Wales and England. The reports on Wales and England both include a detailed analysis of the rationale for devolution: overload at the centre, responsiveness to local concerns, recognition of a sense of identity, scope for regional economic development, democratisation of existing regional bodies, breaking the centre's monopoly on public policy to allow for experiment. The case for Scottish devolution can be made in the same general terms. But there are three factors of particular importance in the Scottish context: Scotland's distinct institutions, in particular Scots law and the institutions supporting it; the sense of national identity; and the democratic deficit. These are considered below.

### 'A World of Dense Scottishness'

9  Without going into the full history of Scotland's past as an independent sovereign state, it is important for an understanding of the present case for home rule to review at least the development of Scottish government since the Acts of Union of 1707. It is helpful to see the developments as a process, a bargain between Scotland and England which has been periodically renegotiated and renewed.

10  The Acts of Union abolished the Scottish and English Parliaments and established in their place a Parliament of Great Britain. This was an 'incorporating union'. But the Acts nonetheless allowed Scotland to retain many of its distinctive features: the position of the Scottish established church was outside the remit of the negotiations, and the continuing autonomy of Scots law and the legal system (on which see the extensive discussion in paragraphs 180 to 199 below), organisation of local government (the Royal Burghs), and distinctive education system were maintained.

11  Lindsay Paterson has argued the case for seeing the maintenance and development of such distinctive institutions over the years since 1707 as having secured for Scotland a considerable degree of 'autonomy' within the Union: "not a fully independent state, of course, but far more than a mere province".[2] He describes a managerial and technocratic response to perceived deficiencies in the treatment of Scottish public affairs by the Westminster Government. He notes the establishment of the Scottish Office and a Scottish Secretary in the UK Government in 1885 as typical of this approach: "Repeatedly...nationalism was about the inadequate treatment of Scottish business by the state, not about imposed policies, far less about oppression. A nationalism of this sort is satisfied if it gets the instruments which it thinks it needs".[3]

12   Whether or not Paterson's thesis is correct, the resulting nexus of institutions designed to respond to distinctive Scottish needs is indisputable. The growth of the welfare state in the first half of this century served to increase the importance of the Scottish Office and made it the primary focus of government in Scotland even when technically the responsibility lay with London departments. The Gilmour committee report on Scottish Administration in 1937[4] noted that "there is an increasing tendency among Scottish people to appeal to the Secretary of State on all questions affecting the social and economic life of Scotland". Whilst the *ends* of post-war consensus government might have been shared throughout the Union, there was considerable autonomy in Scotland to decide about the *means* of achieving them.

13   That remains the case today - an expression of the considerable administrative devolution to Scotland which has accumulated over the years. James Kellas led the way in identifying the result as a distinct 'Scottish political system' in his book of that title published in 1973. In it he described a symbiotic relationship: "The Scottish system is both dependent and independent within the British system, and the latter emerges as a less homogeneous entity as a result, since it is modified by the existence of the Scottish and other systems within it".[5]

14   Paterson describes the landscape of distinctively Scottish institutions which support this political system:

> *"they are the schools, universities, media, churches and the myriad daily practices that develop informally and slowly. In that sense nationalists have been successful: they...have created a world of dense Scottishness which creates a feeling of natural allegiance in nearly everyone who has been brought up here, or who has lived here for an appreciable length of time".[6]*

## National Identity

15   Paterson's thesis is that over the years Scotland gave up just so much of its distinctiveness and capacity for self-government as necessary to secure the best bargain from the Union, starting with the initial settlement of 1707. He describes a self-managing and self-limiting civil society with a clear and observable institutional identity of its own within the UK.

16   But there is another side to that identity which goes beyond Paterson's rational, managerial analysis. As Tom Nairn has pointed out, there had to be a prior sense of Scottishness to defend in the bargaining process, and there still is. Paterson, he observes, shows "how the deal was meant to work out amongst the living, but [he does not account] sufficiently for the illustrious cadaver of the seven-century-old Kingdom. In 1707 it was decreed undead, not dispatched to genuine oblivion. Embalmed by Union, it has not ceased to exert the most profound influence on each new generation".[7]

17   David McCrone explores this deeper sense of national identity in his book *Understanding Scotland: the Sociology of a Stateless Nation*. He notes that the sense of nationhood "draws very thinly on cultural traditions; there is virtually no linguistic or religious basis to nationalism. As a consequence, the tariff for being a nationalist is much lower [than in Ireland or Wales]". Many Scots are still apparently happy to pay it, or at least to acknowledge what John Mackintosh referred to as 'dual nationality' - Scottish for some purposes, British for others.[8]

18  In 1992 the Rowntree Reform Trust conducted a survey in Scotland, Wales and England to explore the sense of national identity. They asked the question: 'Which of these [options] best reflects how you regard yourself?' The results are recorded below.

| Table 1 Sense of National Identity by Country (X=Scottish/Welsh/English) | | | |
|---|---|---|---|
| **Statement Agreed With By Respondents (%)** | **Scotland** | **Wales** | **England** |
| X not British | 37 | 28 | 16 |
| More X than British | 27 | 20 | 12 |
| Equally X and British | 25 | 30 | 43 |
| More British than X | 4 | 7 | 10 |
| British not X | 6 | 14 | 15 |
| None of these | 2 | 1 | 3 |
| Sample sizes | 1664 | 656 | 5057 |

Source: Dunleavy, Margetts and Weir, ICM/Rowntree Reform Trust, 1992.

19  The Rowntree data on Scotland take their place in a series of surveys gauging the relationship between Scottish and British identity dating back to Luis Moreno's study in 1986. The sense of 'dual identity' is strong, but over 60 per cent of Scots in the Rowntree survey give priority to being Scottish rather than British, and a further 25 per cent give equal weight to both identities. As a recent study noted: "It is quite remarkable that, after nearly 300 years of Union in a large and centralised state with no separate legislature, Scottish identity is so strongly held across a wide spectrum of people living in Scotland."[9]

## Democratic Deficit

20  The two quotations which stand at the head of this chapter, from an unidentified respondent to the Kilbrandon Royal Commission on the Constitution and from Burke, encapsulate the two strands which have always run through the impetus to reform Scottish government. The first identifies the practical problems associated with distant government, problems which have been addressed by making government in Scotland more visible through the establishment of institutions like the Scottish Office and the Scottish Grand Committee. But those same institutions encouraged the development of the sense of a separate Scottish political system with its own needs and processes, a sense reinforced by the feeling of national identity. That sense is identified in the second quotation, and has led to demands that Scottish government should not only be more visible and available, but that it should also pursue different policies more representative of the wishes of Scottish people.

21  There has thus always been an element in the home rule case for making the Scottish system more democratic, allowing the Scots the opportunity legitimately to choose different ends as well as different means. This element in the case has strengthened from the 1960s onwards, perhaps as the promise of material well-being offered by the post-war consensus began to fail. Voters moved away from the parties of the consensus, Labour and the Conservatives, and the

SNP vote grew. At the same time, dissatisfaction with the Scottish Office as a mechanism for administrative devolution but not the devolution of democratic choice grew. As James Mitchell notes: "As the era of planning emerged in the late 1950s, and particularly through the 1960s, almost imperceptibly accretions to the responsibilities of the Scottish Office were building up, sustaining the notion of a Scottish economy while not allowing it to tackle Scotland's underlying social and economic problems".[10] In other words, there was clearly a political debate to be had about the management or otherwise of the Scottish economy, but the political system did not permit a distinctively Scottish answer to emerge.

22    Up until the mid-1960s voting patterns for Labour and the Conservatives were pretty even in Scotland and England. But, as **Table 2** below shows, thereafter there has been a marked divergence between levels of support north and south of the border.

## Table 2 Conservative and Labour post-war general election performances in Scotland and England.

Note: years when the UK election result matched the result in Scotland are highlighted in bold script.

| Year: Government | Conservative, as % | | Labour, as % | |
|---|---|---|---|---|
| | England | Scotland | England | Scotland |
| 1945: Lab | 40.2 | 41.1 | 48.5 | 47.6 |
| 1950: Lab | 43.8 | 44.8 | 46.2 | 46.2 |
| 1951: Con | 48.8 | 48.6 | 48.8 | 47.9 |
| 1955: Con | 50.4 | 50.1 | 46.8 | 46.7 |
| 1959: Con | 49.9 | 47.2 | 43.6 | 46.7 |
| 1964: Lab | 44.1 | 40.6 | 43.5 | 48.7 |
| 1966: Lab | 42.7 | 37.7 | 48.0 | 49.9 |
| 1970: Con | 48.3 | 38.0 | 43.4 | 44.5 |
| Feb 1974:Lab | 40.2 | 32.9 | 37.6 | 36.6 |
| Oct 1974:Lab | 38.9 | 24.7 | 40.1 | 36.3 |
| 1979: Con | 47.2 | 31.4 | 36.7 | 41.6 |
| 1983: Con | 46.0 | 28.4 | 26.9 | 35.1 |
| 1987: Con | 46.2 | 24.0 | 29.5 | 42.4 |
| 1992: Con | 45.5 | 25.7 | 33.9 | 39.0 |

Source: Magnus Linklater and Robin Denniston eds., *Chambers Anatomy of Scotland*, 1992.

23    The significance of these figures lies in the fact that Conservative support in Scotland has fallen away since the high point of 1955 (the only occasion on which a party has polled 50% of the vote), and the Party has not won a majority in Scotland since.[11] Yet the Party as a whole has formed the Government for over 70% of that period and for all of the last 17 years - even though its vote in Scotland has almost halved. This is not the place to speculate about the causes of the 'Englishing of the modern Conservative party'.[12] It is sufficient to note the effect this has had as a spur to re-examine the constitutional settlement:

> *"If the different political rhetoric deployed in Scotland inspires voters to vote for one political party, that party gains no prizes unless it has secured victory elsewhere in the UK.*

*That matters not at all if the party system is able to transcend the border, and by and large since 1707 the party system has done so.... Two conditions have produced constitutional stability: first that the party winning power has always enjoyed support throughout the UK, and secondly that both parties have had broadly equal chances of gaining power".[13]*

24    Since the late 1950s the first condition has not held; and throughout the 1980s the second failed too.

## The Conservative Response

25    Between 1912 and 1965 the Conservatives in Scotland were formally the Scottish Unionist Party. Even so, they somehow managed to combine Unionism with nationalism for much of this period, campaigning against socialism in the 1950s as a specifically centralising menace, and keeping the constitutional settlement under constant review - for example, the Balfour Royal Commission on Scottish Affairs set up in 1952 to examine the system of administrative devolution.  Under Edward Heath's leadership the party moved further in the direction of legislative devolution, advocating in 1970 a directly elected Scottish Convention to undertake functions then performed by the Scottish Grand and Scottish Standing Committees (discussed in more detail in chapter 2).  But after Margaret Thatcher took over the leadership any form of devolution or devolved Assembly fell from the agenda.

26    The Conservative response to the case for devolution since the repeal of the Scotland Act in 1979 has focused on the argument about managerial and institutional efficiency, making Scotland's government more visible and accessible.  The Scottish Conservative manifesto in 1979 called for "an all party conference or committee to see if we can reach agreement on improvements in our system of government". Following the election, the Government established a Select Committee on Scottish Affairs as part of the wider St John Stevas reforms instituting specialist committees to shadow the main Government departments.  The Government also instigated a series of amendments to the Standing Orders of the Scottish Grand Committee to permit it to meet in Edinburgh (it had previously met in Scotland on only a few occasions during the war), and to remove its 'additional members' - thus confining its membership to all Scottish MPs.  The orders were amended in 1981.  The Committee met in Edinburgh in February 1982.

27    In the run-up to the 1992 election Prime Minister John Major, campaigning on the basis of a vigorous defence of the Union, nevertheless hinted that a review of the constitutional position might be forthcoming: "after the election we will take stock".[14]  The conclusions of the 'taking stock' exercise were published in a White Paper, *Scotland in the Union: a partnership for good,* in March 1993, fleshed out in a Scottish Office Note published in February 1994.[15]  These documents proposed that a wider range of business should be taken in the Scottish Grand Committee, including questions to Scottish Office Ministers - including the House of Lords - adjournment debates, short debates, Ministerial statements etc.  They  suggested that the Committee might meet more frequently in Scotland and in places other than Edinburgh, and that the special standing committee procedure (taking evidence on a bill) might be used more.  But Scottish Secretary Ian Lang made clear that:
> *"The arrangements enabling the Committee to handle Scottish legislation will remain unchanged, with any Second Reading vote being taken on the Floor of the House.  The Report stage and the Third Reading debate will also continue to be taken on the Floor of the House in the usual way",*

28  He summed up the effect of the reforms as follows:

> *"Taken together, I believe that these measures will lead to a significant improvement in the handling of parliamentary business relating to Scotland, in a way which is less remote, which is more responsive to Scottish priorities and concerns, and which may relieve some of the pressures on the Floor of the House. I stress however that... Scottish Ministers will still remain fully accountable to the House, and the Scottish Grand Committee will remain a Committee of the House. The integrity of Parliament will and must remain intact".*[16]

The amendments to Standing Orders were passed on 11 July 1994.

29  On 29 November 1995, Scottish Secretary Michael Forsyth announced a further series of reforms to parliamentary business which he suggested should be seen as part of a broader initiative to improve 'the governance of Scotland': "plans to devolve power to local government, to create a new forum based on the Scottish Economic Council, and to give the people of Scotland more control over their own lives". He proposed that Scottish bills should have their second and third readings in the Grand Committee "whenever it makes sense that that should happen", that there should be greater recourse to the special standing committee procedure (as was used in the 1994-95 Session for the Children (Scotland) Bill), that a new procedure would be introduced allowing a House of Lords Committee to take evidence in Scotland on legislation introduced in the House of Lords, that Standing Orders would be changed to allow all UK Ministers (rather than only those in the Scottish Office) to take part in debates in the Grand Committee, and that the Committee would meet more frequently and in Scotland.

30  In commending these proposals to the House, the Secretary of State summed up:

> *"What the people of Scotland want is Government close to them, Government listening to them, and above all Government accountable to them. This historic Parliament embodies our great Union. It is the only Parliament that can effectively and powerfully secure Scotland's interests and future".*[17]

31  It can be seen that the Conservative response to the factors identified earlier in this chapter has maintained 'the integrity of Parliament' at all times. Within that framework there has been a steady development of proposals to make Parliament more responsive to Scottish interests when it legislates for Scotland alone (principally by conducting such business in Scotland: in the 1994-95 Session four out of eleven meetings of the Grand Committee were held in Scotland; in the present Session it is intended that all fourteen meetings should be held there). The latest innovation has introduced a new dimension in holding UK Ministers to account for UK policies as they affect Scotland.

32  These changes have certainly addressed some of the technical problems associated with the provision of distinctively Scottish legislation within a unitary Parliament. But there are limits to how far they can go. Apart from anything else they require considerable ingenuity in the planning of the Parliamentary timetable at Westminster, in order to ensure that Scottish MPs may still play a full part in business there as well as in Scotland. They also do nothing to address the problem identified above as the 'democratic deficit'. As Michael Forsyth pointed out in elaborating on the most recent proposals in a speech on St Andrew's Day 1995:

> *"The reforms which I have announced could be used by a Labour government with a majority on Grand Committee, to pass legislation and hold the executive to account. There is nothing further which a Scottish parliament could do which could not be done by Grand Committee except raise a Tartan Tax".*[18]

33   The claim does not hold if there is a Government in Westminster *without* a majority on Grand Committee.  This is precisely the problem: the proposals fail to provide for the democratic expression of political preferences in Scotland different from those represented by the governing party at Westminster.  The scope for the exercise of the powers of the Grand Committee still rests with Westminster.  The reforms depend crucially for their effectiveness in meeting the concerns of the Scottish people on a return to the first condition for constitutional stability quoted above, namely that the party winning power in Scotland should enjoy support throughout the UK.

## The Scottish Constitutional Convention

34   A very different response, based primarily on the democratic rather than the managerial argument, has been adopted by the parties to the Scottish Constitutional Convention (SCC): Scottish Labour and the Scottish Liberal Democrats.

35   Following the Conservatives' victory in the 1987 election, and with it the loss of any hope of reviving the devolution proposals of the 1970s, the Campaign for a Scottish Assembly set up a group of eminent Scots to draw up plans for a constitutional convention.  The committee, chaired by Sir Robert Grieve, issued a report in July 1988, *A Claim of Right for Scotland*.  The report (paragraph 12.1) recommended that a convention should be established:
    *"i) to draw up a scheme for a Scottish Assembly.*
    *ii) to mobilise Scottish opinion behind that scheme.*
    *iii) to deal with the Government in securing approval of the scheme, or an*
    *acceptable modification of it".*

36   The Claim noted the special institutions and procedures which have developed over time in recognition of Scotland's distinctive place in the Union.  But it saw the problems which the changing party political environment in Scotland posed to them, both in principle:
    *"...the political arithmetic of the United Kingdom means that the Scots are constantly exposed to the risk of having matters of concern only to them prescribed by a government against which they have voted not narrowly but overwhelmingly"*
and on a practical level:
    *"Even this unsuitable and inadequate 'government' of Scotland is no longer working.  There is a constitutional flaw in the present machinery of Scottish government:  it can work only within a limited range of election results.  Providing a Scottish Ministerial team, Scottish Whips and Government representation on Standing and Select Committees, requires a certain minimum number of Government party MPs from Scottish constituencies.  There is no guarantee of such a number being elected."*

The Claim concluded that:
    *"Scotland can no longer live with [the present constitution] and has nothing to hope from it.  Scots have shown it more tolerance than it deserves.  They must now show enterprise by starting the reform of their own government.  They have the opportunity, in the process, to start the reform of the English constitution, to serve as the grit in the oyster which produces the pearl".*

37    The Scottish Constitutional Convention duly held its first meeting on 30 March 1989.  All political parties in Scotland were invited to take part.  The Conservative Party declined the invitation.  The SNP took part in the initial preparations but ultimately could not accept the principle of consensus by which the Convention was to make all its decisions and therefore did not participate.  In addition, the Convention drew in representatives from local government, the churches, the Scottish TUC, business groups, ethnic minority groups etc.  It adopted its own Claim of Right at its inaugural meeting: "We gathered as the Scottish Constitutional Convention, do hereby acknowledge the sovereign right of the Scottish people to determine the form of Government best suited to their needs, and do hereby declare and pledge that in all our deliberations their interests shall be paramount".

38    The Convention presented its first report to the Scottish people on St Andrew's Day 1990.[19] Following the 1992 election the Convention established a Scottish Constitutional Commission to work on some of the detailed aspects of the scheme they were proposing.  The Commission reported in October 1994.[20] The Convention's final report, incorporating the work of the Commission, was presented on St Andrew's Day 1995, entitled *Scotland's Parliament. Scotland's Right*.  The scheme contained in that report is summarised below.

---

**'Scotland's Parliament. Scotland's Right.'**

- the Scottish Parliament's powers to include all areas within the remit of the Scottish Office, so that the Parliament would have sole or shared responsibility for all functions except those retained to the Westminster Parliament e.g. defence, foreign affairs, immigration, nationality, social security policy and central economic and fiscal responsibilities.
- the subsidarity principle to apply where a function is shared between the Scottish Parliament and Westminster.
- Scotland's Parliament to be represented on UK Ministerial delegations to the EU Council, and to have the power to appoint representatives to the Committee of the Regions and the Economic and Social Committee.
- the Scottish Parliament to be responsible for the system of local government in Scotland, its financing and its provision of local services. The Convention supported Article 4 of the European Charter of Local Self-Government that local authorities shall, within the limits of the law, have full discretion to exercise their initiative with regard to any matter which is not excluded from their competence nor assigned to any other authority.
- the role of quangos operating in Scotland to be examined by Scotland's Parliament which would "bring their activities under democratic control where it considers this necessary". The Parliament would also have powers to ensure that where such bodies remained they would be subject to greater accountability and accessibility.
- One Member of Scotland's Parliament each for Orkney, Shetland and Western Isles to ensure separate representation.
- acceptance that entrenchment could not be achieved within the concept of supreme parliamentary sovereignty.  Instead, in advance of the relevant Scottish legislation, there should be a clear commitment by the Westminster Parliament made through a Declaration that the Act founding the Parliament should not be repealed or amended in such a way as to threaten the existence of the Parliament without the consent of the Scottish Parliament and people directly consulted through general election or referendum.
- an existing body such as the Appellate Committee of the House of Lords or the Judicial Committee of the Privy Council to resolve disputes as to the relative powers of the UK and Scottish Parliament.
- a Charter of fundamental rights to be adopted by Scotland's Parliament encompassing and improving on prevailing international law and conventions. An expectation that a Freedom of Information Act would be passed by Scotland's Parliament.

---

- a Parliament of 129 Members to be established, electors to have two votes, one for 73 constituency Members of the Scottish Parliament (MSPs) elected from Westminster constituencies with the addition of one extra representative from the Islands elected on a 'first past the post' system, and one for a candidate from a regional party list of additional members. These additional votes to elect 56 members in all from the 8 European Parliament constituencies. These to be counted within the 8 Euro-constituencies and the 7 seats available in each to be allocated so that the total representation from each region would correspond as closely as possible to the share of the votes cast for the party (i.e. the 'additional' votes) in that area.
- a review of the electoral system by the Parliament after the first election, with the assumption that the main principles remain intact.
- endorsement of the cross-party Electoral Agreement which accepts that there should be equal numbers of men and women as members of the first Parliament, and commits the parties to select and field an equal number of male and female candidates for election distributed with a view to the winnability of seats (the cross party agreement has been signed by Scottish Labour and the Scottish Liberal Democrats only).
- a single chamber legislature with no role for the House of Lords.
- a Speaker to be elected by vote of the full Parliament.
- a fixed term of four years for the Parliament unless two thirds of MSPs agree otherwise.
- Executive to be headed by a chief Minster normally, but not necessarily, being the leader of the largest party: Cabinet membership to be drawn from a party or parties forming a working majority in Parliament (exceptions for Law Officers). All Ministers would need to be confirmed by simple majority of the full Parliament. Their role would be to administer Government departments, and to initiate legislation (to be shared with Parliamentary Committees) and to represent the Scottish Parliament.
- adoption of standing orders to provide for the Parliament to operate through a system of Parliamentary Committees, oblige MSPs to devote themselves to the business of the Parliament, and to make appointments to public bodies as open and democratic as possible. Only in the first term of the Parliament would MSPs be able to hold a dual mandate i.e. be a member of the Westminster Parliament, or European Parliament, or a local authority councillor.
- the principle of financial equalisation to be embodied in the establishing Act, with the Barnett formula being used as the basis for the allocation; this would be known as the assigned budget, which would not require annual negotiation.
- the Scottish Parliament to take over the powers currently exercised by the Secretary of State over public expenditure in Scotland.
- a power to increase or decrease the basic rate of income tax by a maximum of 3p in the pound to be given to the Scottish Parliament, but with any tax cuts financed from within the assigned budget. No powers to vary corporate taxation.

## The Constitution Unit's Agenda

39    The Constitution Unit's remit is to inquire into the implementation of constitutional reform in the UK. It is not a campaigning organisation, pressing the case for change. Instead it seeks to contribute to a debate about how change, once agreed, might be put into practice in a coherent and practical fashion. In Scotland it can be assumed that a Labour or Lib/Lab coalition Government would take as its starting point the proposals of the SCC in seeking to implement the commitment to establishing a Scottish Parliament.

40    The Unit's approach has been to consider how these proposals might be implemented. In particular:
- How much more detail might be needed to draft a Scottish devolution bill?
- What elements might need to be added or subtracted to make the proposals work in practice?
In doing so, we have drawn on lessons from other devolved systems, the detailed provisions in

the 1978 Scotland Act and the extensive discussion in the 1973 Report of the Royal Commission on the Constitution (the Kilbrandon Commission) and the Memorandum of Dissent accompanying it.[21] The aim has been, drawing on the benefit of hindsight and the work of the SCC over the past several years, to suggest how a future Scotland Act might differ from the 1978 version in order to promote a more stable, workable and lasting constitutional settlement compatible with reform of the UK constitution as a whole.

# Chapter 2

## The Lessons of
## the Past

## Introduction

41    We have been here before. The Labour Government elected in February 1974 promised a White Paper on devolution to be followed by a bill. When it set out detailed proposals for devolution in a September White Paper and then gained a small overall majority in the October election, the stage looked set at last for the establishment of a Scottish legislative Assembly. Nearly five years later, in June 1979, the Scotland Act 1978 was repealed by a Conservative Government which had come to power in an election forced on the Government by a no confidence motion originally tabled by the SNP. What went wrong?

42    This chapter reviews the experience of legislating for devolution in the 1970s with a view to providing some answers to that question. It covers the bare bones of the political history of the rising pressure for devolution from the 1960s onwards. But its principal focus is the machinery: how the policy was made in Whitehall and how it was enacted in Parliament. The source for this section is largely the personal recollections of a number of those involved at the time, particularly within Whitehall and the then Constitution Unit in the Cabinet Office.

43    Although the political context might be different, it will be this same official and parliamentary machinery which has to be used to deliver devolution today. The final section of the chapter draws some of the lessons from the 1970s experience to suggest how the machinery might be deployed more effectively this time around.

## History

44    The home rule movement in Scotland has a long history (the all-party Scottish Home Rule Association was formed in 1886) to which this chapter does not attempt to do justice. It is well recorded elsewhere.[22] There is, however, a brief chronology at Appendix A, running from 1885 and the establishment of the Scottish Office through to the 1979 vote by which the 1978 Scotland Act was repealed. This might at least provide some corrective to the impression, which might otherwise be gained from what follows, that devolution in the 1970s was simply a response to the rise in political popularity of the SNP. There was more to it than that - and still is.

45    Nevertheless, to understand at least the immediate political context in which the devolution proposals of the 1970s emerged it is necessary to look no further back than to the early 1960s and the revival of the Scottish National Party. For, although the Party had achieved its first parliamentary breakthrough in 1945 when Dr Robert McIntyre won the Motherwell by-election (he lost the general election twelve weeks later), the Party had fought only five seats at the 1959 general election and saved only one deposit. Yet within two years they were doing well again in by-elections. In November 1961 the SNP candidate in Glasgow Bridgeton won 18.7% of the vote and nearly beat the Conservative into second place. In June 1962 their vote went up to 23.3% in the West Lothian by-election where they came second to Labour's Tam Dalyell. At Glasgow Pollok they were third (to a Conservative victor: no Conservative has won a by-election in Scotland since) but with 28% of the vote. Finally, in November 1967, the breakthrough came: Winnie Ewing took the Hamilton seat with 46.1% of the vote.

46    There was more to the SNP's revival than support for home rule. There were other factors which gave the party a wider appeal, especially to the young and upwardly mobile. The 1960s were a time of change across the UK. One interpretation at least of the SNP's rise during the period is that it caught this wider tide of political energy, capitalising at: "the level of everyday life (mobile privatism), the level of communications media (the arrival of television), and the level of state activity (the Scottish growth project). The SNP captured the generation entering the electorate in the 1960s and 1970s who, in England, might have tended towards the Conservatives or the Liberals."[23]

47    It was at the level of the constitution that the other parties responded to the Hamilton result. The Opposition acted first. At the request of Scottish Conservatives, Edward Heath had set up a Scottish Policy Group to examine the machinery of government in Scotland in June 1967. At the Scottish Conservative Conference in May 1968 Heath formally endorsed the Group's proposed elected Assembly in what came to be known as his 'Perth declaration'. A Scottish Constitutional Committee was established under the chairmanship of Sir Alec Douglas-Home to work out the details.

48    The Government responded in December 1968 by appointing a Royal Commission on the Constitution under the chairmanship of Lord Crowther. Its terms of reference were:
   • *"To examine the present functions of the central legislature and government in relation to the several countries and regions of the UK;*
   • *to consider... whether any changes are desirable in those functions or otherwise in present constitutional and economic relationships;*
   • *to consider also whether any changes are desirable in the constitutional and economic relationships between the UK and the Channel Islands and the Isle of Man".*

49    The Douglas-Home Committee's report, *Governing Scotland,* was published in March 1970. It advocated a directly elected Assembly with powers to participate in the framing and passage of legislation but which would not be able to enact legislation itself. The steam by then seemed to be going out of the devolution debate. Labour were beginning to reclaim their support, voters were drifting away from the SNP as they saw it in action in local government, and membership almost halved from 1968 levels.[24] The party did not fare as well as it hoped at the June 1970 general election, taking only 11.4% of the vote and losing Hamilton. But this was nevertheless its best showing, and the first time it had ever won a seat (Western Isles), in a general election.

50    The discovery of North Sea oil, and the highly successful 'It's Scotland's Oil' campaign launched by the SNP in September 1972, gave the party a further boost. A year later the huge oil price rises following the Yom Kippur War made this an ever more potent symbol in the Party's appeal. The Royal Commission on the Constitution, now chaired by one of the two Scots on the original Commission, Lord Kilbrandon (following the death of Lord Crowther early in 1972), finally published its report on 31 October 1973. The Report canvassed a number of options for devolution ranging from legislative Assemblies for Scotland and Wales, down to Co-ordinating Committees of Local Authorities for England. In all there were six different schemes proposed in the report, plus a further scheme for elected Assemblies for Scotland, Wales and five English regions contained in a 'Memorandum of Dissent'[25] signed by two members of the Commission, Lord Crowther-Hunt and Professor Alan Peacock.

51    Reactions to the report were varied. The Liberals welcomed it but were disappointed that it did not embrace federalism. The Scottish and Welsh Nationalists were highly critical since it had dismissed separatism. The Government were reluctant to take a position, and the Scottish

Conservatives were sceptical having dropped their own commitment to the Douglas-Home proposals only at their Conference in May. But the month after publication the SNP won another by-election victory, Margo MacDonald taking Glasgow Govan with 41.9% of the vote.

52    Labour campaigned in the February 1974 general election on a policy of holding meetings of the Scottish Grand Committee in Edinburgh. But when the SNP's vote held up in that election (they polled 22% and seven seats, a gain of six) Labour's policy became more forthcoming. In the Queen's Speech debate on 12 March Harold Wilson responded to prompting from Winnie Ewing: "Of course we shall publish a White Paper and a Bill". A Green Paper[26] outlining the seven schemes proposed by Kilbrandon and Crowther-Hunt was published on 3 June. By September the Party had been brought painfully into line behind firm proposals for legislative devolution to Scotland and executive devolution to Wales, published in a White Paper[27] shortly before the October election. It was sufficient at least to protect Labour's Scottish vote in the polls: but the SNP gained four seats from the Conservatives and their share of the vote rose to 30%, only 6% behind Labour. It was in this political setting after the general election that Whitehall set about producing a devolution bill.

## Whitehall

53    The climate in which the considered report of the Royal Commission was distilled, between the February and October elections, into a specific set of proposals for devolution was an intensely political one. The civil service machinery was not much involved: the Green Paper of June 1974 was handled more as a party matter at Transport House than as a piece of Government business processed through Whitehall. The Government's principal source of advice at this stage was Lord Crowther-Hunt, whom they had taken on from the Royal Commission as Minister responsible for advising on the constitution.

54    It is worth commenting on this choice in passing. Lord Crowther-Hunt had been the prime mover behind the Memorandum of Dissent. The preface to that Memorandum made it clear that neither signatory could accept any scheme for devolution which was not uniformly applied throughout the UK ("to provide equality of political rights for people in all parts of the United Kingdom") and opposed any scheme which "akin to the old Stormont system of government, would devolve to Scottish and Welsh Parliaments and Governments 'sovereign' or 'autonomous' powers in a wide range of subjects - with the Westminster Parliament normally precluded from legislating in these matters". It is clear where Crowther-Hunt's sympathies lay at the start of the process, even if they were completely at odds with Government policy a few months later.

55    The June Green Paper recited the options. The September White Paper took some crucial decisions about the sort of scheme that could win support:
●  legislative devolution to Scotland, executive devolution to Wales.
●  'first past the post' elections.
●  Assemblies funded by block grant: no powers of taxation.
●  retention of the Secretary of State and existing representation at Westminster for both Scotland and Wales.
Thus the framework for the devolution bills which followed was clearly set in September 1974 and did not fundamentally change thereafter.

## The Constitution Unit

56 Only in November 1974, following the election, was the civil service brought fully into the policy process. The Government established a Constitution Unit within the Cabinet Office under the direction of Ted Short, Lord President, Leader of the House and Deputy Leader of the Party. The Unit was headed by an official with Permanent Secretary rank, assisted by three Under Secretaries, and totalled in all between 30 and 40 staff. In addition, both the Scottish Office and the Welsh Office assigned an Under Secretary to devote much of his time to devolution and a dedicated unit to work on the subject, and in most other departments (bar the FCO and the MOD) there could be found at least a middle ranking official whose time was mostly devoted to the topic. This was a formidably large Whitehall machine.

57 The Constitution Unit's task was to take the proposals of the September White Paper and prepare a bill for introduction to Parliament. This took far longer than Ministers had expected (although officials in the Unit had always known the process would take some time). Ted Short was very much the driving force behind the legislation. He had been very keen to introduce it in the first session following the October election, i.e. before the end of 1975. He accepted only with extreme reluctance the advice that the Government simply were not sufficiently ready to do so. The November 1975 White Paper, *Our Changing Democracy: Devolution to Scotland and Wales*[28] was in part a means of keeping up the political momentum, but also a genuine attempt to air the many difficult questions which had by then emerged.

58 Some of the steam went out of the push for legislation when Jim Callaghan replaced Harold Wilson as Prime Minister in April 1976. He himself had previously been sceptical about devolution. Michael Foot, the new Deputy Leader who had come second to Callaghan in the leadership election, asked to become Leader of the House and therefore succeeded Ted Short as Lord President and Cabinet Minister responsible for the devolution bill. But he was more engaged in other issues - managing the House by then with a minority[29] - and less energetic in pushing devolution than Ted Short had been. The motive force from then on was largely supplied by John Smith as Minister of State in the Privy Council Office. The August 1976 White Paper[30], billed as a 'Supplementary Statement' to that of November 1975, was again a means of maintaining political momentum after the change of leadership, and an opportunity to test a slightly less generous form of devolution on a sceptical English public before eventually introducing a bill three months later.

59 Why did the process take so long? There were some difficult technical issues to be resolved, and it did not help that the Government were lukewarm towards devolution in any case. But the bulk of the time was taken up in negotiating between Ministers and their departments precisely which functions and powers could be devolved and which not.

60 That required a huge investment of time and a complex machinery for policy making and negotiation. The Prime Minister himself chaired a committee which held about ten meetings, including three away-days at Chequers, to set strategy, to resolve the major difficulties and to try to maintain collective responsibility in a Cabinet which was divided on the wisdom of devolution. Ted Short chaired a Ministerial committee which met fifteen times. The head of the Constitution Unit chaired a committee of Permanent Secretaries. And a network of Whitehall committees at official level met almost constantly, and were still doing so - filling gaps, drafting amendments - after the bill had been introduced.

61    The Constitution Unit's remit was simply to deliver a bill on the lines Ministers wanted. This circumscribed their room for coming up with fresh ideas, for example on the financing arrangements (where they pressed the case for revenue raising powers: 'No representation without taxation'), or the West Lothian question (as the question of the future role and level of Scottish representation at Westminster came to be known:  see chapter 7). It also dictated a very detailed specification of the powers that were to be devolved: Ministers wanted to be clear about precisely where the dividing line had been drawn.  The Royal Commission's report, while accepting that "absolute precision in definition has not been attained in any constitution" (paragraph 739), favoured the listing of transferred rather than reserved powers[31] and this was the method adopted by the Government.

62    In practice the Constitution Unit found that the only way to achieve the precision Ministers desired was to go through the statute book as it applied to Scotland and Wales and to decide, Act by Act, and sometimes section by section, which could be transferred to the Assemblies and which needed to remain the responsibility of Westminster.  Whilst the aim might have been to devolve as much as possible, this means of going about it meant that the choice between transfer and retention had to be made in each case and was arrived at by bargaining within Whitehall rather than on any clear basis of principle.

63    The Constitution Unit, under the direction of the Lord President, was responsible for conducting the Whitehall negotiation and steering it to a conclusion.  The Scottish and Welsh Offices pressed for a greater devolution of powers, while the other departments generally resisted.  The Lord President was in overall charge of the policy.  He was in the lead in the sense that it was his bill: his responsibility to agree the policy, and to get it drafted.  The status of other Cabinet Ministers depended on the point at issue. Whatever the ground rules, in practice the Ministers or officials with the most clout or the most determination proved decisive. If the question was, for example, how far responsibility for health might be devolved, the Health Secretary (as advised by his officials) effectively had a veto unless over-ruled at Cabinet level.  Several issues had to go to the Prime Ministerial committee for resolution.

## Parliament: The Devolution Bills

64    Finally, a combined Scotland and Wales Bill was introduced in November 1976.  It gained a second reading only after referendums in both Scotland and Wales prior to setting up the Assemblies had been conceded and a consultation paper was published on the implications for England.[32] The Shadow Secretary of State for Scotland Alick Buchanan-Smith and one of his front bench team, Malcolm Rifkind, resigned their posts when the Shadow Cabinet decided to oppose second reading.

65    The Government had embarked on the devolution project in the expectation of a considerable measure of bipartisan support for the principle.  But this was not forthcoming following Edward Heath's replacement as leader of the Conservative Party by Margaret Thatcher.  The immediate signs had been encouraging.  The new leader visited Scotland only ten days after her election and told a rally in Glasgow that the establishment of a Scottish Assembly "must be a top priority to ensure that more decisions affecting Scotland are taken in Scotland by Scotsmen".[33]  But her support did not last long, if it had ever truly existed at all.  As one commentator put it: "What upset all devolutionist calculations was the election of Margaret Thatcher to the leadership of the Conservative Party.  It was apparent from the very beginning to those who knew her best that she was set on scuppering the whole notion of devolution".[34]

66    On the first day of committee 350 amendments were put down. It was clear from the start that this would be a difficult bill to get through the House. Michael Foot planned to set aside thirty days to debate the Bill, but the Conservatives complained that even this generous allowance would not be enough and refused to accept the voluntary timetable. Foot was nevertheless reluctant to impose a guillotine. Instead he waited until the Bill was obviously bogged down: after nearly 100 hours of debate the committee stage had considered only three and a half clauses. A guillotine motion was tabled but defeated by an alliance of Conservatives, Liberals, Ulster Unionists and Labour rebels in February 1977.

67    The Bill was withdrawn. As John Kerr, Scottish correspondent of *The Guardian,* put it later:

> *"A year ago [1976], all the political parties in Scotland were committed to devolution. In effect Scotland had completed the great debate and made up its corporate mind that the time had come for action rather than words. Then came the extraordinary series of Parliamentary manoeuvrings which threw the whole boiling back into the melting-pot...In essence the Bill was stymied by a lack of will in Westminster. This seemed to derive more from the conventions and cloistered moods of the mother of Parliaments than from any rational appraisal of the bill...The system that the Bill was designed to reform struck back in self-defence and disarmed the threatening mechanism".*[35]

68    On 17 March, following the defeat, Margaret Thatcher put down a motion of censure for debate on 23 March. The prospect of defeat spurred the Government into negotiations with the Liberals (and other minority parties) to secure a working majority. The result was the Lib/Lab pact. The Liberal demands on devolution included separate bills for Scotland and Wales, revenue-raising powers (which the Government promised to introduce if they could identify a workable system), proportional representation for the Assembly elections (on which there was subsequently a free vote) and reduction in the powers of veto and interference by the Secretary of State and Westminster in the Assembly's affairs. Similar changes had been called for by the Scottish Council of the Labour Party.

69    The detailed negotiations and policy-making had by this time passed to John Smith. Jim Callaghan explains in his memoirs:

> *"Michael Foot was heavily engaged in wrestling with the rest of our legislative programme and, in his capacity as Leader of the House, had a full-time job fending off the procedural stratagems of the Opposition...I said [to John Smith that] he had a dual task, firstly to work out a Bill that the Cabinet would accept, and secondly to redesign it in such a fashion that it would secure Liberal support without losing any Labour votes. It was a tall order but John Smith was equal to the task".*[36]

70    Separate Bills for Scotland and Wales were introduced, with Liberal support, in November. Both Bills represented a strengthening of the position of the respective Assemblies. The override powers were further constrained, and in a number of areas the word 'shall' relating to the Assembly (for example the details of its standing orders) became 'may', allowing the elected members more discretion. The changes were enough to win the support of the Liberals, and to reduce opposition from those who had opposed the combined Bill on the grounds that the Welsh did not really want devolution. The crucial guillotine vote this time round was won. As James Naughtie, then of *The Scotsman,* described it:

> *"[John Smith] had no illusion that the Commons approved of devolution any more than it had done before, but he guessed that the Government had found a formula which would link most of his party, the Liberals, the SNP and a couple of stray Tories in a fragile coalition which could stagger through the hours of committee debate on the floor of the House and emerge with a Bill more or less intact. The proposals were far from perfect - for anybody on the devolution side - but they might at least become law".*[37]

71    And so they did. Winning the guillotine motion meant that the committee stage held fewer fears for the Government. That was especially so since the debate even then continued at a high level of generality. 61 of the Bill's 83 clauses and 11 of the 17 schedules were carried undebated, and about 500 of the 638 amendments tabled were not reached. None of the detailed provisions of the Bill was amended by the Commons in committee. Until the referendum clause (see below), the Government suffered only two defeats, both to remove purely declaratory clauses.[38]

72    But the argument returned time and again to the principle of whether legislative devolution was possible within a unitary state. Enoch Powell claimed it was a contradiction:

> *"There is an inherent incompatibility between Home Rule, devolved legislative power, and the maintenance of the parliamentary union of the United Kingdom. We have tried to approach this issue from all directions. Almost every question that has arisen has brought us back to the same conclusion".*[39]

73    His doubts about the bedrock of principle underlying devolution as proposed were widely shared. As one official involved at the time put it to us: "They just didn't like the smell of the Bill". Or, in words made perhaps more relevant in that their author now sits on the Labour front bench:

> *"These Bills [Scotland and Wales] were ad hoc solutions which had precious little grounding in political principle or theory. All that supporters of the Acts could argue was that they were the best the House of Commons was capable of producing (and there was some truth in that)".*[40]

74    As the committee stage was nearing its end, it came to debate the Labour backbencher George Cunningham's new clause on the referendum. It required the Secretary of State to lay before Parliament an order repealing the Act unless at least 40% of the eligible electorate voted yes. 'It was the touchstone' says Naughtie. It polarised the pro-devolutionists and the anti-devolutionists and moved people off the middle ground. "It was either a logical test of the Government's premise for drawing up the legislation or an attempt to fix the result of the referendum and an insult to the Scottish electorate", depending which side of the devolution argument you tended to. The amendment was strongly opposed by the Government, but they lost the vote by 166 votes to 151.

75    The amendment in the end proved fatal to the Act. In the referendum on 1 March 1979 Scotland voted in favour - 52% to 48% - but only 32.9% of the electorate had joined the majority. Prime Minister Callaghan tried to play for time and avoid laying the order for repeal of the Act. The 'Frankenstein solution' became the talk of Westminster: that the Act could be suspended for a number of months to be revived by a Labour Government following a general election. But in the event he could not find the support for this that was needed. On 22 March he made a statement setting the end of April as a deadline for concluding all-party talks on improving the Act. The SNP pounced on this vagueness and put down a motion of no confidence immediately. It was followed by one from Mrs Thatcher. Callaghan lost the vote by one, and then the subsequent general election. The order was duly laid on 6 June and the Act repealed. At the same time the Secretary of State announced that all-party talks on devolution would start soon. Labour had argued that the Act should stay on the statute book while the talks went on, but the Conservative Government insisted on wiping the slate clean.

## The Lessons

76    What then are the lessons of this sad history for attempting to legislate for devolution today? One might draw the following:

- **the size of the task:** on any view the devolution effort in the 1970s was a massive commitment of Ministerial and official time, involving almost every department of Government. It also dominated the 1977-78 Session. The 1978 Scotland Act (guillotined in committee) took 23 days in the Commons and 23 days in the Lords. The Wales Act and the failed Scotland and Wales Bill together took as long again. In the Commons all proceedings were on the floor of the House. Time in preparation might be reduced by drafting the bill in a more coherent way, and the passage through Parliament might be eased either by changes in parliamentary procedures, or more imaginative use of existing ones.[41]

- **thorough preparation:** however well-designed the bill is it will still be subject to detailed amendment. Simply finding something that will work will not be enough: it is also necessary to have anticipated the other options that might arise in the course of debate and to have convincing arguments for choosing differently. That applies particularly to any practical arrangements envisaged which are not included in the bill: they need to be thought through too in order to carry conviction. Otherwise the bill will be amended as if they did not exist.

- **be serious:** the Scotland Bill fared better in Parliament than the Scotland and Wales Bill. While the line up for and against devolution had not changed, the Bill itself had been strengthened to increase the Assembly's autonomy. Given that most of the debates in the House of Commons were about whether legislative devolution was possible in principle, the half-hearted Scotland and Wales Bill seemed more like a demonstration of the anti-devolutionists' case than a bold positive advertisement. The stronger and more principled the settlement proposed, the easier it will be to defend in Parliament.

- **be coherent:** the detailed forms of devolution to which the Government committed themselves in the White Paper of September 1974 (from which they did not subsequently depart) failed to reflect any grounding in institutional or constitutional design. The Bills which flowed from it lacked intellectual coherence. In particular the Scotland Bill proposed the establishment of an Assembly with wide-ranging legislative responsibilities over five million people, but without even the revenue raising powers of a parish council. The refusal to contemplate proportional representation for the Assembly elections also detracted from the attractiveness of the concept in practice. Any future Government should ensure it has a coherent package with wide support - especially within its own ranks - before introducing legislation at Westminster.

- **be inclusive:** starting with the Memorandum of Dissent, there was a constant undercurrent in the debates about devolution that it was only being pursued to appease the Celtic fringes and to halt the advance of the Nationalist parties, and that insufficient attention was being paid to England. The 'English backlash' was surprisingly strong and focused on the referendum (quickly conceded), money (not so much absolute amounts as the potentially destabilising effect of a Scottish Government adopting policies with spending implications beyond the control of Westminster), a general resentment at Scots receiving special treatment, and the West Lothian question. *"Devolution must be taken out of the relatively restricted confines of Scotland and Wales and seen as part of an attempt to make British government more acceptable to the British people... The force for change created by the Scottish and Welsh peoples' move away from the British parties is but a special case of a more general* *disaffection".*[42] It will help to see devolution to Scotland as part of a coherent programme of constitutional change embracing all parts of the UK. Consistency and clarity will be needed between the various elements of the constitutional package to make that claim stand up.

- **central machinery:** some central machinery will be necessary to oversee the inevitable negotiation between departments on the content of the devolution bill. Whether this is a central Unit as in the 1970s, or a full-scale department for Constitutional Affairs, as some have suggested, is less important than getting the right Minister to take charge. He or she needs to be a figure with some weight in the Cabinet in order to steer through a difficult inter-departmental negotiation and achieve the desired result. The aim should not be simply to achieve a Whitehall consensus, but to enter the negotiation with an ideal settlement and preserve it. John Smith had that commitment in the 1970s but was not then a sufficiently senior figure to force the other parties to agree. Even so, a Minister with that same commitment and grasp of detail will be needed this time round too, whoever the lead Minister is in the Cabinet.

- **separate bills:** if the devolution settlement for Scotland is to be different from that for Wales it would be best to separate the bills from the start. Dividing them in 1977 helped to divide the opposition and to secure their passage. But the two were still linked in Parliament's mind, and amendments conceded in one Bill were invariably then inserted in the other. This made it more difficult to distinguish one level of devolution from the other.

- **powers not the heart of the bill:** the precise powers of the Assembly were very little discussed in the Commons (an amendment from John Mackintosh that the reserved powers should be listed instead of those transferred was defeated by 133 votes to 35 - but changing the framework of the Bill at that stage would have been disastrous). All amendments, mostly from the SNP, to increase the range of powers were defeated, while in the House of Lords a number of amendments were carried to reduce the scope of the settlement. The precise range of the powers devolved was by no means the heart of the argument in Parliament: those provisions of the Bill were pretty much accepted as given. Much more attention was paid to the institutional machinery which would allow the overall settlement to work in practice.

- **list reserved powers:** opting to list transferred powers added to the preparation time for the Bill. Had the Government instead chosen to list reserved powers it would have changed the premise of the interdepartmental negotiations and might have introduced some principle into the allocation of powers other than simple horse-trading. In particular, concentrating on what *needed* to be reserved rather than on what *could* be devolved would have reversed the burden of proof in Whitehall. The onus would then have been on *all* Whitehall departments to decide for themselves what interests they had to protect, rather than leaving it to the Constitution Unit to make all the running, with encouragement from the Scottish and Welsh Offices.

The final point above - listing the reserved powers - would also have led to a better, more comprehensible and more workable Bill overall. This point is taken up and discussed in the next chapter - on the form of the devolution legislation and related matters.

# Chapter 3

## The Scotland Act: Form of the Legislation, Resolution of Disputes, Entrenchment

## Introduction

77    Any scheme for the establishment of a Scottish Parliament will have to be embodied in a statute specifying the relationship between it and the Parliament in Westminster. This chapter considers the nature of that Act: the form it should take, the technical mechanism to be used for the allocation of powers and responsibilities, and other related legal issues such as the resolution of disputes and entrenchment.

## Federalism and Devolution

78    In a federal system the essentials of the relationship between federal government and the states or provinces are set down in a basic constitutional document distributing powers and responsibilities within the federation between the different levels of government. In most such federal constitutions the balance between the central and local parliaments cannot be altered unilaterally by either party. Instead there is a mechanism specified for the amendment of the constitution which requires a high degree of consensus in favour of change. Beyond that, all constitutions in practice change over time as political circumstances change or as judges reflect such changes in their interpretation of the founding document.

79    It would be possible to introduce a 'federal settlement' if it were embodied in a written constitution within the United Kingdom. The Institute for Public Policy Research's *Constitution of the United Kingdom* (1991) proposed a model. But such an all round settlement is not on the practical political agenda at present and cannot provide a sensible model for the establishment of a Scottish Parliament in advance of similar developments elsewhere in the United Kingdom.

80    In recognition of this, some have proposed a 'constitutional settlement' between the United Kingdom and Scotland alone, confined to those two parties. The Home Rule (Scotland) Bill introduced by Menzies Campbell in 1995 effectively sought to establish by Act of the Westminster Parliament a Scottish Constitution, amendable only by the Scottish Parliament (subject to a two thirds majority and a referendum). Another proposal brought forward in 1991 was for a Constitutional Provisions Bill which would have established a new category of 'constitutional' legislation subject to special conditions relating to its amendment and repeal.[43] Any subsequent Act of the Westminster Parliament establishing a Parliament in Scotland would have been classed as a 'constitutional' law.

81    All such ingenuities are designed to get around, or at least minimise the effects of, the distinction between devolution and federalism. For a devolved parliament is by definition created by the act of a superior body, devolving some of its own powers and responsibilities to a subordinate one. A consequence is that the Act establishing the Parliament will remain in principle amendable and repealable by the Westminster Parliament.

82    Although the nature of the settlement between Scotland and the UK will undoubtedly be 'constitutional', it cannot under the present system be given any strongly entrenched constitutional status - as it would be under a federal settlement. Some measure of political entrenchment might be feasible, and is discussed below. But short of a written constitutional settlement extending throughout the United Kingdom and thus explicitly superseding the

existing constitutional position (including the sovereignty of the Crown in Parliament), a devolved Scottish Parliament will have to be established by an ordinary Act of the UK Parliament. Working from that starting point, the rest of this chapter examines how best to use that vehicle to establish a lasting and workable constitutional settlement.

## The Scotland Act: Transfer of Powers

83  The provisions for the transfer of powers and responsibilities, the allocation of legislative and executive competence, between the Scottish and Westminster Parliaments, will be a key part of the legislation. Although there are infinite refinements and variations possible in how this allocation is expressed, in both federal and devolved systems, all conform to one or other of two basic patterns:
   - the central authority devolves to the local or subordinate authority all of its powers save for those which it specifically reserves to itself (usually including the power subsequently to reserve other specific matters).
   - the central authority devolves to the local or subordinate authority only certain specified areas of legislative and executive competence, with the implication that all other matters remain reserved to the centre.

84  Examples of both models abound. The US constitution might be seen as an example of the first, in that it specifies only the powers of the federal government. 'Residuary powers', those not otherwise specified, belong to the states. The Canadian constitution adopts the opposite model, with provincial powers specified and residuary powers falling to the federal government. Both examples exist too in the context of devolution within the United Kingdom. The Government of Ireland Act 1920 adopted the first approach; the Scotland Act 1978 adopted the second. Which model is best suited for the establishment of a Scottish Parliament in the future?

### The 1978 Scotland Act

85  The 1978 Act specified in great detail the legislative and executive competences devolved from Westminster. Schedule 10 to the Act is split into three lists: Part I lists the legislative powers devolved under a number of general headings; Part II lists specific exceptions (reserved powers) within these general areas; and for the sake of maximum clarity Part III analyses a number of existing statutes in which the application of the lists in Parts I and II might still be unclear. In addition, Schedule 11 lists areas where executive competence is devolved but not the power to legislate e.g. the power to administer the Race Relations Act but not to change the Act itself.

86  It is tempting to use these schedules as a starting point this time round. But there are strong arguments against:

   - in striving for clarity, the 1978 Act was too detailed for its own good: by basing the division of powers so firmly on reference to existing statutes the Act would have required frequent up-dating to reflect new and amended legislation. The Scottish Office already had a long list of such consequential amendments accumulated during the passage of the Act itself, for which time would have had to be found in the next parliamentary session.

- the schedules were still open to different interpretations. Specifying the devolved powers in such detail still left a large grey area where the right of the Scottish Assembly to legislate might be called in question. In those cases it would have been up to the courts to decide whether to give a broad or a narrow interpretation to the description of a devolved power e.g. 'control of pollution', listed as one of the groups of devolved matters. The Scottish Assembly would have had to point to the specific head of power under which it proposed to legislate in all cases. It is interesting to note, in that context, that the SCC's proposals suggest the Scottish Parliament should enact Freedom of Information legislation, yet it is not clear from the Appendix of transferred responsibilities whether in fact the Parliament could point to any power under which it had the right to do so.

- under the 1978 Act the Assembly was potentially open to challenge in many such cases, for the wording of the Act could never be absolutely clear. Vernon Bogdanor quotes a judgement of Lord Watson in the context of the 1920 Government of Ireland Act: "The world is not big enough to hold the book which would have to be written to contain a precise and exact enumeration of all the things relating to the complexity of human affairs which you meant or did not mean to hand over to any legislative assembly".[44]

- the Act was very difficult to understand. Because of the detailed listing of statutes and provisions, it is impossible from a reading of the Act alone to gain any clear idea of what precisely is devolved, still less any sense of the principles governing whether matters are devolved or not. As Neil MacCormick observed at the time of its enactment: "One fears that only lawyers and Civil Servants, but by no means all of them, will be able to work out or give reliable advice on the full meaning of the affirmations as qualified by the negations. Beyond doubt, this complexity and difficulty of comprehension is a defect of the Act. It infringes the principle of intelligibility of law, a principle most to be prized in constitutional enactments".[45]

- The Council of the Law Society of Scotland feared that the form of the legislation would have made adjudicating disputes about the Assembly's competence more difficult: "[It is difficult to] trace any discernible principle or rationale upon which the subjects to be devolved have been selected.... This will cause difficulty to the Judicial Committee of the Privy Council, or any other court, in attempting to provide a corpus of consistent rulings on the legislative competence of the Assembly".

### The Government of Ireland Act 1920

87 The Government of Ireland Act 1920, which established the Northern Ireland Parliament at Stormont, adopts the alternative approach of listing not devolved but reserved powers. Section 4 of the Act provides that:

> *Subject to the provisions of this Act...the parliament of Northern Ireland shall....have power to make laws for the peace, order and good government of Northern Ireland with the following limitations, namely...*
> 1. *The Crown...*
> 2. *The making of peace or war...*
> 3. *The navy, the army, the air force...*
> 4. *Treaties, or any relations with foreign states...*
> 5. *Dignities or titles of honour...*

6. *Treason...*

7. *Trade with any place out of the part of Ireland within their jurisdiction...*

8. *Submarine cables...*

9. *Wireless telegraphy...*

10. *Aerial navigation...*

11. *Lighthouses, buoys or beacons...*

12. *Coinage...*

13. *Trade marks...*

14. *Any matter which by this Act is declared to be a reserved matter, so long as it remains reserved...."*

There are a number of appealing features in this approach, outlined in the following paragraphs.

88    Listing reserved rather than enumerating devolved powers would provide a single, comprehensible constitutional document which should make clear to the people of Scotland (and the rest of the United Kingdom) precisely how the system by which they are governed is to change under devolution. This is a point of paramount importance if the settlement is to gain the popular acceptance, support and allegiance which it requires to endure. The absence of **clarity** was the biggest failing of the 1978 Act.

89    There might be a **smaller likelihood of litigation** arising under the Act. For the most part the Parliament would not have to point to a specific power in the Act to establish its competence to legislate in that area before proceeding. It would also be open to Westminster, when legislating on a matter of uncertain application to Scotland, to include specific clarification of the Scottish Parliament's powers in the Act in question. This device, uniquely available in a devolved (as opposed to a federal) system, was a regular feature of the operation of the 1920 Act which helped to reduce the likelihood of conflicts over the competence of the devolved Parliament. Harry Calvert's study of the operation of the Act describes this process as "greasing the 1920 mechanism so as to make it work more smoothly in discharging [tasks] imposed upon it [many years] later".[46]

90    The 1920 Act came into force and remained in operation for over fifty years. There is thus a **body of case law** developed under the Act (admittedly not an extensive body) which itself draws on jurisprudence stemming from cases heard by the Judicial Committee of the Privy Council over a longer period e.g. concerning relations between central and state authorities in the United Kingdom Dominions. This will provide some guidance to the operation of a Scotland Act on this model in practice.

91    Whilst it might in theory be just as difficult to draw up the reserved as the devolved list, the **onus of proof in Whitehall would be critically reversed.** As described in chapter 2, in the 1970s it was generally left to the Constitution Unit to support the Scottish Office's case for adding items to the devolved list. Other departments simply had to react to those proposals. If, however, the starting point were a list of reserved powers, the onus would be on each department to justify any proposals to change the list. This might lead to a quicker and more satisfactory process.

92    Either model, if properly applied, should be capable of displaying on the face of the Act the principle(s) on which the division of powers is based. But in practice these principles are more likely to relate to reservation than devolution e.g. the need to comply with UK international

obligations, observance of human rights, maintenance of minimum standards of democracy, demands of equity throughout the UK. The expression of such principles is therefore likely to be easier under the 1920 model, and would assist the courts in reaching predictable and consistent decisions.

## The Choice?

93    The choice between these two models is obviously crucial. The 1920 model was considered in the 1970s but rejected by the Government, largely because the Royal Commission had recommended against it. Kilbrandon decided that "the better method would be to list the powers transferred...with as much precision as possible" for the following reasons:[47]
- it was thought this would provide 'the greatest clarity and precision'.
- it was assumed that although the 1920 Act had worked well in Northern Ireland, other parts of the UK would not be so ready to "reach accommodation with the UK Government on matters which might become the subject of dispute" (hence the need for a carefully specified allocation of powers).
- the fact that 'new matters arising' would fall to the devolved Assembly under the 1920 model and that an increasing range of areas were the subject of European Community and other international obligations both suggested "caution in the selection of matters to be transferred and a preference for the transfer of prescribed matters only", lest Westminster had to spend too much time in the politically difficult task of legislating to take back control of powers originally devolved.

94    All three points can be contested, although the second makes a valid distinction between the political circumstances governing the Northern Ireland/UK and the Scotland/UK relationships. The Scottish Law Commission took issue with all three in its Memorandum to the Lord Advocate of 27 May 1975[48] in response to the September White Paper as follows:
- if a wide series of powers were transferred then specifying them all would be more likely to lead to arguments about the precise scope of the devolved functions than would a shorter enumeration of powers retained.
- the fact that devolution to Northern Ireland worked smoothly was partly a function of the political relationship with the UK (any devolution Act would require cooperation and a desire to make the system work). But it might also have been a consequence of specifying the retained rather than the devolved powers, the fact that the devolved powers were extensive, and the fact that the UK Government was circumspect about using its power to intervene in the devolved areas even though it was permitted to do so.
- although the third point had some force, it was again true of any system of legislative devolution that problems specific to the European Community would arise. They were no less tractable under the 1920 model. As for 'new functions', these would hardly arise so frequently as to cause the Government any embarrassment (and, they might have added, the legislation could include provision for their reservation if necessary when they did).

95    The Law Commission came down strongly against the method adopted by the Government. It noted that it would be impossible for the draftsmen to specify the devolved areas without at the same time specifying exceptions to them: "*any* purported system of specification of devolved powers turns out in practice to be a system of specification both of devolved and reserved powers" and thus a recipe for confusion. By contrast an Act on the 1920 model "would contain no lengthy list of debatable powers. This would reduce the risk of conflicts between the United

Kingdom Parliament and a Scottish Assembly and the difficulties of construing the precise scope of the devolved and retained powers". The Commission concluded:

> *"It is of central importance to select the best method of ensuring legal clarity on the scope of devolution. This...can in our opinion be best achieved, and probably only achieved, by specifying the powers to be retained by the United Kingdom government and, subject to the reservation of ultimate sovereignty to parliament, conferring upon the Assembly residual legislative competence'.*[49]

96    The Constitution Unit strongly backs that judgement today.  It is difficult to find anyone involved in the exercise in the 1970s who would dissent. It may be true that a statute framed on the lines of the 1978 Act could win the approval of Parliament, as it has done before.  But it cannot be assumed that the exhaustive process of scouring the statute books in Whitehall committee rooms will take any less time today given the volume of legislation and the magnitude of other material changes in the way we are governed which have occurred since 1979.  Legislation based on specifying the powers retained would be quicker to draft, easier to understand, more workable in practice, technically more robust and more durable.

97    There is one final point.  It is a political one.  It is widely assumed that specifying the powers retained must imply a more generous approach to devolution.  Certainly part of the case for 'precision' in the 1970s was the desire on the Government's part to know exactly what they were devolving.  But the 1978 Act encapsulates a devolution settlement reached in rather grudging circumstances.  The list of retained functions might well have been as long and complex as the list of those devolved.  The method is neutral: it will not determine the generosity or otherwise of the policy.

98    The debate in Scotland has naturally fallen into a 1978 framework: the Scots have inevitably focused on what it is that the Scottish Parliament should be able to do.  That and the experience of the 1978 Act have influenced policy-makers south of the border to think in the same terms.  Added to which, there is an assumption that the 1920 model by its very nature produces a more generous, less circumscribed settlement which would not be politically acceptable to the House of Commons.[50]  Nobody will know the truth of this assumption until it is tested.  But it is an assumption.  It might turn out that Westminster responds more naturally to debating a list of reserved powers, given that these are the ones which Westminster MPs will retain to exercise themselves.

### Flexibility – 'Shared' or 'Concurrent' Powers

99    The choice set out above has over-simplified the options in order to highlight the two basic frameworks within which the devolution legislation might be drafted.  In reality either model is capable of considerable modification.  The Government of Ireland Act 1920 model, for example, was modified substantially in designing its successor, the Northern Ireland Constitution Act 1973.  Having established the case for listing the retained powers, there are still desirable modifications to that basic framework which could provide a more workable Act.

100   Both models of legislation suggest a firm dividing line between devolved and reserved powers.  But in practice there will always be a grey area in which it is not clear whether the Scottish Parliament is legislating in a reserved area or not, or circumstances in which the sovereign Westminster Parliament feels a need to act in a devolved area in the interests of the United

Kingdom as a whole e.g. to fulfil an international obligation. As noted in paragraph 89 above, the question of extension to Scotland will arise in connection with all new UK legislation, some of which might take the opportunity to clarify areas of doubt about legislative competence. The SCC's report suggests in effect a third category of powers falling in the grey area, in that the Scottish Parliament should have *"sole or shared* responsibility for all functions except those retained to the UK Parliament" (emphasis added).

101 A number of federal constitutions do deal with this need for flexibility by recourse to a list of 'shared' or 'concurrent' powers. These are areas in which both the states and the federal government can legislate, each to achieve either a national or a regional purpose. Two principles generally underlie this 'sharing' of legislative competence: federal legislation trumps state legislation *(Bundesrecht bricht Landesrecht);* and, as in Australia, the federal government may legislate in such a way as to 'occupy the field' and thus change a 'shared' power into a reserved one.

102 In contemplating devolution within the United Kingdom, the concept of 'shared' powers is really a misnomer. The doctrine of the sovereignty of the Westminster Parliament means that in effect, even following devolution, all the devolved powers remain 'shared' in the sense that Westminster retains the right to legislate in those areas if necessary. That point was made explicit in the Government of Ireland Act 1920, Section 75:

> *"Notwithstanding the establishment of the parliament of Northern Ireland....or of anything contained in this Act, the supreme authority of the Parliament of the United Kingdom shall remain unaffected and undiminished over all persons, matters and things in Northern Ireland and every part thereof".*

103 The same will be true of the devolution legislation for Scotland, whether a clause on the lines of the above is included or not.[51] In fact this is a helpful feature in designing the legislation. In a rigid federal system the limits on legislative and executive competence make it generally impossible to cross the demarcation lines without establishing a third category of concurrent powers - and the courts are the mechanism for resolving questions of disputed competence. A devolved system in the UK can avoid that rigidity, since Parliament remains the ultimate source of authority.

104 The devolution legislation should use this flexibility to allow for a blurring of the strict division between retained and devolved powers in certain circumstances. Both Edinburgh and Westminster need to be able to operate across the powers dividing line without it resulting in political crisis or litigation. That means constraining Westminster's right to legislate at will in the devolved fields; and providing a mechanism to allow Edinburgh to operate on reserved territory under certain circumstances.

## Westminster's Flexibility

105 The Westminster Parliament might need to trench on Scotland's legislative competences in order to fulfil an international obligation or treaty commitment which touches on a devolved subject; or in order to ensure that legislation on a certain matter is uniform across the UK; or - a special case involving both points, discussed in detail in paragraphs 114 to 119 below - in order to implement EC legislation. By contrast, there might well arise circumstances in which Scotland wishes to enjoy the benefits of a specific piece of legislation under consideration at Westminster,

or is content for a certain issue to be legislated for uniformly across the UK. The Scottish Parliament might then request that Westminster should legislate for Scotland too, even though the matter has been devolved. This last circumstance could turn out to be quite common in practice when policies are not divergent and it makes no sense to use up legislative time in both chambers.

106 Provisions will need to be incorporated in the devolution legislation to acknowledge the possibility of trenching on powers in both directions. But these cannot be drafted in a way which is inconsistent with the basic proposition that the Westminster Parliament has full sovereign powers. For Westminster's flexibility it might be best to include a clause explicitly recognising Parliament's powers to legislate in stated circumstances despite the fact that the matter has been devolved. The following might be considered:

*(1) A provision of this Act placing a matter within the legislative competence of the Scottish Parliament does not affect the authority of Parliament to make provision, by Act of Parliament, in respect of that matter, and in particular for any of the following purposes:*

*(a) for the purpose of implementing an agreement, convention or treaty between the United Kingdom and another country or countries or giving effect to a decision of an international organisation of which the United Kingdom is a member; or*

*(b) for the purpose of implementing a European Community obligation of the United Kingdom or enabling a right enjoyed by the United Kingdom under the European Community treaties to be exercised or dealing with matters arising out of or related to any such obligation or rights; or*

*(c) for the purpose of giving effect to a request of the Scottish Parliament.*

*(2) An Act of Parliament with respect to a matter within the legislative competence of the Scottish Parliament which contains a provision declaring that it is enacted for any of the purposes set out in paragraphs (a) to (c) of subsection (1) does not come into force in Scotland until ratified by the Scottish Parliament.*

*(3) An Act of Parliament referred to in subsection (1) may be amended or repealed by an Act enacted by the Scottish Parliament.*

107 It is worth noting two features of these clauses. First, section (1)(b) deals with European Community matters: these are discussed at greater length below (the term Community is preferred to Union in this draft since the Community's legal order is a product of the first, 'Community', pillar of a 'Union' which embraces intergovernmental cooperation in two other pillars as well).

108 Second, the 1920 Act prohibited Stormont from legislating to repeal or amend post-devolution Westminster legislation, although it was common to negative that in particular Westminster Acts dealing with devolved matters. The 1978 Act adopted the opposite approach, allowing a general power to amend or repeal post-devolution Acts, but on the understanding that Parliament might restrict that power in specific cases. These clauses adopt the second approach.

## Edinburgh's Flexibility

109 It will be equally necessary to provide for flexibility the other way - for Edinburgh to borrow Westminster's reserved powers in certain circumstances. The purpose would be to attain legislative clarity or coherence in Scots law: no legislation enacted by the Scottish Parliament would apply outside Scotland, even where it trenched on a retained matter.

110 A model for this kind of provision exists in the Northern Ireland Constitution Act 1973. Experience of operating the 1920 Act had shown that some flexibility needed to be built in to allow such encroachment, which otherwise would require legislation at Westminster to create the space for what was usually only a minor and unavoidable technical incursion into a reserved area. The 1978 Bill was introduced with a clause matching the 1973 Northern Ireland legislation, but this was amended in the Lords to constrain the capacity for trenching on the reserved areas further. The section of the 1978 Act (Schedule 2, paragraph 8) reads:

> 8. *Paragraph 1 [defining the legislative competence of the Assembly] does not prevent a provision from being within the legislative competence of the Assembly if it is merely incidental to or consequential on other provisions and those other provisions are within that competence.*

111 The judgement about whether a clause was incidental or consequential would be made in the first instance by the Secretary of State, through his power to vet all Assembly Acts, and ultimately by the courts.

112 The analogous provision in the Northern Ireland Constitution Act 1973 makes the role of the Secretary of State more explicit, and leaves a greater margin for authorised trenching on the reserved areas:

> 5 (1) *The consent of the Secretary of State shall be required in accordance with this section in relation to a proposed Measure which contains any provision dealing with a...reserved matter; and the Secretary of State shall not give his consent...unless he considers that the provision is ancillary to other provisions (whether in that Measure or previously enacted) dealing with reserved matters...*

> 5(7) *For the purposes of this section a provision is ancillary to other provisions if it is a provision which is necessary or expedient for making those other provisions effective or which provides for the enforcement of those other provisions or which is otherwise incidental to, or consequential on, those provisions.*

113 The Scotland Act might incorporate a provision along these lines, but perhaps subjecting the decision of the Secretary of State to parliamentary scrutiny (the laying of the clause in question before Parliament allowing a period of, say, twenty days for the tabling of a motion rejecting the Secretary of State's decision to allow it) in order to reassure Westminster that the limited flexibility in the division of powers is not open to abuse. If the Scottish Parliament chooses to go ahead with such legislation following a rejection of its request, or indeed without having sought the Secretary of State's permission to encroach at all, then it will be for the courts to decide whether they have acted *ultra vires* or not.

## European Legislation

114    The volume and scope of EC legislation either directly applicable or requiring implementation in this country is one of the major developments in the legal context since the 1978 Act. That Act simply sought to ensure that all Scottish legislation should be 'compatible with Community obligations or any other international obligations of the United Kingdom' and gave the Secretary of State the right to strike down any legislation (or any executive act) which failed to satisfy that criterion. But the overlap now between the powers likely to be devolved to Edinburgh and the legislative competences already granted to the European Community is striking - environment, training, public health, transport etc - and may yet grow in the light of the 1996 IGC.

115    Some means will need to be found to deal with the situation that in many cases the United Kingdom, as the member state of the EU, will be negotiating and voting into force EC legislation in areas which have been formally devolved to the legislative competence of the Scottish Parliament. This might mean the conclusion of an intergovernmental agreement between the two Governments embodying principles for information, consultation and dispute resolution in arriving at a common UK negotiating position on these subjects. The content of such an agreement is discussed in Chapter 6 on Scotland's relations with the EU. The substance of the agreement need not go in the Scotland Act itself, although some reference to the need for consultation at least might help to ensure that the UK Government adhered to any agreement in practice.

116    Whilst consultation will be doubly important where regulations are involved (since they have direct effect throughout the UK), it is in the implementation of directives that questions of flexibility in the division of powers arise. Within its devolved powers, the Scottish Parliament will need to have the option of legislating itself for the implementation of an EC directive. That legislation, and all other legislation of the Parliament, will have to conform to Community law. In some cases the Scottish Parliament might deem it better to accept UK-wide legislation from Westminster to implement a directive. On the other hand, the UK Parliament will have to reserve the right to legislate in common for all parts of the UK where it is necessary in order to conform with EC obligations and it judges it desirable to do so by uniform legislation. These circumstances are covered by draft section (1)(b) in paragraph 106 above.

117    In the area of European Community law the Act will also need to recognise that it is the UK as the member state which enters into Community obligations and which is therefore liable in European law for any failure to comply. It will be necessary to make absolutely clear which of the two Governments is liable for such failure if both are given the option of giving it effect in Scottish law. In practice liability might be assumed to lie with the Scottish Executive where the obligation does not fall within a reserved area, unless they had specifically requested that the UK Government give effect to the obligation in Scotland on their behalf.

118    Ultimately the Westminster Parliament will have the power to legislate to give effect to an obligation in Scotland at any time, even in the absence of a specific request to do so. A clause might be included in the legislation effectively to give the Scottish Parliament a period of grace of a year to implement an obligation for itself before Westminster intervenes. The clause, again making clear where liability for inaction lies, might be on the following lines:

*(1) If Parliament legislates to give effect to an EC obligation in Scotland, in the absence of legislation of the Scottish Parliament giving full effect to that obligation as part of Scottish law, more than one year after the obligation has arisen, then any financial liability of the United Kingdom Government arising out of that failure is transferred to the Scottish Executive.*

119   It should be noted that obligations under other international treaties and conventions, for example the European Convention on Human Rights, might likewise give rise to questions of liability.

## Executive Powers

120   The 1978 Act specified in its Schedule 11 a number of statutes under which the Scottish Executive would have had executive powers but no legislative power to amend the statutes in question.   In addition it drew on precedents in the Government of Ireland Act 1920 and Northern Ireland Constitution Act 1973 (sections 63 and 11 respectively) to permit the Scottish Executive to enter into agency arrangements with the UK Government 'and any public or local authority or public corporation' such that either authority could provide services or perform functions for the other.

121   The approach in 1978 was driven by a desire to devolve as much as possible in as specific terms as possible.   Hence even where responsibility for an Act could not be devolved, the scope for devolution of its administration was considered.   This seems an over elaborate approach, especially in the context of an Act which specifies only the legislative competences retained.   A neater solution, incorporating the possibility of agency arrangements and suitable financial arrangements to cover them, might be drafted on the following lines:

*(1) The executive authority of the Scottish Executive extends to:*
*(a) all matters within the legislative competence of the Scottish Parliament; and*
*(b) such other matters in respect of which executive functions are conferred upon the Scottish Executive by or under Act of Parliament.*

*(2) Where any function referred to in subsection (1)(b) is conferred on the Scottish Executive the UK Government shall make such payments as may be agreed with the Scottish Executive for the discharge of those functions.*

*(3) Arrangements may be made between the Scottish Executive and any department of the UK Government and any public or local authority or public corporation for any functions of one of them to be discharged by the other, and for the provision by one of them for the other of administrative, professional or technical services, and such arrangements may provide for the making of payments in respect of any costs incurred under those arrangements.*

*(4) No such arrangements for the discharge of any functions shall affect the responsibility of the authority on whose behalf the functions are discharged.*

## Resolution of Disputes

122 However well the legislation is drafted, where legislative and administrative power is divided between two centres it is inevitable that, at some stage, there will be an argument that one or other of the legislatures/administrations has exceeded, or plans to exceed, its powers.

123 For the most part potential disputes will be identified at an early stage and resolved through consultation between the two Governments. Chapter 7 suggests the types of 'interlocking machinery' at both official and Ministerial level which will be required to allow such consultation and exchange to take place as a matter of course. This is how the Government of Ireland Act 1920 was implemented in practice. There was much coming and going with a view to reaching agreed positions about the interpretation of the legislation. These interpretations were often then reflected in legislative provisions (usually in Westminster Acts) clarifying the point in order to settle potential difficulties.

124 Even so, in the last resort it may be necessary to resolve disputes about the *vires* or competence of the devolved authorities in consequence of devolution through the courts. There are two likely circumstances in which this kind of dispute might arise:
- an outright challenge to a piece of legislation or an administrative act in whole or in part.
- in the course of litigation between non-Government litigants, or in the course of a prosecution, reliance may be placed upon a legislative or administrative act which one or more parties wish to challenge as being invalid.

### Pre-enactment Test of Vires?

125 The 1978 Act accepted that the courts could rule on devolution issues as on any other matters of law. But it also included two different mechanisms for remitting a devolution issue to the Judicial Committee of the Privy Council on appeal. Where such an issue arose in the course of other proceedings (i.e. it had not arisen as a devolution issue alone) then that issue would be referred to the appropriate higher court, from whose judgement appeal would lie to the Privy Council. Otherwise, there was also provision for the Secretary of State to refer a proposed Scottish Act to the Privy Council in advance of enactment where he, or his advisers, thought the vires of the proposed legislation were in doubt. If the Privy Council ruled that the proposed Act, or any part of it, was *ultra vires* then it would not be given approval by the Queen in Council (Royal Assent) and would be returned to the Assembly. The Secretary of State could also prevent a bill receiving assent if he thought it incompatible with European Community or other international obligations *without* reference to the Privy Council.

126 The 1978 Act has been criticised for effectively leaving all Acts of the Scottish Assembly open to challenge as to their validity. Under these provisions, as Vernon Bogdanor noted, "an Act of the Scottish Assembly will be law only insofar as a court has ruled that it is valid, or if it has not yet been challenged".[52] Subsequent versions of a Scotland Act have attempted to eliminate this uncertainty.

127 The 1987 Scotland Bill introduced at Westminster by Donald Dewar, for example, provided that if the Secretary of State had not referred a proposed Act to the Privy Council, or if the Westminster Parliament had not agreed his recommendation that a proposed Act should be referred, or if the Privy Council had opined that the Act was *intra vires*, then no further

challenge to its validity would be admissible. Hence Section 2(5) of Dewar's Bill states: "The validity of any Scottish Assembly Act shall not be called in question in any legal proceedings". The 1991 draft Scottish Parliament Bill (to be enacted following a Constitutional Provisions Act: see paragraph 80 above) went one step further in referring *all* proposed Scottish legislation to the Privy Council to test the **vires** in advance of enactment, again with that test being binding in any subsequent legal proceedings.

128   The force of these provisions lies in the argument that, since Acts of Parliament with effect in Scotland are not subject to challenge on *vires* grounds today, nor should they be when enacted instead by a Scottish Parliament with authority from Westminster. Whilst it is legitimate for Westminster to have a say in whether the Parliament has correctly interpreted the extent of its delegated authority (with the Privy Council called upon to ensure this is a legal rather than a political interpretation), it should not be open to others to question the validity of legislation in a way that is not available to them now.

129   There is some force in this point in the emphasis that it puts on the interest the Westminster Parliament will have in ensuring that the devolution legislation they enact is not infringed. That argues, perhaps, for a special fast-track procedure for judicial challenge of a Scottish Act by the UK Government (in practice the Secretary of State on behalf of Westminster). That would operate as a last resort where some difficulty between the two Governments could not be resolved by other means.

130   But it would be wrong to limit the right of direct challenge to Governments. It might be equally clear to an individual, company or interest group that a specific Act which threatened their interest went beyond the delegated authority vested in the Scottish Parliament. They too should have the right to mount a direct challenge to an Act's validity under the devolution legislation if the UK Government opts not to do so. Doubtless the interest group in question would first seek to stimulate a UK Government challenge. But if none were forthcoming it should remain possible for others to establish the *locus standi* to act, after the time limit for the Government's fast-track procedure has expired.

131   The attempts to limit challenges to the validity of Scottish Acts contained in the bills mentioned above surely go too far in allowing only one opportunity to rule on an Act's validity for all time; and the mechanisms suggested would be unworkable, and possibly unjust, within the British legal tradition. However far-sighted the judges might be, they could never envisage all the possible circumstances in which the validity of a Scottish Act or any of its provisions might be called into question in a real case. It would be a novel experience for British judges to rule definitively on the validity of a piece of legislation in the absence of particular circumstances, yet in the knowledge that specific cases might subsequently arise.

132   Lord Haldane summed up the difficulty in a 1914 case (AG BC v AG Canada [1914], AC 153 at 162): "Not only may the questions of future litigants be prejudiced by the court laying down principles in abstract form without any reference or relation to actual facts, but it may turn out to be practically impossible to define a principle adequately and safely without ascertainment of the exact facts to which it is to be applied".

133   These factors argue for a system in which direct application to the final court of appeal for a ruling on the validity of an Act should be available to Governments immediately following the

passage of an Act through the Scottish Parliament; that this right should be extended to other parties who can establish a *locus standi* once the period for immediate governmental challenge has expired; but that in neither case should this rule out subsequent questioning of the *vires* of that legislation in specific cases. Thus, where a devolution issue arises following implementation of a Scottish Act, or in the course of other proceedings, a mechanism is required for the court hearing the case to get an opinion on the devolution issue quickly - if it needs one. There also needs to be an appeals process.

## The Mechanisms for Testing Vires

134 The procedures in the new Scotland Act for ensuring that the Scottish Parliament only acts within its legislative competence, and for arbitrating disputes where this is in doubt, might include the following elements:

- **before presentation of the bill**: in the case of bills presented by the Scottish Executive and others where the sponsors have been given drafting assistance, the bills' vires will have been checked by the sponsoring department, Government lawyers, the Parliamentary Draftsmen, and perhaps the Scottish Law Officer.

- **after presentation of the bill**: it might fall to the Presiding Officer (Speaker) to take a view on whether *prima facie* the bill is within the Parliament's jurisdiction or not, or to refer it to a Scrutiny Committee of the Parliament in cases of doubt. The Northern Ireland Constitution Act 1973 provided for the Clerk to the Assembly to consider the matter of *vires* both on introduction and again before completion of the legislative process (sections 5(2) and (3)). "This would represent merely an internal measure of restraint on the part of one of the Assembly's own organs, but there is no reason to think that it would not be an effective device for constitutional control".[53]

- **after royal assent but before entry into force**: a fast-track procedure allowing for the Law Officers of either the Scottish or United Kingdom Governments to refer a devolution issue they think arises out of any Scottish Act or any provision of a Scottish Act straight to the final court of appeal for an opinion. This would cater for direct constitutional challenges of principle which will require speedy clarification on enactment. There would need to be a time limit during which this procedure could be invoked - perhaps a maximum of one month, except in cases of urgency. Scottish Acts would have to be framed with this provision in mind. It would be open to the Scottish authorities to implement the Act in any case if they so wished, even if a challenge were pending.

- **following entry into force**: the right for others to mount a direct challenge once the Act is in force. Also a provision, analogous to the Article 177 reference procedure where questions of EC law arise, to the effect that if at any point, in any litigation in any court in the United Kingdom a devolution issue arises, it may be instantly referred to the final court of appeal for an opinion. This would be an advisory opinion, as is the case with Article 177 references. Like any opinion of principle given under the procedure described in the preceding paragraph, it will be binding as an interpretation of the point of law put to the court, but it will remain for the lower court then to reach its own judgement taking that interpretation into account. It will of course be open to the lower courts to decide the matter without a reference, for example if the case were clear-cut, or covered by an existing advisory opinion.

● **at all stages:** a provision to ensure that in the event of any such reference the Law Officers of both the Scottish and United Kingdom Governments will be informed immediately and will have leave to intervene in the proceedings (by analogy, for example, with the provision in the Crown Proceedings Act 1947).

## The Final Court of Appeal

135 Within a federal constitution disputes about the *vires* of legislation would be remitted to the constitutional court empowered to decide questions relating to the constitutional settlement. In the long term the case for such a court in the United Kingdom may become stronger. But there is no appetite for establishing one immediately. Disputes arising out of the application of the Scotland Act will therefore need to be resolved within the existing court system, but in a way that does not prejudice the emergence of a constitutional court in due course.

136 In Scotland appeals in civil cases lie from the Inner House of the Court of Session to the House of Lords. In criminal matters there is no appeal from a decision of the Appeal Court of the High Court of Justiciary. In England, the House of Lords is the ultimate court of appeal for both civil and criminal matters. The Scotland Act 1978 provided for 'devolution issues' to be referred to the Inner House of the Court of Session on civil matters and the High Court of Justiciary on criminal matters with a right of appeal in each case to the Judicial Committee of the Privy Council. In effect the only other option within the existing system would have been the Appellate Committee of the House of Lords ('the House of Lords'). Which court should be the final court of appeal?

137 This is a nice question. In practice the House of Lords and the Privy Council comprise mostly the same personnel, although in theory the composition of the Judicial Committee is both wider and larger. In its judicial capacity the House of Lords comprises the Lord Chancellor and twelve Lords of Appeal in Ordinary who may be supplemented by former Lord Chancellors, retired Lords of Appeal and any other peers who have held high judicial office. By convention, two of the Law Lords are Scottish, but no special recognition is given to judges with Welsh or Northern Irish connections. The Privy Council has no permanent judiciary of its own. It draws upon a panel of persons appointed as Privy Councillors who currently hold or have held high judicial office in the UK (and a small number of senior judges from Commonwealth countries from which appeals still lie). In practice, however, the Judicial Committee is usually made up from the twelve Lords of Appeal in Ordinary.

138 The question is really whether or not devolution issues should be dealt with in the course of standard legal procedures, in which case the House of Lords would come in as the final court of appeal. There are good reasons for not departing from standard practice. If final responsibility for ruling on devolution issues were given to the Privy Council, then the position could arise in which a devolution issue came up in the House of Lords in the course of other proceedings. The Lords would then need to decide whether to refer it to the Privy Council. Given that the panel of judges in either event would be drawn from the twelve Law Lords, the court would in effect be referring the issue for final adjudication to those Law Lords who were not selected to hear it in the first instance.

139 Apart from this practical problem, there is also the theoretical risk that some dispute would arise between the two courts as to which had ultimate jurisdiction. The 1978 Scotland Act required that a devolution issue should be referred from the House of Lords to the Privy Council "unless the House considers it more appropriate, having regard to all the circumstances, that they should determine the issue" (Schedule 12, paragraph 24).

140 Against these arguments is the fact that the Privy Council enjoys the weight of precedent as a final court of appeal for devolution issues. For nearly a century it heard appeals on jurisdictional disputes between the federal and provincial governments in Canada, and it was the final court of appeal for the determination of constitutional issues under the Government of Ireland Act 1920. The 1978 Act followed this precedent.

141 But the judicial role of the Privy Council is in decline, and the time may not be so far off when it comes to an end altogether. Appeals will no longer lie from Hong Kong after 1997, and New Zealand may follow. There is also some dissatisfaction with appeals arising from the Carribean countries. Giving the Judicial Committee a role in devolution issues would breathe fresh life into it. On balance therefore it seems more sensible to avoid the risk of conflict at the top of the judicial hierarchy, to accept the decline of the judicial role of the Privy Council, and to leave the House of Lords as the final court of appeal for devolution issues. The convention by which two Scottish Law Lords invariably sit on appeals emanating from Scotland should continue.

## Entrenchment

142 It is a consequence of the constitutional framework in which the Scotland Act establishing a Parliament will have to take its place, described at the beginning of this chapter, that procedural entrenchment of legislation is problematic. Volumes have been written on the subject, but the point comes down to whether Parliament may bind its successors by:
- preventing its successors from enacting certain legislation at all e.g. repeal of the Scotland Act.
- requiring Parliament to follow a special procedure in subsequent legislation that amends earlier legislation.
- requiring Parliament to use a special form of words if it is going to repeal earlier legislation (normally the rule is that a later Act of Parliament impliedly repeals earlier Acts to the extent of the inconsistency).

143 In practice the first of these options would not be acceptable to the sovereign Westminster Parliament. But the other two might be. A version of the second option was included in the Northern Ireland Constitution Act 1973 (section 1). This stated that "in no event will Northern Ireland...cease to be part of...the United Kingdom without the consent of the majority of the people of Northern Ireland voting in a poll held for the purposes of this section". It is possible to imagine a similar provision in the Scotland Act requiring a referendum in advance of any legislation brought forward subsequently to amend or repeal it. Alternatively the Act could prescribe special procedures to be followed by the Westminster Parliament in legislating for amendment. Neither measure could impinge on the right of the Westminster Parliament to decide for itself how it conducts its business or what decisions it might reach.

144 The third option suggests a 'notwithstanding clause' in the Scotland Act. This clause would provide that if a subsequent Act of Parliament were inconsistent with key provisions of the Scotland Act then it should be ineffective, unless it contained express provision that it was to take effect notwithstanding its incompatibility with the Scotland Act. This kind of clause is generally associated with entrenching Bills of Rights where there is no obvious institutional guardian to appeal to outside the legislation itself. It is less useful in the context of devolution where the condition for repeal or amendment might also be expressed in terms of the Scottish people's consent (as in the second option).

145 Finally, it would be possible to include in the legislation a purely declaratory clause. An example is to be found in the Union of Great Britain and Ireland Act 1800, which claimed to "be in force and have effect for ever". Likewise the Acts of Union of 1707 purport in many respects to be effective "for ever after".

146 Any of the clauses suggested above might be ignored in practice. It is possible that the courts would rule action in breach of them invalid in strict legal terms, but unlikely given the over-riding assumption of Westminster's sovereignty. Nor would there be any mechanism for judicial enforcement of such decisions. As Lord Cooper remarked, "it is of little avail to ask whether the Parliament of Great Britain 'can' do this thing or that, without going on to enquire who can stop them if they do" (1953 SC at 412). The declaratory provision in the 1800 Union with Ireland Act did not in practice prevent the creation of the Irish Free State in 1922 by an ordinary Act of Parliament, and in fact every Article and section in the 1800 Act (or the corresponding Act of the Irish Parliament) has by now been repealed or amended.[54]

147 Even so, such declaratory clauses, or other entrenchment provisions as discussed above, can create powerful political inhibitions against change. The Union with Ireland Act proved remarkably durable in practice, remaining effective for over 100 years. Most of the 'unamendable' provisions of the Acts of Union too lasted for centuries before yielding to change. As the 1988 Claim of Right for Scotland (paragraph 2.1) says:

> *"The [Scottish] state was wound up by a Treaty [in 1707] which clearly recognised the nation and its right to distinctive government in a fundamental range of home affairs. The fact that institutional forms, however empty, reflecting these distinctions have been preserved to the present day demonstrates that no-one in British government has dared to suggest openly that the nation no longer exists or that the case for distinctiveness has now disappeared".*

148 Thus, any attempt to entrench the position of the Scottish Parliament would be effective only to the extent that it provides a political (rather than a legal) obstacle to change. But such obstacles might be effective in practice, even in the context of Westminster's sovereignty. It would therefore provide a measure of protection for the Parliament if the Scotland Act contained either a procedural clause on the Northern Ireland Act 1973 model, or a declaratory clause, seeking to constrain Westminster's ability to repeal the Act or to amend it in such a fundamental way that the Parliament's existence was threatened. The constraint might be that the Scottish people themselves should have voted for change in a referendum or a general election.

## Declaration of Westminster

149 The SCC also concluded that "there could, and should, be some way of formally embedding the powers and position of Scotland's Parliament", and that any provision to this effect would have political rather than legal force. They therefore propose a Declaration of the Parliament of the United Kingdom to the effect that the devolution legislation "should not be repealed or amended in such a way as to threaten the existence of Scotland's Parliament, without the consent of the Scottish Parliament and of the people of Scotland, directly consulted through general election or referendum".

150 Like the legislative clauses discussed above, the Declaration will rely on having a deterrent effect, but it makes this more explicitly political. If the Declaration were subsequently ignored and a case brought before the courts it would arguably carry less weight than a statutory clause

would do. But as noted above, neither could have any judicial effect in practice without some means of enforcing a judgement. It may be right to conclude that, given these practical limitations and the issues of principle that *any* entrenchment clause might be thought to raise, Westminster would accept such a clause in the Act only reluctantly and following lengthy debate. The costs of attempting to establish a clause in the Act therefore might be seen to outweigh the marginal gain in terms of effectiveness that it might have over a Westminster Declaration.

## Referendum

151 The arguments for and against the holding of referendums to give greater legitimacy to constitutional change were canvassed in an earlier report from the Constitution Unit, *Delivering Constitutional Reform*. The precedents are inconclusive: there have been referendums in some cases (e.g. on continued membership of the EEC in 1975) but not in others (the Single European Act and the Maastricht Treaty). Whilst a referendum can be a device to secure popular consent for fundamental changes in the political system - and is often explicitly provided for that purpose in written constitutions - it has equally been used in the UK context simply to solve political problems where the normal mechanisms for doing so break down (party splits, sectarian divisions in Northern Ireland etc). The 1979 referendums on devolution were of this sort. Ultimately the decision whether to hold a referendum is a political one in the absence of any constitutional principle.

152 The political case for and against in Scotland is well known. Those against argue that the referendum in 1979 was decisive. They note that opinion polls today show overwhelming support for constitutional change: the 1996 System Three poll puts support for devolution at 51%, with only 21% content with the *status quo*. The general election in Scotland, they claim, will deliver a mandate for change (a stronger argument the closer to the election result the legislation is introduced). And there are serious technical drawbacks to holding a referendum which does not result in a vote influenced by a host of other factors including the question at issue. Those for suggest that the political pressure to hold a referendum will in any event be irresistible, that the general election mandate will not be specific, and that a fundamental change in the way Scotland is governed requires the explicit support of the Scottish people.

153 At a constitutional level, the strongest argument for a referendum might be in the context of entrenchment. The recent work on devolution by the Institute for Public Policy Research puts the case clearly:

> *"A positive referendum result cannot deliver constitutional entrenchment, but it might be seen as a tactical resource in strengthening moral and political entrenchment. [But] if the Scottish Parliament cannot convince the public it is relevant to their lives, entrenchment will neither be possible nor deserved. A convincing vote in favour of devolution through a referendum...would not alter that reality".*[55]

154 There is no doubt that a strong and explicit popular endorsement of the principle of establishing a Scottish Parliament would add to the political inhibitors already mentioned - and should be considered for that effect. But the second IPPR point is equally true. The referendum, whether held in advance of the legislation or following Royal Assent, would take place before the Parliament is established. Experience of the Parliament in practice might cause the Scottish people to change their mind, undermining the political force of their earlier consent. Just as no

referendum result could be binding on the Government (given the doctrine of parliamentary sovereignty), so neither could it be binding on the Scottish people - who would reserve the right to declare the Parliament ineffective and unnecessary once they had seen it in operation.

155　Even so, the *timing* is significant.　If the Government decided to hold a referendum there are arguments for doing so in advance of the legislation rather than afterwards.　The question of principle is less likely to be clouded by other concerns if addressed early in the Government's term of office.　A positive popular endorsement in advance of the legislation's introduction (and recorded in the preamble to the bill) might also help to smooth its passage through Parliament.

156　This last point could prove the decisive factor: popular consent less as entrenchment for the statute once enacted than as necessary support to secure its enactment in the first place.　That decision is a highly political one, which cannot reasonably be taken in advance of the general election.　Another factor in the political calculation is the fact that if it were considered desirable to hold a pre-legislative referendum a short bill would need to be passed to authorise the expenditure, set the question etc.[56]　That would entail some delay in the legislative timetable, especially if the referendum bill were tactically opposed.

## Royal Assent ?

157　There would technically be no need for Royal Assent for Acts of the Scottish Parliament.　Even so, the 1978 Act and the Government of Ireland Act 1920 both provided for legislation to be approved by Her/His Majesty in Council. The new Scotland Act should follow this precedent. Important subsidiary legislation is commonly made in the same way - by Order in Council. Ratification by the Queen in Council is conventionally seen as a formality.　Similarly the signification of Assent could be seen as a formality which confirms the status of the legislation as a legislative act of the State, albeit that of a devolved body.

158　It would ordinarily fall to the Secretary of State formally to put a bill before the Privy Council. It was into this gap, between enactment in Edinburgh and Assent, that the 1978 Act inserted the provisions for political override of draft legislation.　To avoid the possibility that the Secretary of State might similarly refuse to submit a bill for assent on policy grounds, it might be better to transfer this role to the Speaker of the Scottish Parliament (as suggested in Bernard Crick and David Millar's draft standing order 19[57]).　That would be consistent with the Speaker taking on other 'viceregal' functions from the Secretary of State (discussed in paragraphs 378 to 385 below).　But even if the role were left with the Secretary of State, and the Act were silent on whether he or she could refuse to put it forward for Assent, the convention against that power to interfere should quickly be established.

# Chapter 4

## Powers of the
## Parliament

## Introduction

159 This report does not attempt to define the precise extent of the legislative powers which could be devolved to a Scottish Parliament. As described in chapter 2, that task is a complex one which can only satisfactorily be completed with the assistance of all Whitehall departments involved. It is not possible outside Government, and certainly not within the timescale of the Constitution Unit's work, to draw up anything like a definitive Schedule. The Royal Commission on the Constitution reached the same conclusion (paragraph 703):

> "At this stage we are not attempting to identify functions which ought to be devolved....Our immediate object is the more limited one of making a realistic assessment of the practical scope for devolution, and for this purpose we have necessarily to state our conclusions in general terms. We consider in Parts VII and VIII the functions which might be devolved under particular schemes, but even there we are unable to reach any very precise conclusions, since firm decisions could be taken only after more detailed enquiry and consultation with the various interests concerned than it would have been appropriate for us to undertake".

160 Instead this chapter discusses four aspects of the subject:
- the Royal Commission's treatment of the question of powers.
- developments in thinking about the range of the Parliament's powers since 1978.
- what a list of reserved powers might look like today.
- how such a list might be framed, with reference to the particular examples of the Parliament's electoral system and maintaining the integrity of Scots law.

## The Royal Commission's Approach

161 The Royal Commission considered whether it would be sufficient in the Act simply to transfer all those functions then exercised by the Secretary of State or by the Scottish Law Officers under any Act of Parliament, law or custom, with additions or deletions as required. The Commission's report noted that when the office of Secretary for Scotland was first established in 1885 specific functions were transferred to the new Minister. But by an amending Act of 1887 he was given all the functions of the other Secretaries of State so far as they related to Scotland, with only specific exceptions noted. The Commission concluded that this apparently simple method would not be acceptable:
- because it would not be clear on the face of the statute precisely what powers had been devolved.
- because the method would not work if the range of powers devolved differed in practice significantly from the powers of the Secretary of State.
- because the method would not work in the English regions, where there was no Secretary of State to refer to.

162 The general idea that transfer of the Secretary of State for Scotland's responsibilities to a Scottish Assembly might be the ideal solution for Scotland was thus considered, but finding a way to express in legislative terms that apparently simple concept defeated both the Commission and the Government.

163 Instead, the Commission approached Government departments responsible for functions in Scotland (all except those relating to defence, foreign affairs, finance and taxation) and asked for a thorough inventory of those functions, together with a note of the extent of regional or local devolution at the time. The Commission then made its own assessment of the scope for further devolution from within the lists supplied. The results are contained in Appendix D to the Commission's report.

164 It is easy to see how the form of the detailed schedules 10 and 11 to the 1978 Act arose out of this methodology. This way of assessing the scope for devolution already pointed to a bill based on devolution by groups of functions. The Commission's further conclusions about executive devolution (paragraph 870) drove this idea towards more precise definition by reference to statute:

> "The drawing up of a scheme for the devolution of executive power would involve a great deal more than the selection of subjects suitable for devolution. We have seen that for each subject all the relevant statutes and statutory instruments would have to be reviewed and amended so as to distribute powers between the Ministers and the regions".

Thus the 1978 Act enumerated the functions to be transferred by reference to statutes in force. The result was a less generous settlement than had all the Secretary of State's powers been transferred.

## The Scope for Devolution Today

165 The SCC have proposed that the Scottish Parliament's powers should "include all areas of policy currently within the remit of the Scottish Office". This would represent an advance on the settlement contained in the 1978 Act, and indeed that in Donald Dewar's Scotland Bill of 1987 which updated it. The scope of the devolution settlement in each of these three cases is recorded in the comparative table at Appendix B. It demonstrates how complex a piece of legislation there would have to be if the approach adopted in the 1978 Act (exhaustive enumeration of the devolved powers) were followed today.

### Powers Reserved to Westminster

166 The previous chapter suggested that expressing the reserved functions would be a better way to express the division of legislative competence in a devolution Act. The Government of Ireland Act 1920 did just that. Its list of reservations looks rather idiosyncratic today (it is quoted in paragraph 87 above). The Royal Commission looked at it in 1973 and concluded that "the list of matters reserved under the 1920 Act is, with minor exceptions, the minimum that would need to be reserved under any new arrangement for the devolution of powers. Indeed the range of matters reserved would almost certainly have to be greater" (paragraph 551). The SCC have suggested that 'the primary matters to be retained' should be:

- defence
- foreign affairs
- immigration
- nationality
- social security policy
- central economic and fiscal responsibilities

167 A legislative schedule defining the reserved powers would in practice be much longer, as the Royal Commission on the Constitution suggested, and would have to be drawn in far more detail. Something of the same process went on in drawing up the 1978 Act, detailing the specific statutes or sections of statutes which could not be devolved even when there was agreement that in general the matters they dealt with were suitable for devolution. In drawing up a list of reserved functions the premise would be different: the principle should be to keep the list as short as necessary. It should detail not what *can* be devolved, but what *needs* to be retained in order to maintain coherence and a sense of common purpose throughout the UK.

168 The process of refinement which went on in the 1970s policy process should thus be reversed: modifications to broad areas should be such as to increase the devolved matters, making sure that no more is reserved than is necessary. The prime purpose of this chapter is to suggest that a debate on these terms needs to take place. It is time there was some more detailed thinking not just about what a Scottish Parliament might be empowered to do, but what it should not or will not be able to do i.e. what needs to be reserved to Westminster.

169 The remainder of this chapter looks at two specific areas to see how in practice the choices within each as to what should or should not be reserved might be made.

## Reservation in Practice

### The Electoral System

170 One particularly sensitive subject is likely to be the power to determine the Parliament's electoral system. The SCC's proposals imply that this power should rest with the Parliament, although hedged about with qualifications (emphasis added):

> "[the electoral system] should not be easily challenged or changed without careful and democratic scrutiny. A mechanism should therefore be devised so that technical and corrective changes *in the electoral arrangements for the Parliament, as agreed by the Parliament itself, can be carried through without undue delay*".

171 This was not the view taken in the 1970s when responsibility for the electoral system was retained at Westminster. The precedent of Northern Irish devolution was not encouraging. The Stormont Parliament abolished proportional representation in local government in 1922 and then changed its own proportional representation electoral system to 'first past the post' for the elections of 1929 onwards. Every general election from the first in 1921 produced a majority for the Unionist Party, which always formed the Government and had a majority in the Senate.

172 These are not circumstances likely to be reproduced in 21st century Scotland. One should not race to the conclusion that because an additional safeguard for proportional representation might have been needed in Northern Ireland in the 1920s, so it should be applied to Scotland now. Given that one of the primary motivations for devolution is to bring democratic decision-making closer to the people of Scotland, there seems no reason in principle to suggest that this should not extend to determining the electoral system too.

173 Nevertheless there might be an argument for reservation on grounds of a need for uniformity across the UK. But this will be breached in establishing the Parliament with a different electoral system from Westminster, and is breached already within the UK with the system of proportional representation which operates for local and European elections in Northern Ireland. The other argument for reservation would be that the Westminster Parliament is a better guarantor of the electoral system than a Parliament in Scotland. This assertion too is open to question. Proportional representation has been abandoned in other European countries before now at the behest of central government: in France in 1958, Greece in 1952, in Mussolini's Italy, and attempts were made too in Austria and Ireland in the 1960s.[58] There seems no reason to suppose that Westminster should be a better guarantor of Scotland's democracy than Scotland herself.

174 These arguments apply to the power to change the electoral system fundamentally, ie to move from a system of proportional representation to 'first past the post'. But there are a whole host of other issues relating to the administration of elections which may or may not have to be reserved: rules governing the compilation of the electoral register, procedures for absent voting, rules requiring the counting of votes to take place at a central point in each constituency, the level of deposit required to stand for election. All of these are aspects of the present state of UK electoral law which have come in for criticism, notably by the Hansard Society's Commission on Election Campaigns in 1991[59].

175 It is quite conceivable that a Scottish Parliament might want to take steps to remedy some of these deficiencies for elections taking place in Scotland. In particular, the state of the electoral register might command attention given the new voting system (which will need to allocate sets of seven seats by a mathematical process rather than simple majority) and the fact that the more complete the register the better the case to put to any review of Westminster parliamentary constituencies. Other practical steps to address some of the problems identified in the previous paragraph might also be adopted by a Scottish Parliament given the power to do so.

176 None of these administrative changes would fundamentally alter the electoral system. But most (a more up to date electoral register, for example) would have a knock on effect when used in general or European elections, for which Westminster will remain responsible. The question is whether the absence of uniformity that might be introduced in this way is tolerable within a single state. The answer is probably yes, so long as other fundamental aspects of the system remain common - eligibility to vote, for example, voting age, one person one vote.

177 Whilst central government might determine who has the vote and the system under which it can be exercised in general and European elections, there should be no objection to a Scottish Parliament devising better ways to ensure that as many of those eligible to do so actually vote and that the election is run as efficiently and fairly as possible, even if the prime motivation is to improve the conduct of Scottish elections rather than UK-wide ones. The rest of the UK might learn from Scottish experience and follow suit.

178 As for the electoral system itself, it is difficult to determine where responsibility for fundamental change should lie. Clearly, as the SCC suggest, there should be strong democratic backing in Scotland for any change - it should not be imposed from Westminster. That argues for reserving the power to change the nature of the electoral system to Westminster, but to specify that this is an area in which the Scottish Executive should first request Westminster to legislate for a change in the system (using the procedure described in paragraph 106 above). Further, it might require that any change requested by the Scottish Executive should have the prior endorsement of a majority of the Scottish people expressed in a referendum.

179 The treatment of the electoral system in this way in the devolution legislation is an illustration of how reservation might work in practice. In this area, as in others, the reserved list might be more detailed, but less constraining, than a simple reservation of an entire topic would suggest.

## Scots Law and Legal System

180 As noted in Chapter 1, it is a strong argument for legislative devolution that Scotland has its own law and legal system but no legislature of its own to improve them and keep them up to date. The list of reserved powers in this area will need to be carefully considered to ensure that a Scottish Parliament is not inadvertently denied the full range of powers it will need to maintain and improve a coherent body of Scots law and thus remedy the present deficiency.

181 In relation to law and the legal system, in particular, it would be a mistake to think in terms only of what it might be prudent to devolve in the future to a Welsh Assembly or to English regional government. In this field the powers appropriate to a Scottish Parliament are those which would be appropriate to a separate Parliament for the other mainland jurisdiction, namely the whole of England and Wales.

182 The existence of a separate law and legal system in Scotland is thus a reason for devolution, a reason for lop-sided devolution and a reason for careful specification of the reserved areas. This last point, the need for careful definition, can be illustrated by reference to commercial law and international sources of legal change, as described below.

### Commercial Law

183 Much of the law relating to commerce is ordinary private law. It would include, for example, the law on contracts of all kinds, including contracts for the sale or supply of goods or services, contracts for the carriage of goods or passengers, contracts of loan or deposit, contracts of agency and insurance contracts, much of the law on natural and legal persons, including the law on the formation and internal relations of partnerships and companies, and law on the acquisition and transfer of property of all kinds, including shares, bonds and intellectual property.

184 Some commercial law, on the other hand, is general criminal law. For example, offences such as theft, fraud or embezzlement are important in a commercial context. Some relates more to the courts and the legal system, for example the law relating to the evidential effect of entries in bankers' books is part of the law of evidence. The law on arbitration in commercial matters is part of the general law on arbitration.

185 Finally, some of the law relating to commerce is public law of a regulatory nature. Most of the statutory provisions relating specifically to banks, building societies, insurance companies or the provision of financial services are of this nature. So are provisions on legal tender, or the regulation of interest rates or the availability of credit. Company law is a mixture of private and public law. Provisions relating to the legal personality of companies, the relationships between the company and shareholders or directors, contracts by companies, or the execution of documents by companies, are matters of private law. Requirements of registration, accounting, audit or disclosure in the public interest are probably best regarded as matters of public law, as are provisions, backed up by criminal or other sanctions, on dishonest trading, insider dealing and similar matters. Laws on safety and other standards for goods or activities of various kinds are generally matters of public law. So are laws on restrictive trading practices, mergers or monopolies.

186    The above analysis makes it clear that simply devolving or reserving the broad subject of 'commercial law' would be impractical. It is not mentioned as such in the SCC's proposed list of 'principal areas' to come within the Parliament's powers. Yet reserving commercial law as a whole for the exclusive competence of the UK Parliament would make the powers of the Scottish Parliament in relation to Scots law and the Scottish legal system paltry and fragmented and could hardly be seriously proposed. The more sensible approach would therefore be to reserve certain specified areas of commercial law.[60]

187    The reserved areas of the Scotland Act 1978 (those 'matters not included in the Groups' of devolved powers) included the following: "Corporate bodies other than public bodies related to devolved matters. Insurance. Banking. Legal tender. Intellectual property. Safety standards for goods. Restrictive trading practices and monopolies. Regulation of interest rates and credit."[61] But even this apparently restricted list of reservations would be likely to create difficulties and absurdities.

188    Suppose that the private law relating to companies, insurance, banking and intellectual property were excepted from the general private law competence of the Scottish Parliament. And suppose that the Scottish Parliament wanted to enact a Contract Act dealing with the general Scottish law of contract. Would the legislation have to have a provision saying 'This Act does not apply to contracts of insurance or contracts entered into in the course of banking'? That would make no sense. Insurance contracts and contracts entered into in the course of banking would have to remain governed by the old, unreformed Scottish law until the UK Parliament found time to legislate on the matter for Scotland.

189    If it did eventually do so (the matter might not have high legislative priority) it could either adopt the solutions of the Scottish Parliament (in which case why should the Scottish Parliament not have been allowed to legislate directly?) or it could enact something different (in which case there would be one new Scottish contract law for banking and insurance contracts and another new Scottish contract law for other contracts). There would be difficult questions of definition. There would be the danger of distortion of the competitive positions of different institutions within Scotland. The result would be confusion, complexity and incoherence. The position would be even more absurd if the view were to be taken that the reservation of 'corporate bodies' meant that the Scottish Parliament could not legislate on contracts entered into by companies.

190    The same applies to the general criminal law. It would be anomalous if the Scottish Parliament could not include provisions on the criminal liability of corporate bodies in a new criminal code. It would be wrong to have, say, a new law on fraud applying in Scotland generally and an old, unrevised law on fraud applying in relation to banking, insurance and corporate bodies.

191    The difficulty of reconciling a reservation of some commercial law matters to Westminster in the interests of conformity with granting adequate powers for the Scottish Parliament in relation to Scots law and the Scottish legal system is not insurmountable. A solution might contain two elements, as follows.

192    First the reserved area could be defined more carefully. The formulation in the 1978 Act is not satisfactory. It applies too widely. It is a strange jumble of persons, activities, legal concepts, things and regulations. It has not worn well. It seems strange now, in the light of the Financial Services Act 1986, to single out banking and insurance for special treatment. What about

Building Societies and Friendly Societies? What about independent financial advisers? It also seems strange to single out corporate bodies when a level playing field argument would suggest that restrictions ought to be considered in relation to business enterprises engaged in similar activities whatever their legal structure. The area of reservation might be better expressed in more functional terms, confined to public law regulation, perhaps on the following lines:

> *Regulation of currency, interest rates and credit. Regulation of competition policy, monopolies and mergers. Regulation of registration, accounting, disclosure and other requirements imposed in the public interest on business enterprises. Regulation of the provision of financial services, including banking and insurance services. Regulation of the requirements and effects of registration in relation to intellectual property.*

193 This is not to express a definitive view on the policy of reserving all these matters but, as a matter of legislative technique, something on these lines would cover the same sort of ground as the equivalent paragraph in the 1978 Act but would be expressed in a more functional and coherent way. It would be easier to see the limitation to public regulatory law (which was possibly meant to be implicit in the 1978 Act) and the underlying theme of the preservation of a level playing field in various important areas. There would be much less danger of conflict with the Scottish Parliament's general powers in relation to Scots law and the Scottish legal system.

194 Second, there could be a special saving provision. However carefully the reserved areas are framed, there is always the risk that a reserved area will unintentionally limit the competence of the Scottish Parliament in relation to legal matters which ought to be devolved as a coherent whole. To guard against this risk, which might arise at the stage of last-minute amendments to the bill when there would be little opportunity for consequential changes elsewhere, it would be worth considering a provision to the effect that nothing in the list of reserved areas would prevent the Scottish Parliament from legislating on matters relating to the courts and legal system in Scotland, the criminal process in Scotland, Scottish private law or the general Scottish criminal law.

### International Sources of Changes in the Legal System

195 Foreign affairs would be a reserved area under any conceivable scheme of devolution. But here too a blanket reservation of 'foreign affairs' without further qualification might damage the Parliament's ability to maintain the system of Scots law. Many legal reforms, often of a nature which would be clearly within the proposed competence of a Scottish Parliament, originate in international conventions like the Brussels Convention on Jurisdiction and the Enforcement of Judgements, the Hague Conventions on Private International Law or the United Nations Convention on Contracts for the International Sale of Goods.

196 It would be anomalous if the mere fact that the stimulus for a desirable reform was an international convention meant that the UK Parliament had exclusive competence. The reservation of foreign affairs should not deprive the Scottish Parliament of its competence to legislate on matters relating to Scots law and the Scottish legal system: the general saving provision suggested above would safeguard the Scottish Parliament's powers.

197 A further source of change might come through treaties presently ratified under the Crown's powers of Royal Prerogative. A standard provision in treaties dealing with private law matters is that:

> "If a Contracting State has two or more territorial units in which different systems of law are applicable in relation to matters dealt with in this Convention, it may at the time of signature, ratification, acceptance, approval or accession declare that this Convention shall extend to all its territorial units or only to one or more of them and may modify this declaration by submitting another declaration at any time".

This is article 40 of the Hague Convention on the Abduction of Children, but similar provisions are standard in other conventions.

198 The devolution legislation might contain a provision to ensure that, where a treaty relating to a devolved matter could be extended to Scotland without necessarily being extended to the rest of the UK, the Scottish Parliament could recommend that the treaty be ratified in relation to Scotland. In the case of private law, for example, because Scottish private law is often more like continental European private laws than English law is, there are cases where it would be very much easier to extend a treaty to Scotland than to the United Kingdom as a whole. Consequently there are cases where the benefits of a treaty, in reciprocal treatments, could be achieved at very little cost for people coming under Scottish law by virtue of domicile or habitual residence. It would be unfortunate if an unnecessary linkage to English law prevented these benefits from being obtained.

*Communication and Co-operation*

199 Finally, in order to maintain the integrity of Scots law there would still be a need for communication and co-operation between UK and Scottish Government departments, and other bodies, on legal matters and for adequate legal advice to be available on both legal systems. A United Kingdom department dealing with, say, the regulation of financial services, if that were a reserved area, would need to have access to Scottish legal advice as the implications of any legislation would not necessarily be the same in Scotland as in England and Wales. UK legislation should be prepared on the basis of a proper legal input from all parts of the country. This, however, is nothing new, is a matter of good legal practice, and should not require any provision in the legislation.

## Conclusion

200 This chapter, while not attempting a full enumeration of powers which might be reserved in a new devolution Act, has attempted to show how such a list might be drawn up. It is likely to be complex, but the aim should be to keep it as short as possible. It should express what needs to be reserved in order to maintain the integrity of the UK, and should be careful not to constrain the Scottish Parliament more than that principle implies simply through inadvertent drafting.

201 The debate about the scope of devolution has been conducted to date almost exclusively in terms of precisely what powers and functions should be devolved (down to the inclusion of 'the licensing and control of dogs' in Appendix I of the SCC's report). Perhaps the devolution bill will be drafted in these terms - although this report argues strongly against that. But even so, the public debate - in Scotland and in the rest of the UK - cannot sensibly be conducted at that level. The sooner it moves on to consider what powers it is necessary to retain at Westminster in order to maintain whatever it is the UK and its Parliament stand for, the better.

# Financial Provisions

# Chapter 5

## Introduction

202 The heart of the devolution settlement will be the arrangements for financing the Scottish Executive's actions. At present some 95% of the Scottish Office's total budget is determined through the application of a formula which relates changes in Scottish planned spending to changes in equivalent spending on English programmes. This is a method pioneered by a Labour government and applied by Conservative governments for 15 years. But translating it from an internal allocation mechanism *within* government to an external transfer *between* separate administrations will not be easy and will expose the system to a level of technical scrutiny and political pressure which it has largely avoided to date.

203 The design of the financing provisions for Scottish devolution is crucial. The danger is that central government control of the purse strings will lead to control, or at least undue influence, over the Scottish Parliament's policies. Ideally, therefore, the financial provisions might satisfy the following criteria:

1. they should be equitable as between the nations and regions of the UK.
2. they should respect the principle of equalisation according to need between the nations and regions of the UK.
3. they should be politically sustainable, providing reasonable financial certainty for the Parliament even when political relations between Edinburgh and London are not good.
4. partly to redress point 3, they should leave the Scottish Executive as little dependent on detailed negotiation with HM Treasury as possible.
5. they should operate within the financial constraints imposed on and from the centre (national and international constraints of macroeconomic policy).
6. within those constraints, they should provide for maximum policy and spending autonomy for the Scottish Executive.
7. they should ensure accountability to the Scottish electorate for spending decisions. This is closely related to point 6 about autonomy, and also requires the allocation mechanism and other data to be publicly accessible.
8. they should be practical, and not so complex or time-consuming that they introduce unmanageable delay into the budget process either in the UK or Scotland.

204 Points 1 and 2 are both necessary. The first dictates a process for distributing revenues within the UK which is fair. The second goes further in arguing for a settlement which attempts to match resources to needs throughout the UK. This implies some redistribution from richer to poorer areas in order to maintain a similar quality of public provision for all.

205 It would be possible to design financing mechanisms without this quality. But that approach would cast aside a principle already underlying the allocation of revenues within the UK, and one which is arguably crucial to the concept of Union itself. The Scottish Office report of October 1995 on Government Expenditure and Revenue in Scotland makes the same point: "It is to be expected that, within any State, the level of public expenditure will differ from one constituent part to another. Needs vary and public expenditure should reflect needs, rather than the wealth or taxable capacity of the area in question".[62]

206 The remainder of this chapter falls into three parts:
- consideration of the present financing arrangements: the Barnett formula.
- a description of the financial provisions proposed by the SCC and how they measure up to the criteria outlined above.
- some suggestions for measures to complement the financial provisions proposed in order to enhance their durability.

207 The chapter concludes that formula-based allocation, as the SCC propose, is a sensible basis for the financing of devolution. But the detailed arrangements will need to take account also of monies which are not presently channelled through the block and the formula; the need for a limited overdraft facility to facilitate financial management; and the possibility that the application of the formula, and even more so any review of it, will come under a much greater degree of public and political scrutiny under devolution than they have to date. It suggests that the establishment of an independent Commission to act at least as the guarantor of reliable and objective data, and to conduct a new needs assessment exercise, could be the key to the SCC's financial proposals commanding respect in the longer term.


## The Present Arrangements

### The Barnett Formula

208 In the autumn of 1976, in anticipation of devolution, the Treasury undertook a study of relative expenditure needs in England, Wales, Scotland and Northern Ireland. The study took two and a half years and involved a complex set of judgements - some disputed more than others - about how to measure objective levels of need across a range of spending programmes. It covered not all government spending but a subset of those services proposed for devolution. The study concluded that, taking data from 1976-77, the relative amounts of expenditure per capita required to provide 'the same range and levels of service as in England' for the devolved services were as set out in **Table 3** below (actual spending levels are in brackets).

| Table 3: Public Expenditure Relatives for Devolved Services 1976–77 | | | |
| --- | --- | --- | --- |
| England | Scotland | Wales | Northern Ireland |
| 100  (100) | 116  (122) | 109  (106) | 131  (135) |

Source: H M Treasury, *Needs Assessment Study Report* (para 6.5), December 1979.

209 The study noted that, "since the underlying principle of enabling similar policies to be pursued in each country is not new, it might be presumed that this was reflected in past expenditure allocations". However, it discovered that the per capita figures available from 1959-60 onwards showed a consistent bias in favour of Scotland for the range of services ear-marked for devolution, rising to a peak of 34% above the English level in 1968-69, and standing at 22% above for the year 1976-77. The reasons for these disparities were not elaborated in the study:

*"No systematic record exists of the reasons for these relationships; and there is no basis on which the pattern for any one year could be presented as being the "correct" pattern for the*

*foreseeable future. It is not therefore possible to infer from them what future allocations should be or what factors should be taken into account in their determination".*

210 Although the devolution debate and the legislation of 1978 did not lead to the establishment of Scottish and Welsh Assemblies, the spotlight which fell on territorial public expenditure did lead to a restructuring of the way spending in Scotland and Wales was allocated. Up until then the Scottish Office budget had been the result of detailed programme by programme negotiation between the Scottish Office and the Treasury. In order to regularise the financial relationship between the Treasury and a Scottish Assembly, to simplify the annual budget-setting exercise, and to address the apparent bias in favour of the other territories in the UK over England, the Labour Government devised a new approach.

211 The then Chief Secretary to the Treasury, Joel Barnett, devised a formula which ensured that any future changes in the Scottish or Welsh budgets should be calculated as a proportion of the changes in equivalent English spending. The formula allocated increases or decreases in public expenditure to Scotland, Wales and England in the ratio 10:5:85, the rounded share of GB population for the three nations concerned in 1976[63]. This became known as the 'Barnett formula': for every £85 *change* in planned expenditure on comparable English services, Wales would receive £5 and Scotland £10.

212 One of the objectives of the formula, and certainly its effect in theory, was to bring about some convergence over time between relative spending in Scotland, Wales and England. Since the formula applied only to *changes* in spending, if population shares remained constant the effect of the formula would be to reduce spending in Scotland and Wales as a proportion of English spending. The historical base - that quantum of spending in Scotland and Wales to which the changes would apply - would slowly assume less importance in the overall budget.

213 There appears to be no published documentary record of precisely how far this convergence effect was intended to go. In theory the operation of the formula would in time bring about per capita parity throughout Scotland, Wales and England (a separate formula applies for Northern Ireland). But it seems reasonable to assume that the formula was rather intended to bring about convergence to the level of assessed need, as measured by the 1979 Treasury study. It was applied for the first time, it appears, in setting the Scottish budget for 1981-82; although this too is not confirmed by any published documentary record.

214 In any event, the aim of convergence does not appear to have been realised. Scotland's population has fallen both absolutely and relative to England, undermining the convergence bias in the formula. Added to this, the squeeze on public spending through the 1980s meant that the changes in the English budget were not dramatic and so the cumulative effect of the formula on changes in relative spending was limited. This became an issue in the 1992 general election campaign when "Scottish Office Ministers loudly proclaimed Scotland's public expenditure differential over England as a reason for rejecting constitutional change, without any regard for the inevitable repercussions at the hands of the Treasury".[64] The new Chief Secretary Michael Portillo revised the formula following the election so that it now guarantees Scotland changes in comparable English expenditure or in combined English and Welsh expenditure (on programmes like law and order) strictly proportional to its 1991 population share, rather than its share in 1976.

215 Whilst this recalibration of the formula went some way to restore the original basis of the figures, the population trend in Scotland remains downwards. Scotland's share of GB population was 9.57% in 1976 (Barnett), 9.14% in 1991 (Portillo), and is projected to fall to around 7.60% over the next 35 years.[65] Over the same period total population in England and Wales is set to increase. The effect of Scotland's declining population trend on per capita data used for making comparisons is magnified in that the formula uses historical data, while per capita relatives are always expressed in terms of up-to-date population figures. In addition, the squeeze in public spending has been maintained since 1992 and further inhibited the convergence effects of the formula. At the least, with or without devolution, there must be some prospect of further reviews of the formula in the future simply to reflect changes in relative population.

## Government Revenue and Expenditure in Scotland

216 In October 1995 the Scottish Office published financial statistics for the year 1993-94[66]. This is the most recent year for which full data are available. The report details all public expenditure in Scotland, both identifiable and non-identifiable. The figures show that while Scotland's share of non-identifiable public expenditure per head may be lower than the UK average, identifiable expenditure is much higher.

217 The relative per capita weights for identifiable public expenditure in England, Scotland, Wales and Northern Ireland for 1993-94, as recorded in the Scottish Office report, are set out in Table 4 below.

| Table 4: Identifiable Per Capita Public Expenditure Relatives 1993–94 | | | |
| --- | --- | --- | --- |
| England | Scotland | Wales | Northern Ireland |
| 100 | 121 | 113 | 138 |

Source: Scottish Office, Government Expenditure and Revenue in Scotland, 1993-94 (Table 2c).

218 The report further estimates that total spending in Scotland i.e. identifiable and non-identifiable for 1993-94 was £5,553 per head, 14% higher than the UK average figure of £4,971 per head. It also estimates a shortfall in the balance between revenues and expenditure of some £8 billion: £20.4 bn in tax revenues to £28.4 bn estimated total public expenditure. These figures exclude revenues for North Sea oil, since the North Sea is treated as a separate region (the UK Continental Shelf) for accounts purposes. If the £1.7 bn revenues from the North Sea were allocated to Scotland the shortfall would have been £6.4 bn.

219 These figures are open to differing interpretations and debate. There are doubts about the accuracy of the revenue side of the equation (notably the once-for-all step change in Scottish income tax revenues which appears to have occurred in 1986-87). The treatment of North Sea oil revenues is often disputed (although the fall from a peak of £12 bn in 1984-85 to a forecast £2.4 bn in 1995-96 is not). The allocation of non-identifiable public expenditure - Scotland's share of services like defence and overseas service - is a matter for judgement (the Scottish Office allocates it in line with Scotland's share of UK GDP). 1993-94 was also not a typical year - the depth of a UK recession in which the overall UK deficit was unusually large at around £50 bn. The Scottish deficit was likewise greater than the norm.

220 A further complication in acquiring a true picture of the Scottish budget in 1993-94 is the fact that the Treasury has recently published a new set of figures for spending in Scotland in that year which show substantial differences from the Scottish Office report. According to the *Statistical Analyses 1996-97* published in March this year, the figures in **Table 4** above should instead read as in **Table 5** below.

| Table 5: Identifiable Per Capita Public Expenditure Relatives 1993–94 (revised) | | | |
|---|---|---|---|
| England | Scotland | Wales | Northern Ireland |
| 100 | 124 | 118 | 140 |

Source: HM Treasury, *Statistical Analyses 1996-7*, (Table 7.5B), Cm 3201, March 1996.

221 Whichever estimate is taken, the figures indicate that:
- Scotland still receives a relatively larger proportion of per capita identifiable public expenditure than England.
- the prospect of Scotland financing all current services out of its own revenues appears, on the present tax basis, unrealistic. The recent Institute for Fiscal Studies commentary reinforces that view by suggesting that to do so a basic rate of income tax of 37% would be required in Scotland and a higher rate of 58%.[67]

222 These figures also mask variations in identifiable public spending relatives between programmes. Taking English spending as 100, the relative spending in Scotland on agriculture, fisheries, food and forestry in 1993-94 was 205; on health and personal social services 125; on housing 151 (Scottish Office figures). The significance of these variations is that the *overall* relative will depend on the range of services and spending programmes included in the calculation. Social security spending accounted for 35.7% of identifiable spending in Scotland in 1993-94, but was only 3% higher per head than equivalent spending in England. If this element in the spending block is removed (as it would be in calculating relatives for devolved services, since the social security system will not be devolved) the overall relative with England for all other identifiable spending was 131 in 1993-94.[68] Using the revised Treasury statistics that figure rises to 134.

223 The figures thus tell us something about the nature of any convergence that has occurred since the introduction of the Barnett formula. It can be argued that in the absence of any assessment of relative need it is impossible to say for certain that the formula has not brought about convergence towards that level. What these figures indicate however, in particular the last, is that if there has been convergence since 1979 it must be a product of increased need in Scotland rather than any significant reduction in relative expenditure compared with English levels.

224 This is the context in which financing provisions for the Scottish Parliament will have to operate.

## Financial Proposals of the SCC: Assigned Budget

225 The SCC propose that the Scottish Parliament should continue to be financed largely in the same way as the Scottish Office is now:

> "*The principle of equalisation will continue. This means resources will be pooled on a UK basis and distributed on the basis of relative need.... The current formula for the calculation of government expenditure in Scotland - the Barnett/Goschen formula[69]- will continue to be used as the basis for the allocation of Scotland's fair share of UK resources*".

The formula will give Scotland an annual 'assigned budget'. In addition the SCC propose that the Parliament should have the power to vary the basic rate of income tax for Scottish taxpayers by a maximum of three pence in the pound.

226 The tax variation element in these proposals is discussed in more detail below (paragraphs 287 to 303). The maximum amount of revenue it might raise would only represent about 3% of the total Scottish budget. This section concentrates instead on the main element in the SCC's proposals - the assigned budget. In particular it considers whether existing financing arrangements based on the Barnett formula are robust enough to survive the transition from an internal allocation mechanism within government to a much more public transfer mechanism between separate administrations.

### Monies Outside the Block

227 Aside from the tax variation power, there is no mention in the SCC's proposals of sources of finance outside the assigned block. But the 'Scottish block', i.e. that part of the Scottish Office budget determined by the Barnett formula, in normal circumstances comprises only some 95% of the total budget. Spending on agriculture, fisheries and food and the nationalised industries is not, and has never been, calculated according to the formula - originally because these services were not intended to be devolved.

228 In addition, central government may choose not to channel new spending initiatives through the block, but to distribute spending between the regions and nations on a different basis. For example, when a package of construction-related projects to stimulate the economy was announced in the 1992 Autumn Statement the expenditure was allocated so as to maximise the intended macroeconomic effects by choosing the right investment location rather than any consideration of regional per capita spending.

229 Finally, the Scottish Office has no contingency reserve to meet unforeseen expenses, but the Treasury does. Data about how often Scotland has benefited from this reserve is very hard to come by, but cases will arise in any government where strict financial planning cannot cope with actual circumstances. For example, a pay award to NHS staff or to teachers would apply throughout the UK, but since the numbers of such staff in Scotland exceed the average in England and Wales, funding on a population basis through the formula would leave Scotland relatively disadvantaged and perhaps unable to meet the cost. That might entail a call on the contingency reserve, but with consequentials for subsequent years having to be absorbed within the block settlement.

230 These instances ring warning bells about the wisdom of relying on the formula *tout court* as the basis for financing devolution. In practice the Scottish Office has had recourse up to now to a variety of funding practices *outside the block* in order to maintain its position. A Scottish Parliament will need access to similar levels of flexibility.

## Durability of the Formula Under Scrutiny

231 Adapting the present practice of allocating public expenditure in Scotland according to a formula is certainly a practical and a sensible approach to financing devolution. But the SCC's proposals do not acknowledge the extent to which the existing allocation mechanism is likely to come under scrutiny when applied in the new circumstances of devolution. In order to maintain support and legitimacy in Scotland and in England, and to withstand the new political pressures to which the formula might be exposed with an elected administration - and opposition - in Edinburgh, all relevant data will surely have to be made more widely available and the process by which the Scottish spending allocation is then calculated made more comprehensible and visible.

232 The lack of clarity surrounding the operation of the Barnett formula - the point at which it was introduced, the precise objectives it was intended to achieve, the reliability of figures estimating revenues and expenditure in Scotland - has already been remarked upon above. A further factor is the lack of published Treasury data identifying the equivalent 'English block', the sums and the programmes of spending in England (and in some cases England and Wales) to which the Barnett formula is applied.

233 Official figures *are* published for 'identified' and 'non-identified' General Government Expenditure broken down between the four UK territories - England, Scotland, Wales and Northern Ireland - and beyond that, so far is possible, to the eight standard English regions.[70] This analysis gives some idea of the English/Welsh data underlying the Scottish settlement. But in practice there is some variation between identifiable expenditure in England and that part of it which is treated as an 'equivalent' for the purposes of calculating the Scottish block. Most departments' spending will include elements which are GB-wide as well as spending specifically related to England. But no attempt is made to separate those elements out in the published figures for identifiable expenditure, which means that the 'English block' can only be estimated.

234 This lack of precise definition is one means by which the Treasury maintains control of the game by determining where the goal posts should be placed each year. This can be a vital source of flexibility in the arrangements where there is a significant change in the make-up of the 'English block' which is not matched in Scotland. For example, the privatisation of the regional water authorities in England and Wales removed from the 'English block' a quantum of public expenditure which still required to be met from public funds in Scotland. So long as there is some flexibility in the precise definition of what constitutes English equivalent spending, this kind of problem - the lack of an analogue - can be overcome through internal negotiation between the Scottish Office and the Treasury. But that kind of tolerant pragmatism, coupled with the room for manoeuvre provided by imprecise data, might not survive in a more public atmosphere with a potentially vocal elected opposition in Edinburgh.

235 That is especially true if Scotland's relatively favourable spending position is to be maintained for any length of time, since public and political scrutiny might also then intensify from those in England resentful of Scotland's treatment. The Barnett formula does not appear to have brought about convergence; and the public debate about the establishment of a Scottish parliament has brought this fact back on to the political agenda. This is Chancellor Kenneth Clarke speaking at the Focus on Scotland lunch on 24 March 1995:

> *"Identifiable government expenditure in Scotland in 1993-94 was 21 per cent higher than in England. That is over £600 more per person a year and over 16 per cent more than the*

*United Kingdom average. If a devolved Assembly were set up in Edinburgh many English taxpayers would undoubtedly expect more of this higher public spending in Scotland to be raised in Scotland."*

236 The same argument about the operation of the Barnett formula and public spending relatives will arise with or without an Assembly. The allocation of public spending has been changed twice in recent years in response to the devolution debate - with the introduction of the formula and its recalibration in 1992 - even though no Parliament has been established. It is difficult to believe that even the Portillo formula will fare any better while public spending remains tight. As Arthur Midwinter and Murray McVicar put it:

*"A Scottish assembly would have to be 'aware' of the retaliatory measures of Whitehall and Westminster (although greater attention to expenditure relativities will likely occur, even with the continuation of the status quo) and the prospect of the needs formula being revisited to Scotland's disadvantage is a very real one."*[71]

Their message is that if the formula does not deliver an obviously fair and equitable division then it will come under pressure with or without devolution. In these circumstances, and given the other points identified above, a continuation of the existing formula as a long term means of financing a Scottish Parliament cannot be taken for granted. At the very least thought needs to be given to the mechanism for any future review which would have to take place under the changed circumstances of devolution.

## Block Grant Finance and the Assessment of Need

237 This section will consider in detail how the existing financing mechanisms based on the Barnett formula and the Scottish block might be adapted for devolution in a way which meets the points identified above. It will concentrate on two key issues:

- the assessment of relative need which must underpin any judgement about appropriate relative levels of per capita spending.
- the need for transparency and public confidence in the allocation mechanism and the data to which it applies.

### Needs Assessment

238 It is impossible to avoid the conclusion that the long term stability of the financial settlement will require a further needs assessment exercise to up-date the one completed in 1979. Ian Lang, then Secretary of State for Scotland, stated the case against such an exercise in evidence to the House of Commons Scottish Affairs Committee on 21 June 1995:

*"The formula itself is designed to achieve very slow but gradual convergence. That is happening. You mentioned the question of a needs assessment. There has not been one since the time the formula was established. If there were to be another obviously that would be a focal point for reappraising the relative spending positions...I do not see the need for it at the moment because I am confident that expenditure per head reflects fairly well the relative differences between Scotland and the United Kingdom".*

239 The decision whether or not to conduct a new needs assessment will clearly be influenced by a political judgement. Ian Lang may have been right that existing expenditure in Scotland reflects

relative need. So long as that is a generally accepted view on all sides, as it may be for now and the immediate future, then the political case for a needs assessment exercise is weak. However, should the position change, a number of other technical arguments for a needs assessment might then be brought into the debate:

- continued application of the Barnett formula would **in theory** reduce Scottish spending to per capita parity with England i.e. to below the level indicated by the last assessment as required for equalisation on the basis on relative need.

- although the Barnett formula has not threatened that result to date, it might begin to do so if the formula is recalibrated or otherwise adapted in response to public scrutiny, relative population changes or general debate about the lack of convergence it has so far achieved (as happened in 1992). Some new assessment of need is ideally required to inform *any* recalibration.

- the SCC propose that: "The principle of equalisation will continue. This means resources will be pooled on a UK basis and distributed on the basis of relative need". To put these words into practice must involve some assessment of 'relative need' on which to base the distribution.

- the Barnett formula does not apply to the allocation of resources to English regions, nor could it. Thus if devolution does proceed to Scotland, Wales, Northern Ireland *and* the English regions then a UK-wide assessment would be a necessary part of the financial infrastructure.

## Local Authority Spending Assessments

240 In England, Scotland and Wales a form of needs assessment already takes place every year in deciding how to allocate revenues to local authorities in those areas (slightly different systems are used in each). What are the lessons to draw from this experience for conducting any needs assessment exercise undertaken to inform the financing of devolution?

241 The objective of the local authority grants systems in Scotland, England and Wales is to ensure that if people in different parts of each country were provided with all local authority services at a standard set by central government then the council tax rate (or rather the eight rates for the various property bands) in each authority should equal a notional standard rate calculated by central government (known as the Council Tax for Standard Spending: CTSS). The system is slightly different in Wales, and very different in Scotland. All share the basic aim of equalisation, although there is no attempt to equalise between the three countries of GB (Northern Ireland is outside the exercise as there is no comparable local government role in the province).

242 In England and Wales each area's Revenue Support Grant (RSG) is calculated by first determining the money the area would need, net of any specific grants, to provide the standard levels of service. This is the area's Standard Spending Assessment (SSA). From this sum are subtracted the tax revenue the area would raise if council tax were set at CTSS and the area's per capita share of non-domestic rates (revenue sharing). The result is the area's RSG.

243 The SSA is the sum of 13 separate elements representing blocks or sub-blocks of local authority services. For each element a monetary sum representing standard cost of provision is multiplied by various needs indicators to provide a total cost for providing the service in question. The Scottish system is similar but even more complex. There are over 40 separate elements in the system, some of them covering services with very low total spending like registration of births

and school crossing patrols. The indicators of need applied to each element also vary according to the special circumstances of Scotland. For highway maintenance, for example, they include weighted road lane lengths for different types of road, with extra amounts allowed for roads built on peat if they are 600mm or less in depth and carry 20 or more commercial vehicles a day.

## The 1979 Treasury Needs Assessment Study

244  The Needs Assessment Study conducted by the Treasury in 1976-79 adopted a similar approach.[72] The study took the six main spending programmes which were intended to be devolved (Health and Personal Social Services, Education and Libraries, Housing, Other Environmental Services, Roads and Transport, and Law, Order and Protective Services), split them into identifiable spending blocks for which comparisons could be made between the four territories and then drew up a list of objective indicators of need for each expenditure block. Since most of the services in the six programmes were provided to individuals the main indicator in most cases was the number of people supplied with the service. But other factors like population sparsity or the age of school and hospital buildings, factors which might affect the cost of providing the service, were also taken into account.

245  The next step was to determine for each relevant factor what information was available under consistent definitions for all four territories. This caused some difficulty. Where information was not available on a uniform basis the figures were adjusted to the same scale by statistical experts. Where insufficient information was available proxy measures for the same indicator were used. Mortality ratios were, for example, taken to represent morbidity (the general level of illness in the population) - a decision which led to considerable controversy in the working group studying the health area resulting in a majority view of Scotland's relative need of 104% (relative to England) and a minority view setting the figure at nearer 125%.

246  This last example serves to show that needs assessment is by no means an exact science. Health was one area where a disagreement about the weight of objective needs indicators could not be resolved in the group: countless other similar arguments - about both the methodology and the reliability of the data - lie beneath the surface of the study, many of which are still open to question.

247  The report of the study readily acknowledges the rough and ready approach it was forced to take:

> "[This has not been] an exhaustive study. The work undertaken was limited by the time available and there is considerable scope for carrying it forward to provide more soundly-based conclusions". (paragraph 8.4); and

> "At one extreme the significance of the study may be exaggerated and the claim be made that its results should be reflected directly and without qualification in the actual expenditure allocations for future years. At the other extreme, admitted weaknesses in the methods and data might lead to argument that the results are meaningless and should be totally ignored. Neither view is correct: the study does not provide a method of determining allocations, but is a display of relevant data intended to help towards better-informed judgements". (paragraph 7.8)

This is precisely the role a future needs assessment exercise would have to play: the provision of relevant data, as objective, consistent and fair as possible, to allow a better-informed judgement about spending allocations to the devolved territories and regions of the UK.

The English Regions

248 The 1976 Treasury exercise did not break England down into regions for the purpose of assessing relative need. There was no realistic prospect then of devolution to the level of the English regions. The prospect is stronger now, although the introduction of directly-elected Assemblies with a wide range of powers requiring substantial transfer of financial responsibilities from the centre is still some way off.[73]

249 Even if the figures for relative need for the English regions will have no immediate operational consequence, however, it might still be desirable for the needs assessment to determine them. The overall aim of the exercise would be to provide some objective underpinning to formula-based allocation of territorial public expenditure, and to make that process transparent for all interested parties. The English regions will certainly have an interest in the allocation mechanism - particularly those bordering Scotland and Wales. It might be a sensible innovation in the context of an overall financial settlement to expose spending variations *within* England on the same basis as those between England and other parts of the UK. That might encourage a more sophisticated understanding of regional variations in public expenditure and the reasons for it, and promote a political debate centred on notions of 'equity' rather than 'subsidy'.

250 The pattern which might emerge within England can be estimated by looking at available data for the 85% of identifiable public expenditure in England which the Treasury is now able to 'allocate' to a particular standard region. The figures, quoted in the recent IFS Commentary, are shown in **Table 6** below. As for Scotland and Wales, the relative spending levels vary from programme to programme.

## Table 6: Per Capita 'Allocated' Government Spending in the English Regions, 1992–93

| | | Index, England (regionally-allocated) = 100 | | |
| --- | --- | --- | --- | --- |
| | Total | Social Security | Health and Social Services | Education |
| North | 107 | 115 | 101 | 101 |
| Yorks & Humber | 100 | 101 | 100 | 103 |
| E Midlands | 90 | 92 | 91 | 97 |
| East Anglia | 88 | 91 | 90 | 95 |
| London & S East | 103 | 96 | 105 | 100 |
| South West | 92 | 98 | 95 | 92 |
| W Midlands | 97 | 99 | 93 | 100 |
| North West | 107 | 112 | 104 | 107 |

Source: HM Treasury, *Public Expenditure: Statistical Supplement to the Financial Statement and Budget Report 1995-96*, (Table 7.9), Cm 2821, 1995.

251 These variations are to be expected. The UK is a fiscal union in that the same rules of taxation apply throughout, irrespective of the diverse needs, consumption patterns and income levels in different regions and territories. A progressive system of taxation and public expenditure

distributed in accordance with need has provided for an automatic process of regional redistribution and stabilisation. Richer regions contribute more per head to the national exchequer than poorer ones; but the latter, especially if they have high unemployment, poor infrastructure and industries in need of support, get more per head in public expenditure.

252 Another recent study has estimated the scale of this redistribution in terms of the balance between revenues raised and expenditure received in the territories and regions of the UK. **Table 7** below expresses these transfers in per capita terms. Figures below the line represent a net transfer of funds from those regions - London, the South East, East Midlands and East Anglia - above it.

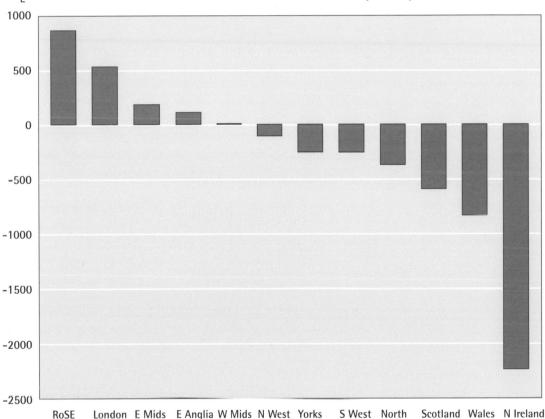

£ Table 7: General Government Current Balance (per capita) 1991

Note: The figures in this diagram relate to current expenditure only and do not include capital investment
Source: Neil Blake, 'The Regional Implications of Macroeconomic Policy', *Oxford Review of Economic Policy*, Vol II, No 2.

153 These figures are estimates taken from available data published in a variety of places. But they provide a picture of the operation of the UK tax and spending system on a region by region basis which gives valuable insights for those contemplating devolution. The establishment of a Scottish Parliament and of Assemblies elsewhere in the UK will place an emphasis on the territorial and regional effects of the existing financial system. Charts like Table 7 and the IFS study of regional finance will proliferate. The needs assessment could recognise this development by introducing a greater objectivity and transparency into English regional transfers as well as those between the four countries.

## The Next Needs Assessment: Institutions and Mechanisms

254 The paragraphs above have made the case for a needs assessment covering the whole of the UK and described relevant recent experience in assessing needs in the UK. Three questions arise:
- What needs should be assessed and how?
- Who should assess them?
- What should be done with the results?

255 The first question is the one which the Treasury started with in 1976, and which they still thought would repay further study over two years later. The answer will depend on the extent of the devolution settlement proposed, although since health and education spending alone comprise over 60% of the present Scottish block, variation in the settlement at the margins should not greatly affect the overall result.

256 The answer also needs to draw on the 1976 study, in particular its detailed methodology and the points in that process where improvements are suggested for next time around. In particular the assessors should take to heart the Report's strong encouragement to simplify the process. The full assessment involved measuring need against a range of about 130 different factors. But replaying the exercise after the study was concluded with only about 45 of the key indicators produced results which differed by only a single percentage point from those of the full study. The goal of maintaining public and political confidence in the allocation mechanisms would also be assisted by making the assessment process itself as simple and comprehensible as possible. The 1979 Report concluded:

> "We would recommend strongly against attempts to refine the calculation by adding a lot of further factors which could have only a negligible effect on the results. In fact, we have wondered whether the proposed method should not be simplified...In particular, cutting down the number of objective factors would mean confining the exercise to the main features where, in general, the external evidence is strongest".[74]

257 The second question - who should conduct the assessment? - arises out of the complexity of the first and in particular the need at all stages in the exercise to make crucial judgements about the relevance of various 'objective' factors and the relative weight to assign to them. The example of health services quoted above from the 1976 study is the tip of the iceberg.

258 For the needs assessment to be accepted by all parties as a truly objective presentation of relevant data on which to make judgements about spending allocations, it cannot be right for any one of the parties to be responsible for determining the data provided. This argues for an independent body to be responsible for overseeing the conduct of the needs assessment exercise. It would step into the role the Treasury played in 1976: co-ordinating work in a number of Whitehall departments, resolving disputes about methodology, legitimising decisions taken about the factors to be included in the assessment and the weights to give them, and assuring the objectivity of the data.

259 Initially this body, an independent Commission, might comprise a number of persons appointed by central government and a number appointed by the Scottish government. As devolution to other nations and regions progressed, so appointments could be made by other devolved areas too. The Commission would remain neutral and impartial, the servant of no one party in the negotiation. Its role would be purely advisory. It would remain the responsibility of the UK government, subject to the approval of Parliament, to take all necessary decisions.

## The Allocation Process

260 The third question - what should be done with the results of the needs assessment? - is the most complex. It would be difficult to establish the Commission in advance of the Scottish Parliament, and certainly in advance of Royal Assent to the devolution legislation. The needs assessment may take two to three years on the 1970s precedent. That means that, in any event, the Scottish budget in the early years of the Parliament would need to be allocated roughly on the existing basis, the Barnett formula, as the SCC propose.

261 But the role of the Commission in the allocation process might be three-fold:
- to conduct a UK-wide needs assessment.
- to make recommendations about the allocation formula in the light of that assessment.
- to conduct an independent audit of the results of applying the formula each year in order to ensure the objectivity of the data and the process, and to highlight any areas of difficulty in the strict application of the formula (eg the loss of English equivalent spending).

## Application of the Formula

262 The Treasury presently enjoys considerable control at the margin in determining the make-up of the block and the precise definition of English equivalent spending to which the formula is applied. If this same process is to enjoy the confidence of a number of different administrations within the UK, possibly of different political persuasions, then there will need to be some guarantee that this flexibility in the present system is not used to prejudice the interests of one territory against another.

263 Ideally the independent Commission would be responsible itself for the application of the formula to the data, thus introducing some rigour into the process, especially the public identification of the 'English block'. But in practice there simply is not time in the budget setting cycle to allow this to happen. The precise allocations within the 'English block' would not normally be known until announcements in the November budget. If the Commission had to wait until then to begin applying the formula the Scottish financial cycle would get seriously out of line. Hence the suggestion that instead the Commission should be given the power to audit the application of the formula by the Treasury 'post hoc'.

264 The audit might reveal errors in the application of the formula, or inconsistencies in its application from year to year, which the government would be obliged to make good. But its other function would be to identify any areas in which the application of the formula had caused difficulty, or inevitably involved some subjective judgement. The most likely such cause might be the lack of English equivalence brought about by different choices about spending priorities by the various devolved administrations in England and Scotland.

## Lack of English Equivalence

265 Allowing such differences to occur is the object of the devolution exercise. But the financial arrangements need to allow for them to be possible in practice. The arrangements might need to cope with the emergence of different concepts of the range of services appropriate for public provision North and South of the border.

266 There are clearly limits to the degree of policy divergence that a system based on central pooling of resources and allocation on the basis of relative need can logically tolerate. If the gap in political and economic philosophy on either side of the border becomes too wide there might no longer be *institutional* means to hold the Union together. This is David Heald's view: "Maintenance of the Union does indeed require a measure of common aspirations: no financing framework could sustain, for example, the abolition of the NHS in England but its continuation in the other three countries".[75]

267 But even if extreme variations might prove too much for the system, there will have to be mechanisms in place to cope with less dramatic differences between concepts of the public sector in Scotland and the rest of the UK. In the longer term, as it becomes politically feasible, this might mean that devolved parliaments be given more scope - along with local government - to determine their own level of resourcing through local taxation. In the meantime it will be part of the independent Commission's audit role to identify such problems as they occur, to comment on the methods chosen for their resolution, and to make recommendations for the future. The Commission might recommend some change in the overall allocation system if the cumulative effect of such problems becomes significant. The following suggestions might help, if they are not features of the allocation mechanism from the start:

- the mechanism for determining the grant might contain a compensating formula whereby changes in the UK part of the equation of more than 10% brought about by UK policy change would trigger compensating payments for a transition period and the recalibration of the allocation formula.
- the equalisation grant, rather than being based on providing English levels of service in other areas of the UK, could instead be based on average service levels across the UK (which will reflect the differing priorities regional governments with full spending autonomy have given them in practice). This might be particularly effective once the English regions have devolved government, diluting to some extent the inevitably dominant impact of English practice on the rest of the system.

## Determination of the Formula

268 The aim of the needs assessment exercise would be to provide a bench-mark against which to measure the success of the Barnett formula in bringing Scottish spending closer to the level indicated by Scotland's relative need. The recalibration of the formula in 1992 simply updated the population ratios. It is fair to assume that the change was intended to make the formula more effective in bringing about convergence, although there was no attempt made to reassess how Scottish spending then compared with relative need.

269 A new needs assessment, however flawed, questionable or judgemental, would provide a common estimate of relative needs throughout the UK. In particular, it would allow an objective appraisal of the operation of the Barnett formula in bringing about convergence to relative need. The rate of convergence will become more important as devolution is extended throughout the UK. For it is only by bringing about such convergence that extensive devolution can be financed on an equitable basis without entailing a significant increase in public expenditure - raising spending throughout the UK, for example, to Scottish levels.

270 The needs assessment would indicate levels of relative need. It would show the gap, if any, between Scotland's actual spending and the level of spending that is justified by higher levels of need. The question that would have to be decided following the assessment is how quickly that gap could in practice be closed: the rate of convergence? That is an intensely political question. Ultimate responsibility for setting the formula would have to rest with the Westminster Parliament, acting on a proposal from the UK government. That proposal would have to reflect consultation with the Scottish Parliament and Executive, and it would need to be based on a recommendation from the independent Commission.

271 This last point is important. The agreed formula would inevitably result from a political process involving negotiation between the Edinburgh and London governments, parliamentary debate in Edinburgh and Westminster, and a vote - preferably in both the House of Commons and the House of Lords. The principal issue in the negotiations would be the rate of convergence required. But this is also a highly technical question. The rate of convergence would depend on overall economic conditions in the UK. In periods of higher growth or higher inflation the rate of convergence under the Barnett formula is increased. The opposite is true in a recession. The rate of convergence that might be feasible - given that cuts in public spending would inevitably be painful - would depend crucially on the size of the gap between actual spending and the level indicated by relative need. That is something that the Commission would be responsible for identifying.

272 The Commission would also have identified during the course of auditing the application of the formula over a number of years weaknesses, contradictions, special circumstances and other factors which had hamstrung its operation in practice. For all of these reasons it should be for the Commission to recommend changes to the formula as necessary, and in any event following each new needs assessment.

273 The first needs assessment might be conducted in the immediate two to three years following the establishment of the Parliament. Thereafter, the exercise might be repeated at intervals of between five and ten years. The report of the Commission following each such exercise, incorporating data on levels of relative need, a critique of the operation of the formula in previous years, and any recommendations for reviewing the formula, would provide a focus for the political debate which must then take place.

274 The report would be a public document which would allow an informed debate in Westminster, Edinburgh and elsewhere. The levels of need and the precise configuration of the formula will always be contentious political issues. Establishing an independent Commission with the roles described above would at least remove as many as possible of the technical aspects of the issue from the political debate. More importantly it would remove the monopoly of understanding of these issues from one party, and one alone, in the complex negotiations that financing devolution will require.

## Flexibility: Sources of Finance Outside the Block

275 The budget assigned to Scotland under the allocation formula will cover the majority of the Scottish Executive's needs. But it will still need additional sources of revenue, to meet special circumstances, for example, to cover existing spending which falls outside the block, perhaps to

pursue a special project, or simply to give some flexibility in balancing the budget from year to year. This section considers three sources of additional revenues:

- funds from central government.
- borrowing.
- independent revenue raising powers.

## Funds from Central Government

276 At present about 5% of the Scottish Office budget falls outside the block, and therefore outside the formula. Spending on the Common Agricultural Policy and domestic agriculture is outside the block. So is spending on remaining nationalised industries in Scotland. These monies are a small percentage of the Scottish budget, but arrangements will need to be included in the financial provisions for devolution to ensure that they are still covered.

277 The treatment of EU funds, in particular monies from the European Regional Development Fund, might also need to be re-examined in the light of devolution. The principle of additionality requires that European finance is matched by funds provided by the recipient. In theory, public expenditure provision for those matching funds in Scotland is included within the Scottish block. But the precise operation of this element in the block is far from clear. In order to satisfy the additionality requirement after devolution the financing arrangements would have to distinguish between funds from central government and funds from Europe, and would need to ensure that additionality occurred at the Scottish, rather than at the UK, level.

278 Finally, there is a case - as already suggested in paragraph 229 above - for allowing the Scottish Executive continued access to the UK contingency reserve. That might be required to cover unforeseen circumstances like flooding or other natural disasters. It would be odd if, following devolution, Scotland were the only part of the UK state denied access to the reserve.

279 But access to the reserve, as now, would come with conditions attached. The Scottish Executive would presumably need to demonstrate to the Treasury that the monies required could not be found through savings elsewhere in the budget, and would have to make necessary adjustments to the budget in subsequent years if there were continuing financial implications. Thus, although access to the contingency reserve should be provided for in principle, the Scottish Executive might want to use it as little as possible if it wished to avoid any Treasury involvement in policies devolved to Scotland.

## Borrowing

### Borrowing for Revenue Smoothing

280 The 1978 Scotland Act made explicit provision for the Scottish Executive to be able to borrow up to £75m to cover short term problems in managing its finances. The sum was intended to represent about 10 days' expenditure: the figure would have required an increase in line with inflation had the Act come into force. The provision amounted to a temporary overdraft facility to assist financial management.

281 The SCC proposals do not mention borrowing, but some means of covering temporary shortfalls or in-year contingencies will be needed, especially if the assigned budget is to be paid in monthly instalments. Two options might be considered:

- prior arrangement with the Paymaster General's Office - which would pay the block grant - that shortfalls should be covered, perhaps up to a certain limit and with guarantees that the shortfalls were only temporary. This would amount to a rolling float from central government in addition to the block grant.
- borrowing, up to a certain limit, by analogy with the 1978 Act, either direct from central government or - if the Scottish Executive's revenues are managed by the Scottish commercial banking system - from a commercial bank, or both.

282 The second option provides a more secure arrangement in the long term. It would be feasible to allow both borrowing from central government and from commercial banks (the interest charges would affect the choice). In any event the sums available to the Scottish Executive through this means should be strictly limited to cover only short-term contingencies.

*Capital borrowing*

283 The issue of borrowing for capital investment is more complex. Scottish local authorities may only incur capital expenditure with the consent of the Secretary of State. Since such spending in government accounting terms counts as public expenditure (even though it is not specifically voted in Parliament) these 'capital consents' are included within the Scottish block. Thus the actual monies available to the Scottish Office in any year will consist of the Scottish block *less* the value of capital consents it needs to give to local authorities in that year. After devolution therefore, the status quo might be maintained by the Scottish Executive determining what proportion of its assigned budget it wishes to allocate to capital consents for local authorities.

284 Capital spending by the Scottish Office itself is at present also financed out of the block. Investment in road building, for example, would come largely from that element in the block which reflects the existence of a road building programme in England/Wales. The advantage of this arrangement for Scotland is that all debt interest on central government spending falls to the Treasury and is not allocated by region. There is thus no charge levied for monies used for capital investment. So long as these arrangements continued, the Scottish Executive would be most unlikely to fund capital investment in any other way.

285 There are changes on the horizon. The Government have proposed to introduce by the year 2000 a new system of 'resource budgeting' which will involve changes in the treatment of capital spending, debt interest and capital assets in the government's accounts. The new system will apply throughout the UK. It might be that as a result of the new system it became relatively more attractive for the Scottish Executive to finance its own capital spending externally. The Treasury's concern in that instance would be to limit the potential consequences of such borrowing on tax payers in the rest of the UK. Their overall attitude might also depend on the nature of the formula in existence at that time: if it required particularly tight control of spending to bring about convergence the case for access to other sources of finance for capital investment might be stronger.

286 The conclusion for the moment must be that the devolution legislation will not need to provide for capital borrowing by the Scottish Executive, but that the arrangements should be amendable by secondary legislation should developments in the Government's accounting process require some adjustment.

## Independent Revenue Raising Powers

287 Powers to raise revenues independently are crucial for the Parliament. Running throughout this chapter has been the notion that no Parliament can enjoy any degree of policy autonomy unless the financial arrangements are designed to allow it. The constraints on that autonomy will be felt initially at the margins - when even a minor policy initiative is stifled through lack of funds. Crucial expenditure decisions will likewise occur at the margins. Further, it is desirable that the Parliament should be accountable to the Scottish people for those spending decisions at the margin, rather than being able to pass the responsibility for their decisions about priorities on to Westminster. So long as there is no power for the Parliament to raise revenues independently the political debate would be in danger of degenerating into cross-party attacks on the attitude of the UK Exchequer.

288 The recent Institute for Fiscal Studies commentary concluded both that independent tax raising powers were necessary and that they were feasible in practice:

*"If regional governments are to function as genuine democratic units, with the power to make free decisions concerning the level and pattern of public services, they will need to have access to some form of tax revenues under their control. Reliance on fiscal transfers from central government will undermine the ability of regional governments to make their decisions free from central influence"*; and

*"It is unlikely that there would be major administrative difficulties in operating a regionally-varying income tax now, although it would be necessary to incur the additional administrative cost of registering the place of residence of each income tax payer".*

289 The *power* to raise additional revenue is important even if it is heavily constrained and even if it is never used (the difficulty of raising direct taxation in an environment where there will always be an election in the offing, either in the UK or Scotland, should not be underestimated). The former Prime Minister Lord Home made these points in the second reading debate on the 1977 Scotland Bill:

*"I am quite certain that an Assembly must be given some ability to raise revenue, otherwise we shall be asking for trouble. It need not be a great deal. The cry for the right to tax is very popular before the taxes have to be applied. If I had had my way, and it had not conflicted with regulations in Europe...I would have applied a sales tax. It would have been immensely unpopular, and no Assembly would have wielded it except in the most moderate way".*[76]

290 The SCC propose that the Parliament should have the power to vary the basic rate of income tax by up to three pence in the pound. It is estimated that each penny on the basic rate would raise around £150m in Scotland: hence what is proposed is a power to vary spending in Scotland by less than 3% of the present Scottish Office budget. It would not have any significant macroeconomic effects in the UK as a whole and, so long as it were levied with a clear and accepted purpose, there should be little danger of it introducing incentive effects which distort the Scottish economy. This power has raised an astonishing volume of comment given its relative insignificance in the overall financial settlement. It should be welcomed in principle for the reasons given above. But there are a number of technical points which will need to be addressed in implementing the proposal which are discussed below.

## Variation in the Basic Rate of Income Tax

291 The basic rate of income tax was chosen by the SCC as the vehicle for independent revenue raising on the grounds that it would be easily identifiable as an extra tax by those paying it and the burden of the additional taxation would be spread reasonably widely throughout the

population. These are important qualities relating to accountability and equity. They satisfy the 'accountability' criteria for regional taxes suggested by the IFS: "The incidence of the tax should be broadly distributed across tax payers, and the amount of the tax and the government authority responsible for charging it should be clearly perceived by taxpayers".

292 Other options cannot match the criteria. The council tax operates on a relatively narrow tax base, too narrow to support demand both from local government and a Scottish Parliament. Problems of equity also arise. A regional sales tax would spread the burden of taxation more widely through the population, but would therefore relatively disadvantage poorer households and would be less 'visible' as a specifically Scottish tax. Added to which any changes in national VAT arrangements would probably require the agreement of our EU partners.

293 Even so, the British tax system is a relatively centralised and streamlined one in which major taxes, excluding council tax, and business and water rates, are collected by central authorities and the vast majority of tax transactions occur automatically without the need for the individual to complete a detailed tax return. This makes the variation of income tax in one part of the UK alone a potentially troublesome measure to implement.

*Taxable Income*

294 It will be necessary to reach a tight definition of taxable income for the purposes of variation in the basic rate. This will need to recognise the inter-relation between the various elements in the tax system (corporation tax, capital gains tax and income tax). Some definitions might lead to a more equitable distribution of the tax burden than others. If the variation power applies only to the basic rate of income tax, as proposed, then it means that the Parliament will neither be able to lower taxes for the poor (who do not pay that rate anyway), nor to increase taxes on the incomes of higher rate payers in excess of the basic rate band. As it stands levying the tax would be a regressive measure: the higher one's income the smaller percentage of it would be taken in tax by the Scottish Parliament. That too might become a factor in the political decision whether to use the power or not.

*Changing Tax Base*

295 The notion of a 'basic rate' of income tax was introduced to replace the 'standard rate' in 1973-74. It was intended to be the basic tax rate around which the tax system as a whole operated. But that concept has been eroded in recent years: MIRAS no longer relies on the basic rate, and tax credits on dividends, purchased life annuities and interest are now assessed at source at a lower rate. Also, now that there is a lower rate of tax, each time that rate or the range over which it is levied is changed, the number of people in the basic rate range falls. The width of the basic rate band may have to be narrowed to offset increased tax relief at the lower end of the scale. The tax base available to the Scottish Parliament to exercise the three pence option would therefore be wholly at the mercy of the UK Chancellor. It could not be otherwise: the needs of a tax system in Scotland, covering only 10% of the population, could not dictate to the perceived needs and progressivity of the UK tax system as a whole.

*Administrative Costs*

296 As the IFS study concludes, there will be a need for Scottish taxpayers to provide the Inland Revenue with a greater degree of information than now (declaration of residence - and of change of residence). Systems will need to be devised to accommodate the new tax, but they will certainly add to the administrative cost in terms of time, money and convenience of the

system. There will be judgements to be made too in terms of the practicality of collecting the tax in all circumstances. It might be that the administrative costs do not justify attempting to levy the tax on people moving to Scotland within the tax year, for example, or those resident in Scotland for only a portion of the tax year. Some of those decisions too could have consequences for the overall equity of the system.

*Making Local Tax Work*

297 These are complex issues which any Government implementing the SCC's proposals would have to think through with the aid of the expertise then available to them in the Inland Revenue and elsewhere. It will be important to make the power a workable one, even if it is never used.

298 One possible modification to address the points about equity and application might be to apply the power of variation to *all* income tax rates, rather than just the basic rate. The Parliament might even so have to be restricted from changing the lower rates in view of the inter-relation with the benefits system (which will not be devolved). If there is a poverty trap in the system then it will have to be addressed at Westminster. Alternatively, it might be possible to place a limit on the power by reference to a different ceiling, eg the size of the permissible *overall* yield, or the *equivalent* to three pence on the basic rate, however the Parliament decided to distribute the tax burden in practice. In either case, the incentive effects which might operate in varying higher tax rates might persuade the Scottish Government in any event to confine itself to varying the basic rate alone.

299 It should be possible by clarifying such points of detail to ensure that the proposed revenue raising power is both workable and equitable: visible to the taxpayer and levied across a wide portion of the Scottish population. But if devolution is to proceed throughout the UK then a deeper analysis will be needed. Fiscal devolution would be a lot easier to implement in the context of devolution all round - or of full-scale federalism. But federalism is not realistically on the political agenda. Systems developed to finance federal government elsewhere cannot be transferred wholesale into the very different context of asymmetrical devolution in the UK.

300 What is really required is a thorough analysis of the operation of a fiscal Union, which includes a number of devolved governments, within the broader framework of the EU. Even if devolution were extended only to Scotland there would be implications for the whole of the UK. Scots derive income from England and English derive income from Scotland.

301 To conduct such an analysis the first requirement would be accurate data about the levels of tax revenues raised in the UK and how they are derived. For example, it is difficult to decide whether the collection of an additional marginal rate on investment income in Scotland would be economic when there are no disaggregated figures for the sums of revenue involved.

302 Second, it is necessary to relate the magnitude of the tax power (and therefore the variety of instruments which might supply it) to the likely additional spending needs of the authority in question. There are thus wider questions about independent revenue raising powers for devolved administrations which will have to be addressed in the longer term: the relationship between independent revenues and the assigned budget, the appropriate range over which a revenue raising power might vary in the light of that relationship, and the mechanisms by which revenue might be raised - not just in Scotland but potentially in time across the UK.

303 These are points for the future which the Constitution Unit hopes to return to in a later report.

## Assignment of Scottish Tax Revenues

304 The fact that Scottish expenditure at present is financed for the most part by allocation from Westminster can obscure the fact that a large proportion of this revenue was raised originally in Scotland. It is tempting therefore to suggest that the Scottish Parliament should be financed simply by retaining all its own tax revenues, cutting out the allocation function of the centre.

305 This was the approach adopted for financing devolution in Northern Ireland from 1921. Stormont was originally assigned all revenues raised in the province from which it was required to pay an Imperial Contribution to cover the cost of services retained at Westminster (foreign affairs, defence etc.) with the remainder at the disposal of the Parliament to spend as it saw fit. But it soon became apparent that tax yields in the province were too small to finance a level of service comparable to that in the rest of the UK and the financial arrangements were recast so that the UK would make good any deficit in Northern Ireland so as to guarantee services of a UK standard in the province.

306 This is a salutary lesson for Scotland. Depending on the assumptions made in calculating revenues and expenditure, it is clear at least that Scotland would risk falling into the Northern Irish position - unable to finance all its spending needs - if such a system were adopted (see paragraphs 216 to 224 above).

307 Even so, there is scope for attempting to assign all or part of Scottish tax revenues to the Parliament as part of the financial package. This would not alter the overall size of the Scottish budget. It might also make the equalisation grant look more like a subsidy than if it covered a larger proportion of the total budget. But such assignment nevertheless might have two potential benefits:
- it would give the Parliament, and the Scottish people, a greater sense of entitlement to revenues raised in Scotland which would be retained in Scotland as of right, rather than negotiated out of the central exchequer. This is an important element in the fiscal psychology of the relationship between central and regional government[77].
- it would reduce the size and therefore the significance of the block grant element. The gearing effect would then mean that any percentage reduction in the block grant would have a smaller impact on the Scottish budget overall and could more readily be compensated for through other mechanisms.

308 'Assignment' could either involve retention of revenues actually raised by a tax in Scotland, or - preferably - Scotland's share of the total revenue generated by the tax across the UK, allocated on a per capita/per household/per adult basis. The latter form of assignment is more accurately termed 'tax sharing'.

309 A good deal of thought has been given to the assignment of tax revenues, notably by David Heald. His 1990 study *Financing a Scottish Parliament: Options for Debate*[78] provides a full analysis of taxes raised in Scotland and their suitability or otherwise for assignment. The SCC's earlier proposals published in the same year contained an eloquent commitment to the principle of assigned taxes and identified income tax and VAT as the most suitable.[79] And the Scottish Office's report on the 1993-94 budget provides estimates of Scottish tax yields from all sources:
> "The four main classes of revenue raised in Scotland are income tax (raising an estimated £4.62bn in 1993-94), social security receipts (£3.45bn) VAT revenues (£3.35bn) and local

*authority revenues, which includes non-domestic rates and council tax (£1.98bn). These taxes are highlighted for two reasons: they are the largest revenue earners in Scotland; and they can be estimated with reasonable accuracy. Illustrative calculations suggest that these four sources of revenue raised £13.39 billion, or two-thirds of total Scottish revenues, in 1993-94".*

310    Of these four sources, social security receipts are inappropriate for assignment given that the social security system will not to be devolved. The problems involved in precepting on the local authorities' tax base have already been briefly discussed. That leaves two main sources of revenue - income tax and VAT. These are the best candidates for tax sharing. The other taxes are either too small in terms of yield to deliver the benefits described in paragraph 307 above, or are too difficult to disaggregate for Scotland.

311    Tax sharing could well come to play a larger part in the financial arrangements if devolution is established throughout the UK. But that is not the case now, and nor is there sufficient confidence yet in the reliability of the figures for tax yields in the territories and regions to allow it to deliver the benefits in 'fiscal psychology' described. Nevertheless the option of incorporating some element of tax sharing in the financial settlement should be kept open for the future.


## Conclusion

312    The financial arrangements are likely to come in for closer scrutiny than any other aspect of the devolution settlement once the Scottish Parliament is established. Whilst formula-based allocation of an assigned budget to Scotland, as now, will provide a workable financing system, it is by no means certain that present methods of determining the formula or applying it each year (both the prerogative of the Treasury) will continue to command confidence in the changed circumstances of devolution.

313    If that view is accepted, the key to retaining trust in a formula-based system might be the establishment of an independent Commission to take on responsibility for monitoring the operation of the formula and collecting and making public reliable data relevant to its calculation and application. The Commission would have an advisory role only: all decisions would still be taken by the UK Government subject to the Westminster Parliament's approval.

314    The Scottish Executive will need access to monies outside the block, as now, including an overdraft facility to assist financial management. It also needs independent revenue raising powers in order to ensure accountability to the Scottish people for spending decisions. The proposed variation in the basic rate of income tax is probably the best available instrument for that purpose, although points of detail still need to be settled. In time, and as the number of devolved administrations increases, other options might become available which would help to refine the power in the direction of greater administrative efficiency and enhanced equity.

# Chapter 6

## Scotland and the European Union

## Introduction

315 The growth in the impact of the European Union on domestic policy and legislation is one of the biggest changes in the context in which a devolved Scottish Parliament and Government might operate since the passage of the 1978 Scotland Act. Then the UK's membership of the European Community was only a few years old and the Community itself was enduring a period of 'Euro-sclerosis' before the subsequent advances of the Single European Act (1987) and the Maastricht Treaty (1993). These two Treaty revisions added numerous new competences to the Community's remit, including new chapters on the environment, health and safety, culture, training. It is striking how great the overlap is between the list of powers the SCC suggest should be devolved to the Scottish Parliament and the present list of Community competences. It is perhaps not so surprising that powers central government is prepared to devolve to Brussels - in whole or in part - it might also be willing to devolve to Edinburgh. But the overlap does cause difficulties in defining and operating the devolution settlement. This chapter addresses them.

## The European Context

316 The importance of the European framework in which the UK now takes its part cannot be overestimated. Even if the Intergovernmental Conference now in progress promotes no radical new policy changes, the Union already enjoys considerable powers including, according to the Maastricht Treaty, the prospect of the introduction of a single European currency before the end of the century. Then President of the Commission, Jacques Delors, famously told the European Parliament (EP) in July 1988: "Ten years hence, 80% of our economic legislation, and perhaps even our fiscal and social legislation as well, will be of Community origin."[80] We may not have reached that point yet, but the impact of Community law on domestic policy and legislation is already considerable.

317 This matters in the context of devolution because of the unique character of the European Community (EC).[81] For the Community is a community of law, in that it is able to adopt legislation, justiciable before the European Court of Justice (ECJ), which has direct and superior effect in the member states i.e. overrides domestic legislation which conflicts with it. This legislation takes two main forms: regulations which take effect directly, and directives which require to be implemented by the member state i.e. embodied in domestic legislation. The direct effect of Community obligations is provided for by section 2(1) of the European Communities Act 1972 (emphasis added):

> *All such rights, powers, liabilities, obligations and restrictions...created or arising by or under the Treaties...as in accordance with the Treaties are without further enactment to be given legal effect or used in the United Kingdom* **shall be recognised and available in law, and be enforced, allowed and followed accordingly.**

318 It is this provision, coupled with the principle that Community law may prevail over domestic legislation, which led to certain parts of the UK Merchant Shipping Act 1988 being ruled invalid by the House of Lords.[82]

319 The significance of this legal structure is two-fold:
- it is the United Kingdom which has signed and ratified the Community treaties and which therefore enjoys all the rights bestowed by them and the obligations arising from them. The rights include representation in the Community institutions, 10 votes in the Council of Ministers, a formal say in the decision-making process. The obligations include the implementation and enforcement of EC law, even where this has been enacted without the support of the UK.
- where EC legislation is not given effect in domestic law, is implemented in a defective or incomplete fashion or is not enforced, it is the UK (as member state) which is liable in European law for any damages arising out of such error.[83] The Maastricht Treaty introduced a power for the Commission to fine a member state which fails to fulfil its obligations even after an adverse judgement from the ECJ (Article 171).

320 The implications of this legal context for the treatment of EU issues in the devolution legislation itself were considered in chapter 3. This chapter goes on to discuss some of the practical implications of operating the devolution settlement as it relates to the EU within the legal parameters set by the devolution Act. The first section considers the scope for direct representation of a devolved Scotland's interests in the EU; the second considers the policy-making processes within the UK Government; and the third assesses how the Parliament itself might maximise its European role.

## Representing Scotland's Interests

321 There is a wide literature on the impact of European integration on systems of government within the member states, especially federal or otherwise decentralised states.[84] Within that literature it is the experience of the German Länder which probably brings most to a discussion of how Scotland might participate in the EU. Germany has developed the most sophisticated and comprehensive institutional and legal machinery for intergovernmental policy-making within the state to marry the demands of federalism at home and integration abroad. The objectives of the Länder in developing this machinery have been threefold:
- to shelter certain policy fields against excessive EU involvement by emphasising the principle of subsidiarity.
- to promote direct access to policy-making at the EU level.
- to increase their weight in national arrangements for EU-related decision-making.[85]

322 Scotland's aims following devolution can be expected to be the same. Scotland will become a European 'region' like Bavaria or Catalonia, with its own government and Parliament. It will want to add its voice to those of other regions with legislative competences in arguing for greater respect for subsidiarity, not only between the EU and the member states, but within the member states themselves. Whether that argument will prove decisive is another matter, and not the subject of this report. For the foreseeable future Scotland, like even the most powerful of the Länder, will in practice need to concentrate on the second and third objectives above.

## Direct Access to EU Policy-making

323 Scotland already enjoys direct representation in two of the Community's institutions: eight Members of the European Parliament out of a UK total of 87, and five members of the Committee of the Regions out of 24. Scots representation in other institutions (e.g. Judge David Edward in the ECJ, Campbell Christie on the Economic and Social Committee) is an accident of merit rather than any regional distribution. For it is the UK which has the right to representation in all the Community institutions, and it is for the UK Government to decide how to allocate its places between constituent nations and regions.

324 This formal position will not change after devolution. But there are ways in which it might need to be modified in practice. It may not be necessary to embody in the devolution legislation any confirmation of Scotland's existing representation, especially in the case of the MEPs where any change would in any case require primary legislation, redrawing of the boundaries, etc. But some form of general understanding between the Edinburgh and London Governments will be needed about the Committee of the Regions, and about representation in new or enlarged institutions in the future. The widespread suspicion that Scotland's generous representation on the Committee (relative to population) was part of a deal involving SNP support in a crucial division for Maastricht ratification is a warning of how allocation of places might become politicised.

## Committee of the Regions

325 Responsibility for nominating Scotland's five places on the Committee of the Regions should clearly fall to the Scottish rather than the Westminster Government. At present the Secretary of State nominates representatives. Whether nominations are subject to Parliamentary approval will be for the Parliament to decide: they are not at present. Since the Treaty refers to a Committee composed of 'representatives of regional and local bodies' (Article 198a), it is up to the member state to decide how such representatives are to be chosen. The UK legislation implementing the Treaty specified that all UK delegates should be *elected* representatives. But it did not attempt, for obvious reasons, to rule on the balance between regional and local representatives.

326 This has become a point of contention in other countries. In Germany, for example, the German municipalities insisted on retaining the representation they had enjoyed in the Committee's predecessor body, the Consultative Council of Regional and Local Authorities. Hence the Federal Government gave the Länder autonomy to select their Committee of the Regions' representatives only with the proviso that their nominations included three local councillors (and alternates).[86]

327 A similar balance will have to be struck in nominating Scotland's representatives. It is doubtful whether this balance needs to be laid down in central government legislation. The initial balance will reflect the desire for continuity with pre-devolution practice. Other considerations might suggest a different balance in the future. An initial distribution of two local councillors and three MSPs should be a sensible starting point. That balance, ways of changing it in the light of experience (e.g. the workload on MSPs), and perhaps the selection/election process for choosing the local authority nominees might be incorporated in the Concordat between the Scottish Parliament and local government described in detail in chapter 8.

328 The tensions already developing in the Committee of the Regions between representatives of European regional autonomous governments and local authorities may in time lead to the distinction the Scottish Executive will have to draw being formally recognised in the structure of the Committee itself, perhaps through its splitting into two chambers.

## European Parliament

329 Scotland will continue to enjoy representation by eight MEPs. Devolution will not change their status within the EU, but it may integrate them more closely into the political process in Scotland. At the moment, since many MPs at Westminster see themselves in competition with MEPs, it has been very difficult to implement co-operative arrangements between them. But the choice of the Euro-constituencies as regions for the operation of the Additional Member voting system in Scotland will give the European constituencies a greater salience in Scottish politics. There will be seven MSPs (taken from the regional list) representing precisely the same constituents as each MEP. This is bound to encourage links between them. Any move to adopt a system of proportional representation for European elections, to bring the UK into line with the rest of Europe, might further strengthen these links.

330 It will be for the Scottish Parliament to capitalise on these closer links between Scottish and European electoral politics, especially in its rules and procedures. As Bernard Crick and David Millar's draft Standing Orders say: "the Scottish Parliament must throw open its doors to the eight Scottish MEPs and seek their active collaboration in building up its relations with the EP and the Community, in a way never done by the House of Commons and only partially by the House of Lords".[87] Edinburgh should follow Westminster in allowing Scottish MEPs full access to the Parliament building and its facilities. But it might also go beyond that in coopting say two MEPs on to its European Affairs Committee - to encourage the flow of information and to assist in the scrutiny of EC legislative proposals. There will be practical difficulties for MEPs in combining these roles: hence the Committee should be established so as to function equally well in their absence. Beyond that it will fall to the Scottish Government to liaise as necessary with Scotland's MEPs in order to maximise their usefulness as a channel for influencing legislative proposals.

## Scottish Representative Office in Brussels

331 The SCC propose that the Parliament should establish a representative office in Brussels, but that this should be undertaken "through consultation with other Scottish and UK organisations which operate European offices so as to maximise impact and provide co-ordination among agencies". That is to say, the Parliament's office needs to complement the promotion of Scotland's interests in Europe already undertaken by Scotland Europa and by the office of the UK Representative to the European Communities (UKRep).

332 Scotland Europa is an umbrella organisation for the representation of a number of interests and quite deliberately does not include any Scottish Office officials. Its establishment in 1991 was accompanied by assurances that UKRep would include more Scottish Office officials on secondment, that a European central support unit would be established within the Scottish Office and that more Scottish Office officials would be encouraged to learn languages.[88]

333 The choices for the **Parliament** will be:
   1. to establish a new office in Brussels.
   2. to restructure Scotland Europa to make it an office of Parliament, which would thus take over the landlord function presently filled by Scottish Enterprise.
   3. to participate in Scotland Europa like any other client.

On grounds of cost and continuity options 2 or 3 seem more sensible. Either will provide a base in Brussels for the Parliament (i.e. MSPs) to gain direct access to the Community institutions and, more importantly, to gain from the 'intelligence gathering' which the office already undertakes on behalf of its clients. For presentational reasons option 2 appears best. The office should be seen to derive its authority from the Scottish administration.

334 For the Scottish **Executive** the options are more varied. It will retain access to information and some limited influence through Scottish Enterprise's participation in Scotland Europa. The main source of information for the Scottish Office at present is UKRep, where one Scottish Office official is almost always to be found on secondment, and through the Secretary of State's access to reports of contacts and meetings in which UKRep is involved. The new Scottish Government will need to retain access to as much information as possible under devolution. Hence it should:
   • benefit from the facilities and information supplied by Scotland Europa.
   • continue to second officials to UKRep.[89]

335 It is unrealistic to assume, however, that access to UKRep reporting could continue under devolution, especially under administrations of different political persuasions in London and in Edinburgh. The Scottish Executive will therefore need in addition to establish its own presence in Brussels for the purpose of contacts, lobbying and information gathering. This might be separate from the Parliament's office (a reformed Scotland Europa). But given that the electoral system in Scotland should encourage a more consensual approach to politics than is found at Westminster, it is probably better that Parliament and Executive should be housed under the same roof - as landlords to the present clients of Scotland Europa.

## Representation in Other Institutions

336 Apart from the European Parliament and the Committee of the Regions (and the analogous Economic and Social Committee), issues of regional distribution of seats do not arise in the other Community institutions where the UK generally has the right to only one place. That will be true, for example, of the European Central Bank. It is also true of the ECJ, although it so happens that the UK judge on the Court has been a Scot for nearly twenty out of the twenty-four years of UK Community membership. The exception is the Commission in which the UK, in common with the other four large member states, has two places. It is tempting to insist that one of these should fall to Scotland - as it did in practice from 1973-76 (George Thomson) and 1989-94 (Bruce Millan).

337 In practice however, the UK's second Commissioner may well be removed in the interests of streamlining the institutions ready for enlargement. It will still be open to the UK Government to appoint a Scot to the post (as it has done before) after devolution, whether on the recommendation of the Scottish Government or not. But it will be for the UK Government to make the appointment to this and to all other institutions. The Scottish Government should therefore reserve the right to nominate persons for all Community institutions, including notably the Commission and the ECJ, but on the understanding that it will then be for the UK Government to weigh their individual claims against others'.

338 Finally, all member states have recognised the importance of having a good proportion of their own nationals serving within the Commission itself. Scotland should aim for the same result: say one in ten of UK nationals working in the Commission. It should therefore maintain participation after devolution in the UK's civil service Fast Stream scheme which seeks to prepare UK candidates to win posts in the EC institutions' entry competitions. The Parliament might want to monitor performance in this respect.

## The Council

339 The EU is a union of states and peoples. Its heart is the Council in which representatives of the governments of the member states meet to discuss policy and to agree legislation. The pooling of state sovereignty in the Council is mirrored by a pooling of popular sovereignty in the EP. The EP's role in the legislative process has been progressively strengthened through the Single European Act and the Maastricht Treaty. It now has the power to block the enactment of legislation under the codecision procedure. It may also amend legislative proposals. The Commission retains the sole right of initiative to propose legislation, although the Council or the EP can request that it brings forward proposals they desire. It is in this constitutional framework that a devolved Scotland will have to take its place.

340 Scotland will be able to exert a degree of influence on the Commission during the pre-legislative period so that Scottish interests are accommodated in the initial draft (its influence will clearly be stronger if the UK is singing the same tune); and some influence in amending legislative proposals in the EP through its MEPs. But the real decision-making forum is the Council: "neither the assent powers conferred on the European Parliament in the Single European Act and in the Maastricht Treaty nor the codecision of that Treaty (nor, for that matter, Parliament's powers as a joint budgetary authority) can oblige the Council to accept anything which it or a blocking minority of its members does not want to accept".[90] Since a good deal of the legislation the Council adopts will be in areas formally devolved to the Scottish Parliament, the Scottish Government needs to gain influence in this body above all.

## Influence on National Policy-making Arrangements

341 It is helpful to visualise the Council not as a body but as a process of negotiation between representatives of the member states' governments. That negotiation is carried out in a great number of ways: informal contacts, diplomatic demarches, working groups of member states' officials, the Committee of Permanent Representatives (COREPER), and in the Council itself (which, in one or other of its many formations, is in almost permanent session in Brussels). The substance of each member state's position in these negotiations is arrived at through an internal policy-making process within the state. The agents of the state conducting the negotiation - officials, embassies, Ministers - will all follow this agreed policy line. For Scotland therefore it is less important that there should be a Scot presenting the line in the Council than that the policy should be one which is in Scotland's interests.

342 Scotland's interests are taken into account in formulating UK Government policy at present: through the participation of Scottish Office officials and Ministers in the Cabinet Committee structure (including the Cabinet itself), through official level contacts between UK Ministries and

the Scottish Office, through official representation in Council delegations where the subject matter is of particular relevance to Scotland (and in working groups on the same basis), and through the presence on occasions of a Scottish Office Minister on the Council delegation e.g. in the Fisheries or Agriculture Councils - very rarely elsewhere. The aim should be to try to preserve as much as is politically realistic of this existing level of influence after devolution. That means in effect converting the existing machinery from an internal arrangement within Government into an external one between Governments within the same state.

343 The experience of other member states with regional governments is instructive. Experience is mixed. In Spain the autonomous regions have so far failed to gain the influence over EU policy they desire. The Government proposed in 1986 an 'Agreement for Cooperation in Community Matters' based on early German practice. But the negotiations stalled in 1988 because Catalonia and Euskadi in particular wanted too much autonomy in the Council delegation. There is for the moment in practice only co-operation in access to information and in specifically regional policy, although the recent change of Government could presage a greater regional role.

344 Other European regions have been more successful. The federal systems in Belgium and Germany give exclusive competence to the regions in a number of areas, and they have used this influence over changes at the EC level affecting those competences to negotiate participation in the European policy-making process across the board. In Belgium the federal government, the three regional and the three community governments concluded in 1993 a co-operation agreement laying down the composition of the Council delegation and decision rules concerning negotiating strategy and voting when there is no agreement. The co-operation agreement was finalised in an Inter-Ministerial Conference for External Affairs, which is now the main forum for joint EU policy-making. The directorate for EU affairs within the Foreign Ministry and the Belgian Representation to the EU in Brussels act as the 'two diplomatic gatekeepers' of Belgian policy, ensuring that the policy presented in the Community institutions is coherent and has been arrived at in the right way.[91]

345 Since the constitutional changes of May 1993, the Belgian regions and communities are fully competent to enter into international agreements themselves within the scope of their competences. Treaties which affect shared competences require the assent of all assemblies involved. This means that any revision of the Maastricht Treaty is likely to require ratification in the Federal Parliament and in all regional and community assemblies. That has made co-operation in European policy a necessity for the central government.

346 The same is true in Germany, where the Länder have used the leverage they possess by virtue of the Bundesrat's role in the ratification of European treaties to formalise rights in the European policy-making process. The Länder thus made Bundesrat approval for the ratification of the Maastricht Treaty conditional on a number of demands which were met by the inclusion of a new Article 23 in the federal constitution. Among other things, this Article stipulates a qualified majority in both the Bundestag and the Bundesrat for the transfer of any sovereign powers into Community competence, it makes the position of the Bundesrat decisive in those areas which affect the exclusive legislative competences of the Länder, and it provides that the Federal Republic may be represented by a representative of the Länder in the Council where those legislative competences are being discussed.[92]

**347** These arrangements have been negotiated between the regional and national governments in the member states concerned. The Scottish Government will have to do the same with the UK Government. The form that any agreement reached might take is for debate. The German arrangements have developed over the years: they were originally informal (based on an exchange of letters), took on a legislative basis only as a result of negotiations over ratification of the Single European Act, and are now embodied in the Constitution. The devolution Act itself is not the place to entrench arrangements for Scotland which will similarly have to develop over time, according to experience. But the Act should make reference to such an agreement, in order to make sure that something like it is concluded and maintained in practice. The Act might contain a provision along the following lines:

> *The involvement of the Scottish [Parliament and] Executive in the formulation of policy in the European Union in areas outside those reserved to the UK government should be governed by a Cooperation Agreement on European Affairs to be concluded between the two Governments following the entry into force of this Act.*

**348** In any event, a document containing the substance of an agreement between the two Governments should be prepared in the Scottish Office with a view to concluding an agreement as soon as possible after devolution. The agreement might contain the following elements designed to maintain and build on existing Scottish input into the policy-making process:

- attendance by officials at any working group or Council meeting not exclusively concerned with matters reserved to Westminster, including participation in any preparatory meetings of the delegation.
- similar provision for attendance by Scottish Ministers at Council meetings and preparatory meetings. The Maastricht Treaty introduced a new provision (Article 146) permitting any person of ministerial level to represent a member state in Council, provided that person is authorised to 'commit the Government of that Member State'.
- the establishment of an intergovernmental committee at official and ministerial level to co-ordinate European policy outside the reserved areas. In practice this might simply be the existing committees within the Cabinet Office structure reformulated to call them 'intergovernmental'. Participation at Ministerial level could prove difficult: see further discussion below.
- a guarantee of consultation between the two Governments before the adoption by the UK of any measures which trench on the Scottish Parliament's competences.
- provisions relating to Scotland's share of UK representation in the EP and the COR, and the nomination of candidates for the other community institutions.
- observer status at any Intergovernmental Conference called to revise the Community Treaties (conceded to the German Länder in advance of the Maastricht negotiations).
- agreement to maintain the practice of secondments from the Scottish Office to UKRep.
- a commitment on the Scottish side not to do anything to undermine the UK's national interests or to detract from the UK Government's ability to fulfil its responsibilities in the reserved areas (by analogy with the Länder's responsibility to recognise the Federal Government's role in Article 23 of the German Constitution).

**349** Four points are worth drawing out further. First, it is in the interests of both the Scottish and UK Governments that Scotland's officials should be fully involved in the development and negotiation of policy in certain key areas where they have particular expertise e.g. agriculture, fisheries, energy.

350 Second, a guarantee of consultation does not guarantee influence. In practice Scotland's negotiating position in Whitehall will be weak. It might be strengthened in areas where it has major interests by making the Scottish Office the lead department in policy terms i.e. giving it the responsibility to produce the first drafts of policy positions and for brokering a deal around them. That might apply in the areas of fisheries, forestry, whisky production, off-shore engineering and safety, North Sea oil and gas production.

351 Third, there are many who argue that in areas such as these the Scottish Minister ought to lead the UK delegation to the Council as of right. There is nothing to prevent this happening in theory in special cases - and the Maastricht Treaty explicitly permits it. But if this were ever to happen it would be a sign of a great spirit of co-operation between the two Governments. If that state of co-operation does exist, then insisting on a Scottish head of delegation is no more than tokenism; and if it does not then it will not happen in any case.

352 Finally, the political sensitivities of all of the arrangements should not be underestimated. Even a UK Government of the same politics as that in Scotland might baulk at incorporating them into day to day practice. The proposals include an element of aiming high for the initial agreement in the hope that workable compromises can then emerge before the relationship comes under too much strain. Even so, it is important to be realistic about how far the agreement can go. Scotland's position within the UK will not be analogous to the Länder within Germany, or even the autonomous communities in Spain. Scotland will most likely be negotiating for influence for herself alone - and there will be limits to what other regions in the UK will find permissible. The case must be based on Scotland's legitimate interest in EC legislation likely to be adopted in areas falling within the Scottish Parliament's legislative competence.

353 That caveat particularly applies to the thought of involving Scottish Ministers in UK Cabinet Committees. If this *is* acceptable under Lib/Lab administrations in both capitals then it should be written into the agreement, in the knowledge that this element might be changed in the future. If it is *not* acceptable, even from the start, the agreement should specify procedures for invoking an inter-Ministerial committee (including a representative of the Scottish Government) where officials feel the debate needs to be moved to that level, and their Ministers agree. In either scenario official level contacts should be maintained as a minimum. The intergovernmental Joint Council advocated below in paragraph 442 might take on this role; but a specialist forum would be better.

## The Role of the Scottish Parliament

354 It is a consequence of the Council being a forum for negotiation between Governments that national Parliaments for the most part find themselves insufficiently involved in the negotiating process. This is one of the deficiencies in the system that the present IGC will attempt to address. The phenomenon extends also to regional assemblies. It is remarked, for example, that the increased involvement of the Länder in German policy-making has been won by the Länder executives, further marginalising the Parliaments.

355 This might well turn out to be the case for the Scottish Parliament too. To prevent its marginalisation it will need to adopt procedures which give it the best possible opportunity to hold the Executive to account for actions in the European field. The direct involvement of Scotland's MEPs in the parliamentary committee responsible will help, as will the direct access to the Community institutions and information that an office in Brussels will supply. Beyond that the Parliament might include in its procedures a number of elements building on existing Westminster practice for the monitoring of European affairs:

- a debate on the UK Government's policy in advance of every European Council.
- the same service as Westminster in terms of documentation, written reports of Council meetings, perhaps even repetition of Ministerial statements by the Scottish European Minister e.g. following a European Council, the Prime Minister's statement is repeated in the Lords - and could also be repeated - and commented on - in the Scottish Parliament.
- parallel powers to scrutinise EC legislation - with the option of calling for a debate in Westminster or making a report to the House of Commons scrutiny committee in the event of disquiet.
- where the legislation under scrutiny involves an area of devolved power, this process to amount to a formal scrutiny reserve - to be lifted only following a debate in Westminster or a formal response from the House of Commons scrutiny committee.
- close liaison with the scrutiny committees in other European parliaments, including in the regions, for the exchange of information and best practice.
- if the Maastricht review conference agrees further measures for inter-parliamentary co-operation e.g. developing the Conference of Parliaments idea, then the Scottish Parliament should participate.

The formal arrangements for scrutiny of EC legislation proposed would require agreement from Westminster and by the UK Government. They too might therefore find a place in the Co-operation Agreement described above.

# Chapter 7

# Scotland's Relations with Central Government

## Introduction

356   The central institutions of the UK Government will still play a significant part in the government of Scotland even after the establishment of a Scottish Parliament. They will remain responsible for the overall size of the Scottish Executive's budget, for the negotiation and implementation of EC laws, and for the exercise of a range of reserved powers which will continue to have an impact on the Scottish people. The Scottish Parliament will not be operating in a vacuum. There should be machinery and structures in place to promote co-operation between the institutions of government in Edinburgh and London.

357   This chapter suggests ways in which this might be achieved.  It is divided into four parts.  The first three consider relations with the three central institutions of UK Government:  the Cabinet, Westminster and Whitehall.  The last suggests what 'interlocking machinery' it might be sensible to develop to tie them and the Scottish institutions of Government into a co-operative embrace.

## Cabinet: The Secretary of State for Scotland

358   Within the present system the most obvious link between the institutions of Scottish and UK Government is the Secretary of State for Scotland. The Labour Party envisage that this position will continue after devolution, to "ensure that Scotland, with Wales and Northern Ireland, retains a voice in the UK Cabinet".[93]  The Scottish Liberal Democrats on the other hand have said that the post will be redundant and should not be retained.[94]  The SCC is silent on the question, reflecting the lack of consensus and the fact that the composition of the UK Cabinet will rest in any event with the Prime Minister.  It does however envisage the Secretary of State presiding over the first meeting of the new Parliament.

359   In the 1978 Act the post was retained, and in fact carried with it significant powers in relation to policing the devolution settlement.  The Royal Commission on the Constitution's report had suggested that the post be dropped, but the Government rejected that proposal following consultation:

> "There is a strong desire both in Scotland and in Wales to retain an effective Secretary of State.  Major changes and a diminution in their present powers would be an inevitable consequence of a substantial measure of devolution; careful thought will have to be given to their precise role.  They will however retain important executive functions, will act as spokesmen for Scotland and for Wales in the United Kingdom Government for those matters which are not devolved and will contribute to the formulation of United Kingdom policy as a whole".[95]

### The History of the Secretary of State's Position

360   At the very least there will have to be some reassessment of the role of the Secretary of State following devolution.  It might be profitable to start by looking back at the way the role has developed over the last hundred years:  there might be lessons to be learned from the arguments for establishing the role in the first place.

361 In 1782 formal responsibility for Scottish affairs passed to the recently created Home Office. Prior to that, from the Acts of Union onwards, there had always been someone in Scotland responsible for its government, sometimes a 'Secretary of State', sometimes not. It is impossible to resist quoting from Daniel Defoe's attack on the need for a Scottish Secretary written in 1711, in the early years of Union, for the resonance it has with today's debate. The office, he wrote to Harley, the Queen's First Minister, kept up:

> "a kind of a form of separate Management, which being destroy'd by Union, all vestiges of the separate state of things ought to dye with it, and the very remembrance if possible be Taken away; Scotland No More Requires a Secretary Than Yorkshire or Wales. Nor (the clamour of petitions excepted) can it supply business for an office with two clarks".[96]

362 From 1782 responsibility for Scottish affairs in Parliament was transferred to the Home Secretary, but earlier arrangements endured and the role fell in practice to the Lord Advocate. It was dissatisfaction with these arrangements which led to the creation of the post of Secretary for Scotland in an Act of 1885 which also set up a Scottish Office. The post did not at that stage have Cabinet rank. The first holder, the Duke of Richmond and Gordon, did not want to take the post. He had not been in favour of setting up the Scottish Office, and was worried that the Secretary would have nothing to do. But the Prime Minister, Lord Salisbury, insisted that it was necessary that a prominent figure in Scottish society should be appointed since, as he maintained in a letter to the Duke, "the whole object of the move is to redress the wounded dignities of the Scotch people - or a section of them - who think that enough is not made of Scotland".[97]

363 The Scottish Office established at this time was actually an office in London: Dover House. The Scottish Secretary took over responsibility for overseeing the functions of a number of disparate administrative Boards in Edinburgh. The Reorganisation of Offices (Scotland) Act 1939, which established the modern Scottish Office in St Andrew's House, brought the many public agencies scattered around Edinburgh under one roof for the first time. The original Scottish Office presence in London remained at Dover House. It still performs a vital function in providing a London base for Ministers and their officials, especially during the Parliamentary session. It has only a small permanent staff of about fifteen officials.

364 Although the Duke of Richmond and Gordon was not in the Cabinet, all Scottish Secretaries from 1892 onwards were. The convention that they should have a Cabinet seat was thus well established by the time Baldwin's Government formally upgraded the office to Secretary *of State* for Scotland in 1926, claiming this was "giving the country a status unknown since the 'forty-five".

365 It is important to keep the powers and influence the Secretary of State for Scotland might be able to wield in the UK system in perspective. Much depends on the individual. For the most part the Secretary of State's role has been to defend Scottish interests in UK policy formulation, rather than to initiate change in Scotland or in UK policy as a whole.

## The Functions of the Secretary of State

366 The late John Mackintosh set out a powerful case for the abolition of the office of Secretary of State in response to the Government's devolution White Paper of November 1975.[98] His case was made in the context of a proposed devolution settlement which left a wide range of matters reserved at Westminster, and therefore the responsibility of the Secretary of State in Scotland. The SCC's proposal that the Scottish Parliament's powers should "include all areas of policy

currently within the remit of the Scottish Office" suggests the range of the Secretary of State's continuing policy responsibilities in Scotland will be far narrower than envisaged in the 1970s. With that caveat in mind, Mackintosh's analysis provides a good framework for considering the issue today.

367 Mackintosh identified six functions envisaged for the Secretary of State under the Government's plans for devolution:

- as a **UK Cabinet Minister.**
- **'wet nurse'** functions: managing the elections for the Assembly; arranging the first meeting; setting the initial pay and allowances of Members of the Assembly; publishing standing orders and fixing the number of Ministers and their assistants.
- **'viceregal'** or **'continuity'** functions: inviting someone to form a government after an election; formal appointment of the Chief Minister; ratifying changes in composition of the Scottish Government at the request of the Chief Minister; power to appoint a caretaker Government if the Government lost its majority and the Assembly could not decide on a new Chief Minister;
- **'veto'** functions: adjudicating on whether legislation is *ultra vires* and asking the Assembly to remove offending sections; general power to declare a bill unacceptable on grounds of public policy and with the consent of Parliament; to take over and undertake executive acts of the Scottish Executive.
- as the **channel for all communications with the EC.**
- as **chief adviser to the UK Government** on all aspects of Scottish affairs.

368 The remainder of this section deals with each of these functions in turn (except for the penultimate one, which was covered in the previous chapter).

## UK Cabinet Minister

369 The SCC did not take a position on the role of the Secretary of State partly because they could not reach consensus, but also because ultimately the decision whether an individual capable of speaking for Scotland needed to be in the Cabinet or not would fall to the Prime Minister of the day. The point is well made. The office was established as a sop to the Scots. But the calibre of those who held it in the early years established it *de facto* as a Cabinet post. It might happen, after devolution, that something like this process occurs in reverse to prevent any decline in the post. A dedicated Secretary of State might, through sheer force of personality and through his or her value to the Prime Minister, preserve the post even in the face of diminishing formal responsibilities.

370 Overall this seems unlikely. If the relationship with Scotland is a significant factor in the UK political debate the Prime Minister might well want somebody of high calibre in the Cabinet with expertise in the area. But he or she will likewise want to limit the size of the Cabinet, and would likely conclude that the person in question need not necessarily sit in the Cabinet as 'Secretary of State for Scotland'.

371 That is to view the issue from a UK perspective. From the Scottish point of view, the purpose of the post is to represent Scotland's interests in the Cabinet. This has been for the most part a defensive rather than a pro-active role. Depending on the generosity of the settlement, responsibility for the protection and pursuit of those interests will fall after devolution to the

Scottish Parliament and Government rather than the Secretary of State. There will still be a Scottish interest in the reserved areas - defence, foreign affairs etc. - which will need to be represented in Cabinet. But the voicing of this alone does not seem sufficient claim to a seat at the Cabinet table, although it might be a function combined with other responsibilities.

372 Beyond the reserved areas, Scotland will still have a considerable interest in policies pursued at a UK level, or at least in the rest of the UK excluding Scotland, which will be determined in Cabinet. They are bound to have an influence on what is feasible in Scotland. Representing Scotland's interests in the Cabinet across the range of these devolved functions might be seen as a substantial continuing role for the Secretary of State.

373 But there might be practical and political problems in a Secretary of State continuing to play this role after devolution. First, to perform the task properly across such a broad range of policy areas the post would need to be well supported in terms of a reasonably sized office and staff. Second, although it is true that there will be a continuing need to feed Scottish views into the Whitehall policy making process, it is far from clear that a Secretary of State from within the UK Government would be the best channel for doing so. Were there a Secretary of State perhaps of a different political party from the Scottish Executive, the Whitehall machine might be receiving two different views of the Scottish interest and would be bound to give priority to the views of the UK Cabinet Minister. That could bring any mechanisms for cooperation at official level between the Scottish and UK governments into disrepute, which would damage the chances of devolution working.

## Wet Nurse Functions

374 Mackintosh felt that these functions could easily be allocated elsewhere. Most of them are associated with the initial establishment of the Parliament. Having fired the starting pistol, the Secretary of State can hand over such responsibilities to the Parliament itself. These functions are discussed in more detail in chapter 10 (on the transition). However, one 'wet nurse' function, managing the elections to the Parliament, will of course recur at periodic intervals. There are two issues here: fixing the time for an election, and making sure that it is conducted fairly.

### Timing of Elections

375 The 1978 Act specified a fixed term Assembly, with elections on the third Thursday in March every four years. But it gave the Secretary of State the discretion to vary this date by up to two months either way. The House of Lords insisted that what the Government described as 'a matter of simple administrative convenience' should be subject to Parliamentary approval. Their fear was that this limited power to determine the election date could be used to gain political advantage. There were also fears that the Act might permit one postponement to follow another, or that the election could be postponed at the last moment, well into the election campaign. The scope for political manipulation that this clause introduced probably outweighs the advantage of the flexibility it provided. If the Parliament is to be elected for a fixed term, as the SCC propose, then it should really be 'fixed'.[99]

376 A related point is the timing of elections following a dissolution. In the 1978 Act the setting of these dates too fell to the Secretary of State, again within strict constraints. Yet in the case of by-elections the Presiding Officer or Speaker of the Assembly took this role. There seems no reason why he or she should not perform the same function following dissolution, provided that the election has to take place within, say, two months of the resolution to dissolve.

*Management of Elections*

**377** The question here is less about the role of the Secretary of State than about which aspects of the electoral process should be reserved to Westminster. There is a detailed discussion of this complex of issues in paragraphs 170 to 179 above. Briefly, that discussion canvassed various options for ensuring that elections throughout the UK all adhere to common democratic principles, while ensuring that the Scottish Parliament should have a degree of control over - or at least confidence in Westminster's control over - administrative detail relating to how elections are run in Scotland. The devolution legislation itself may well have to set down conditions specific to Scotland relating to the introduction of the additional member system in a UK election for the first time. Whatever the technical method or methods adopted to effect this division of responsibilities, there should not need to be any further involvement of the Secretary of State. Within the framework set by Westminster, the management of parliamentary elections in Scotland can be left to the existing machinery, overseen by the Scottish Parliament.

## Viceregal Functions

**378** The viceregal functions might be summarised as those performed by the sovereign for the Westminster Parliament. They relate to the selection, appointment and dismissal of the Scottish Executive. The UK Prime Minister and Cabinet are appointed formally by the sovereign herself and each one of them enjoys in theory the privilege of direct access. The 1978 Act regarded such direct access as inappropriate in a devolved system of government and delegated the authority to the Secretary of State. But the Act made it quite clear that the Secretary of State would be acting on the advice of the 'First Secretary', the head of the Scottish Executive, in making these appointments. The same safeguards will serve equally well for a future devolution bill: the rubber stamp on behalf of Her Majesty can be delivered by any Secretary of State in the Cabinet. Reference in the legislation to 'the Secretary of State' may be to any one of them.

**379** The real problem is the appointment of the First Secretary or Prime Minister. That appointment may still be formally made by a Secretary of State on behalf of the sovereign, but how is the Secretary of State's choice to be circumscribed? The 1978 Act placed the onus on the Assembly to select the First Secretary, which person would then be automatically appointed by the Secretary of State. But if the Assembly failed to agree on a candidate, the Secretary of State had the power to appoint a candidate of his or her own choosing. It would then be up to the Assembly to decide whether it could live with the Secretary of State's choice or whether to force a dissolution.

**380** The problem of choosing a First Secretary in the absence of a clear consensus in the Parliament is likely to be a real one. The proportional representation voting system will mean that coalition government in Scotland is highly likely. It is easy to imagine the bargaining that will ensue following a particularly even-handed election result. It is right that the choice should be left to the Parliament itself. This could be achieved, even in the most difficult circumstances, by an exhaustive ballot, eliminating candidates at each stage.[100] But the results of such a process are likely to be unpredictable and may produce an unlikely First Secretary commanding little committed support. For that reason the suggestion might not find favour with politicians.

**381** If exhaustive ballot is not acceptable, there will need to be some input from outside to bring about a resolution. As a first step, the devolution legislation might contain a time limit within which a new First Secretary has to be appointed and an administration formed. That should spur the political parties to negotiate.

382 But what should happen if the time limit is reached? Either there could be provision for another election; or the Secretary of State could appoint as First Secretary whomever he or she felt could form an administration in practice. At Westminster this role falls to the sovereign. It is a murky area of the constitution, and one on which many would like to throw more light. A good deal of attention was devoted to it after the formation of the Social Democratic Party when there seemed a good prospect of a hung Parliament at Westminster (and again in the run up to the 1992 election).[101] There are no written rules guiding the monarch in these circumstances: she seeks advice where she sees fit.

383 Someone will have to perform this function in Edinburgh. So long as the sovereign has to operate at one step removed from devolved legislatures (which seems reasonable especially in the context of devolution all round), the power of formal appointment will have to rest with her representative. There might be a technical case in this instance for following the model of the Government of Ireland Act 1920 where a Lord Lieutenant (later replaced by a Governor) represented His Majesty the King in Northern Ireland. His duties included the appointment of the administration and the granting of Royal Assent for bills. It would be possible to transfer all of the viceregal functions to a similar figure appointed by the Queen in Scotland. But this might be seen as an odd consequence of home rule, and really not necessary simply to deal with this one eventuality.

384 On balance it seems right to leave the Parliament itself to resolve any difficulty in electing a First Secretary, whether by exhaustive ballot or by other means. It is after all the Parliament which would have to live with the consequences either of electing a figure commanding inadequate support or, worse, failing to elect one at all. It would not be appropriate for the Secretary of State, a political figure, to play any kind of role in the process of resolving such difficulties.

385 The Speaker or President of the Parliament, a figure above party politics, might be the best person to act as facilitator in a process leading to the Parliament choosing, or confirming in office, a First Secretary for itself. The devolution legislation need not detail the process, but simply provide for the First Secretary to be appointed by the Secretary of State on the advice of the Speaker of the Parliament.

## Veto Functions

386 The 1978 Act contained a series of four provisions (sections 38-41) giving the Secretary of State some degree of policy override in respect of primary legislation, secondary legislation, executive action and the protection of the interests of Orkney and Shetland. The November 1975 White Paper suggested that the Secretary of State could block a Scottish bill 'on policy grounds' even if it were *intra vires* (paragraph 58). In response to criticism of the sweeping nature of this override, the Government made clear in the Scotland and Wales Bill 1976 that the power would only be used to prevent unacceptable repercussions on matters which remained the UK Government's responsibility.

387 This position was further refined following the loss of the Bill. The provisions of the 1978 Act applied only to non-devolved areas. They allowed the Secretary of State to recommend that Parliament strike down a Scottish bill or provisions of a bill (or a subordinate instrument, or an action or inaction of the Scottish Executive) on the grounds that it *both* might affect a reserved

matter directly or indirectly *and* its enactment 'would not be in the public interest'. Since this was the only place in the Act where the concept of a 'reserved matter' was used, it further specified that this was an area outside the Assembly's legislative competence. This made sure that the override could not be invoked simply because Scotland was legitimately following different policies which might have an unfortunate impact on the rest of the UK.

388    These were tightly constrained powers. Nevertheless they do place some emphasis on the political judgement of the Secretary of State: 'If it *appears* to the Secretary of State...that a Bill...*might* affect a reserved matter...he *may* lay the Bill before Parliament...' (section 38: emphasis added). The Secretary of State plays a role Mackintosh described as a 'one-man-House-of-Lords'.

389    Is there a need for that backstop role at Westminster today? The rationale for including it in the 1970s was that it operated at a political level rather than a judicial one. If the judicial process failed to deliver the verdict on grounds of policy that the UK Government wanted, they would have had to invoke their general right to legislate even in the devolved areas to correct the position. This would have been an inflammatory act, and might have taken time in waiting for a slot in the legislative programme. The override provisions allowed for such political disputes to be resolved through an overtly political alternative process to the judicial route.

390    Chapter 3 of this report discussed in detail how the devolution legislation might be framed to keep disputes to a minimum and how those disputes might be resolved. It suggested a judicial process, but acknowledged that there would be a prior and parallel political process involved. Installing the Secretary of State as a one-man-House-of-Lords would allow the political process formally to trump the judicial. That arrangement, by which a Westminster representative enjoying perhaps little support in Scotland has a qualified veto over decisions of the Scottish Parliament, is surely politically unacceptable today. In practice there will be plenty of ways for the UK Government to apply political pressure to protect their interests - through the financial settlement, for example - without recourse to a formal policy override. The formal means for the resolution of disputes should be through the courts. It will always after all be possible, as a last resort, for Westminster to enact legislation effectively repealing Scottish Parliament Acts.

## Chief Adviser on Scotland to the UK Government

391    The first of Mackintosh's functions saw the Secretary of State in the Cabinet to push Scottish interests in the formulation of UK policy. This last sees him or her as a source of expertise on a nation within the UK with which the Government needs to have a political relationship. It is a role that somebody will have to perform - just as the Secretary of State for Scotland performs it today. Post-devolution the role will combine a number of tasks. The UK Government will need a source of political advice on how to manage the relationship with Scotland. Other Ministers might need guidance on the limits of their responsibilities with respect to Scotland following devolution. There will have to be a channel for the flow of information in both directions between Edinburgh and London. At least initially there will also be considerable 'wet nurse' functions to perform within the machinery of government, overseeing and bedding down the co-operative working arrangements required for success.

392    All of these tasks would fall naturally to a Secretary of State for Scotland initially, but in the longer term might suit a Secretary of State for Territorial Affairs responsible also for devolution to Wales and England - and perhaps, depending on the nature of any eventual peace settlement,

Northern Ireland as well. Initially again this figure should probably be a Scot, to satisfy the Chief Adviser role on Scotland, but that convention would doubtless lapse as the responsibilities of the post increased.

## Managing the Transition

393 The role of manager of relations with Scotland and keeper of the devolution settlement may be a real one, and one which may evolve over time to cover other territories and regions within the UK. Other functions identified above are either undesirable in principle (veto), temporary (wet nurse) or easily distributed elsewhere (viceregal). The position of the Secretary of State as Scotland's representative in the Cabinet might also become a less comfortable role in time, especially when different parties are in government in Edinburgh and London.

394 It is important to recognise the possible dynamics of the Edinburgh/London relationship over time. What holds formally at the establishment of the Parliament may well evolve rapidly in practice. That is what happened in Northern Ireland under Stormont. Harold Macmillan reported in 1960:

> "Strictly speaking, the official channel of communication between the Governments of Northern Ireland and Her Majesty's Government is through our Cabinet Offices and the Home Office. That was the original set-up. Since then, for purposes of convenience, for purposes of speed and personal contact, Ministers are in direct contact with their opposite numbers on the other side".[102]

395 In the same way, the authority of the Scottish Executive to speak for Scotland on UK-wide issues may develop over time. James Kellas foresaw this occurring even under the 1978 Act which reserved a substantial role for the Secretary of State:

> "Eventually, the Scottish Executive will emerge as the 'legitimate' spokesman of Scotland, because it is directly elected, to the embarrassment of the Secretary of State, who can speak only for the 'UK interest' in Scotland (albeit from a background of knowledge which his UK Cabinet colleagues will not possess). When that happens the Scottish arm of the UK Government will wither and die, leaving a straight dialogue between the Scottish Government and the UK Government".[103]

396 It will remain for the UK Prime Minister to determine the composition of his or her Cabinet. It could be that a continuing role for a Scottish Secretary will be found desirable in the future, even if only as part of a wider political calculation. But the considerations above suggest a two stage approach to the future of the Secretary of State for Scotland's role:
1. The Secretary of State remains in place to perform the wet nurse functions in establishing a Scottish Parliament and to continue to be responsible for powers (e.g. executive and spending functions in Scotland) left to 'the Secretary of State' under the devolution legislation; but
2. During the remainder of the Westminster parliamentary term (likely to be of the order of less than two years) a key part of the role should be to devise coherent proposals in the light of experience for the future of the post.

397 Proposition 1 should satisfy the political imperative of maintaining Scotland's place in the Cabinet at least as long as Wales has one. Proposition 2 will allow a decision about whether to maintain the role to be taken in the light of experience. It might well lead to the establishment over time of a Minister in the Cabinet with responsibility for intergovernmental relations with

the territories of the UK. The pace of that development is difficult to judge: the role may include Wales from day one, it may include Northern Ireland before the end of the Parliament. Or it may be a role which, following the establishment of the Scottish Parliament, is absorbed into the wider remit of a Cabinet Minister with sole responsibility for constitutional matters - if such a figure is created to tackle the Government's wider agenda of constitutional reform.

## Parliament: the West Lothian Question

398   Scotland will continue to elect representatives to the House of Commons following devolution. They will speak for and represent the interests of their constituents as they do now. They will seek to bring the concerns of Scotland to the attention of the House and to influence UK policy to meet Scottish interests. But they will also vote on the passage of legislation, a point which Tam Dalyell made his own in the 1970s by objecting forcefully and persistently to the proposition that they should be allowed to do so on matters which had been devolved to Scotland and for which the legislation in question would only apply in the rest of the UK.

399   Within a devolved system, there are in reality only two possible answers to this, the 'West Lothian question'. One is to cut Scottish representation at Westminster to zero so that the question would not arise; the other is to develop elaborate parliamentary procedures to prevent the question arising i.e. by preventing Scottish MPs voting on matters that had been devolved to Edinburgh. The first answer is politically unacceptable and patently unjust. Scotland will retain a legitimate interest in all matters reserved to Westminster. Gladstone suggested the equivalent for Ireland in clause 24 of the Government of Ireland Bill of 1886. This was roundly criticised for breaching the principle that there should be no taxation without representation. It is inconceivable that any Government would try to carry such a provision today.

### Special Parliamentary Procedures: In and Out

400   The second answer - special parliamentary procedures - was adopted in the 1978 Act, albeit against firm Government opposition. Section 66 provides for a further vote after fourteen days where a bill which 'does not relate to or concern Scotland' is carried on a vote which makes the number of Scottish MPs in the count decisive. The fourteen day interim was intended 'to give time for people to think again'. The clause was first proposed as an official Opposition amendment at the Report Stage in the House of Lords by Earl Ferrers. It was rejected in the Commons by the casting vote of the Speaker, but returned again by the Lords and eventually carried by one vote.

401   Section 66 hints at a version of the 'in and out' principle, under which Scottish MPs would be in the chamber for some votes but out for others. Gladstone's 1893 Government of Ireland Bill contained a provision with this effect, listing five areas from which Irish MPs would be excluded, among them matters 'confined to Great Britain or some part thereof.' It also provided for a reduction in the number of Irish MPs at Westminster from 105 to 80. The 'in and out' provision was criticised for making Cabinet government impossible (the Government might have a majority for some issues but not for others) and because of the difficulty in practice of defining those areas which would not be subject to votes by Irish MPs. Gladstone offered to withdraw the provision, but maintained the case for reduced representation.

402 The same difficulty of definition can be seen in Section 66. That section does not suggest who should decide whether a bill falls within its ambit or not. That judgement requires an assessment of the extent of the Assembly's legislative competence which elsewhere in the Act is a matter for the courts to decide. Decisions of this nature would be crucial if any version of 'in and out' were put into operation. If it is left to Parliament to decide whether a measure relates to the legislative competence of the Scottish Parliament or not, should Scottish MPs have a vote in that decision? In practice the only way to make 'in and out' work is federalism or home rule all round: that would provide a clear definition of the remaining legislative responsibilities of the federal Parliament for which all MPs would be 'in'. But this too is an unrealistic proposal in 1996.

403 Even if problems of definition were surmounted, the bigger problem of categorising two different classes of MPs would remain. In debates on the Scotland Bill Enoch Powell rejected the 'in and out' solution (as he rejected all other 'solutions' to the problem) partly for this reason:

> "The nature of this House is that it is a body corporate. What concerns any part of it concerns us all. We are, in the best sense of the word, peers in every respect and sit on a basis of equality of responsibility and rights".[104]

Besides, there would be the related problem of governing the UK with two different majorities (or perhaps minorities) in the House of Commons according to the issues under debate. That would make coherent Cabinet government impossible.

404 Some dispute this claim. Professor Bill Miller of Glasgow University, for example, noted in a letter to *The Scotsman* last year that:

> "No UK parliament since the war has over-ruled a majority of English MPs. The Labour governments of 1945-50, 1966-70 and October 1974-79 were all elected with a majority over the Conservatives in England. Only the very short administrations of 1964-66 and February to October 1974 faced a Conservative majority of English MPs...These short parliaments did not inflict major legislative changes on a bitterly hostile electorate".[105]

405 This has been taken as an argument both for the feasibility of 'in and out' (the feasibility of having a majority in both Scotland and the rest of the UK) and for the status quo (Scottish votes have not in practice been decisive of English fortunes). But the figures should be treated with caution as a basis for settling the West Lothian question for the future. They relate to a period when two party politics predominated which is less true today, they say nothing about the cohesiveness of the parties and the practical chances of mobilising either the Scottish or the English majorities *en bloc,* and the excess of Labour seats over Conservative seats in Scotland has grown from parity in the early 1950s to around 40 in the 1987 and 1992 elections. The figures might be very different indeed, and the operation of any special parliamentary procedures radically different in effect, if the UK as a whole moved to a proportional representation voting system following a referendum.

## Level of Representation

406 The problem with the West Lothian question is not that it has no answer, but that none is remotely feasible in practice. As Bill Miller also remarked, the West Lothian question is not really a *question* at all because "no matter how often it is answered, Tam simply waits a while and then asks again".

407 The one precedent for legislative devolution within the UK suggests if not an answer, at least a political response to the question: reduction in the level of representation at Westminster. The Government of Ireland Act 1920 did not attempt to curb the voting rights of Northern Irish MPs at Westminster, but it did cut their numbers by a third. An additional factor in the case of Scotland is the fact that it is clearly over-represented at Westminster compared with other parts of the UK, both in terms of seats per head of population and seats per head of electorate. The average constituency electorate across the United Kingdom is 67,261. In comparison the figure in Scotland is 54,822, Wales 58,476, Northern Ireland 68,373 and England 69,571.[106]   If the 659 parliamentary seats to be contested at the next election were distributed according to the size of the electorates in the constituent nations and regions, Scotland would have 59 seats (actual = 72), Wales would have 33 (40), England 549 (529) and Northern Ireland would have 18 (no change).

408 The Royal Commission's Report came down in favour of reducing representation at Westminster in response to the West Lothian question. It considered the 'in and out' solution but rejected it as impractical. Instead it concluded that "all Members of Parliament, whether or not they come from regions with their own legislative assemblies, must have the same rights of participation in the business of the House of Commons" (paragraph 814). Noting the Northern Irish precedent, it went on to advocate a reduction in Scottish and Welsh representation to bring them into line with the representation of England. "The probable effect would be to reduce Scotland's representation from 71 to about 57 and that of Wales from 36 to about 31" (paragraph 1147).

409 All practical responses to the question thus appear to come down to how far Scottish representation in the House of Commons should be reduced. The Scottish Liberal Democrats have committed themselves to a figure of 'around 60'.[107]   Strict proportionality suggests 59, although the Hansard Society Commission on Election Campaigns in 1991 suggested that seven of Scotland's 72 seats merited special treatment on grounds of  "special geographic factors".[108] The House of Commons Home Affairs Select Committee report on Redistribution of Seats in 1987[109] suggested Scotland should have 66 seats in a House of Commons whose overall size was stabilised as nearly as possible at its then level. Figures below this are beyond the realm of practical politics as a realistic response to the West Lothian question. But for completeness it is worth noting that the Acts of Union provide: "That by virtue of this Treaty of the Peers of Scotland at the time of the Union Sixteen shall be the number to sit and vote in the House of Lords and Forty five the number of the Representatives of Scotland in the House of Commons of the Parliament of Great Britain".  Although both these numbers have been changed since in practice, the figure of 45 MPs is seen by some as an irreducible minimum.

410 Whether or not it 'answers' the West Lothian question, a political response in the form of  some reduction in representation at Westminster may be demanded by the Opposition parties as part of the price Scotland pays for gaining its Parliament. In the 1970s it was a price the Scottish (and Welsh) people were reluctant to pay and in the end were not required to do so. That was partly due to the rules of parliamentary procedure which effectively ruled any amendment to the legislation which dealt with the Westminster Parliament rather than the Scottish Assembly outside the scope of the Bill and therefore out of order. When the Ferrers amendment was passed (the rules on scope in the Lords are different from and perhaps looser than those in the Commons) the long title of the Act was amended to add the words "and in the procedure of Parliament".

411 Another attempt to raise the issue during the passage of the Act was through the suggestion that there should be a Speaker's Conference on Scottish representation convened once the Assembly was established. This too originated in the Lords, but was rejected by the Commons. It had in any event served its purpose by then in putting the prospect of future reduction in Scottish MPs on the agenda before the forthcoming referendum. It may have been rejected partly on the grounds that it would have involved the Speaker in determining what was by then not a technical but a highly political issue. Some rejected it because they doubted a Speaker's Conference could answer the question any better than Parliament had - Tam Dalyell, for example, who voted against the amendment:

> *"If we are to have a Speaker's Conference, we have to try some kind of consensus but a consensus here is a Will-o'-the-wisp - there is not a census to be had. Had there been an acceptable compromise, or a formula in which the nationalists and anti-Assembly Members of Parliament could have acquiesced, it would have been found long ago...But [a Speaker's Conference] will not dig up any solution since there is no possible solution to be had'.*[110]

412 It is likely that the same constraints on scope will apply in trying to raise the issue this time around. Whilst there will be room for ingenious amendments like the Ferrers clause being debated and perhaps even passed, and there will be a host of amendments seeking to delay the entry into force of the Act until the issue of Scottish representation has been reviewed, it is most unlikely that any reduction in MPs could be forced on the Government through the legislative process itself. Which raises the final question: how should a Government implement any decision to reduce representation if it wished to of its own volition?

## Speaker's Conference

413 The conventional mechanism for changing the number of Parliamentary seats would be a Speaker's Conference. An all-party committee of MPs meeting 'under the presiding genius of the Speaker'[111] to take decisions about electoral matters outside party politics has preceded almost every significant change this century.

414 A series of such Conferences are in fact responsible for the distortions in representation which have arisen since 1885 when Scottish and Welsh representation were increased in the context of the third Reform Bill and all parts of the UK were proportionately represented. A Speaker's Conference between October 1916 and January 1917, considering redistribution of seats in advance of the 1918 Representation of the People Act, recommended that "each vote recorded shall, as far as is possible, command an equal share of representation in the House of Commons". This led to instructions to the Boundary Commissions for England and Wales and for Scotland to work for the same average figure of 70,000 electors per seat. At the same time the instructions to Ireland stipulated no reduction in the number of seats. As a result the number of Scottish seats increased by two to 74 in 1918, and Wales gained two seats - up to 37.

415 The Speaker's Conference in 1944 was established to look into the causes of distortions in the levels of representation across the UK and to decide how to review constituency boundaries systematically to reflect changing populations. The Conference came up with a number of recommendations which were then reflected in the Redistribution Act 1944. This included separate Boundary Commissions for Scotland, England, Wales and Northern Ireland, the idea of a target electorate for all seats in the UK, a dispensation to depart from the target if "special

geographical considerations, including the area, shape, and accessibility of a constituency" demanded, and the idea that the overall number of seats in the UK should remain 'substantially as at present'.

416 In view of its broad terms of reference it is surprising that the Conference also resolved that the number of non-University seats in Scotland and Wales should not be cut. The minutes of the Conference are illuminating on this point:

> "It was pointed out that a strict application of the quota for the whole of Great Britain would result in a considerable decrease in the existing number of Scottish and Welsh seats, but that in practice, in view of the proposal that the Boundary Commissioners should be permitted to pay special consideration to geographical considerations, it was...unlikely that there would be any substantial reduction. It was strongly urged that...it would be very desirable, on political grounds, to state from the outset quite clearly that the number of Scottish and Welsh seats should not be diminished. The absence of any such agreement might give rise to a good deal of political feeling and would lend support to the separatist movement in both countries".[112]

417 As this last reference shows, Speaker's Conferences are by no means a reliable means of settling tricky political questions. Quite the opposite. As David Butler has pointed out, "their record is not very impressive either in achieving consensus on controversial matters or in seeing their recommendations translated into law".[113] Nor can it be said, since the Home Affairs Select Committee reported on the redistribution of Commons seats in 1987, that these matters are any longer their exclusive province.

418 Even so, some mechanism would be needed to legitimise a reduction in Scottish representation other than the passage of Government legislation. The key to making a Speaker's Conference - or any other cross-party forum - effective for this purpose would be to have reached a substantial degree of political agreement amongst party leaders about objectives and outcomes *before* the Conference began. Apart from anything else the Speaker could refuse the Prime Minister's request to establish one if he or she felt the issue were too political for the forum.

419 Thus the political parties would need to agree among themselves the objectives and terms of reference for any Conference. It might be held simply 'to review the level of Scottish representation in the House of Commons in the light of the establishment of a Scottish Parliament.' But the remit of the Conference could, and if it is to happen ideally should, be drawn wider, particularly if it is held later in the Government's term when other reforms have become clearer.

420 The Conference should, for example, include Welsh representation in its remit. And it makes no sense to consider Scotland and Wales without taking in England too: note that the same calculations which reduce Scottish and Welsh representation in proportion to population also suggest an increase for England. Northern Ireland should probably not be considered: it is proportionately represented at present which suggests there will be little call for change in the event of a settlement, and if there is no settlement then even 'reviewing' Northern Irish representation at Westminster will be an unwanted complication and too 'political' for the Speaker.

421 The Conference would need to know too whether the objective of the exercise was to place a limit on the overall size of the House of Commons (it has grown with every boundary review), to achieve parity of representation per vote across the UK, to reduce Scotland and Wales' over-representation as a one-off, or to redraw the rules of the four Boundary Commissions to make them compatible and reduce the likelihood of further distortions occurring in the future.

422 This is potentially a very heavy agenda, and a technically complex one. The prospect of a referendum on changing the electoral system for Westminster as well might lead any Conference to postpone its conclusions in any event until after the result of the referendum is known. The concept of constituency size might become irrelevant under some forms of proportional representation. The Conference might also conclude that, should a UK Electoral Commission by then have been established (as recommended by the Plant Committee and the Hansard Society, and supported by both Labour and the Liberal Democrats), it would be better for that body to tackle all of these questions comprehensively.

423 Thus, even having arrived at an 'answer', or at least a response, to the West Lothian question in terms of reducing Scottish representation at Westminster, it will be by no means straightforward to arrive at that conclusion through due process, or to implement it without considering other aspects of the system. The key will be reaching cross-party agreement about the process by which the 'answer' is determined, and the wider objectives the exercise is intended to achieve. The options might be:
- cross-party talks followed by a clear remit to a Speaker's Conference.
- cross-party contacts providing a remit for a Speaker's Conference to develop agreed objectives (e.g. stabilise the size of House of Commons, equal representation per vote) to be worked out in their technical detail by a UK Electoral Commission.

424 An earlier Constitution Unit report, *Delivering Constitutional Reform*, explores in more detail the options for the first part of this process - reaching cross-party consensus.

## Scottish Business at Westminster

425 It remains to consider what might be termed 'the reverse West Lothian question': namely, the role of Scottish MPs at Westminster and in particular their capacity to raise there matters which are formally the responsibility of the Scottish Parliament. The Stormont precedent is clearly set out in Harry Calvert's authoritative study.[114] He makes clear that it was the fact Stormont would be able to handle 'a wide variety of internal affairs' for itself that 'undermined' the basis for full representation at Westminster. In terms of handling Northern Ireland business at Westminster, he notes that there was no restriction on raising Northern Irish business relating to matters excepted or reserved to Westminster under the 1920 Act. But in practice the legitimate areas of interest went wider and "may be taken as including the overall constitutional responsibility, including questions as to the extent to which the machinery provided is adequate to discharge the tasks imposed upon it".

426 The procedure for policing this division varied between parliamentary questions and other occasions. Calvert summarises the position thus:

> "1. So far as questions are concerned, the Chair may refuse to receive a question where it would clearly be purposeless to do so, there being no Ministerial responsibility and hence, no prospect of a useful answer. Otherwise the modern practice seems to be to allow the

*question and leave it to the Minister to whom it is addressed to determine the bounds of his responsibility in his answer.*

*2. So far as supplementaries and other occasions are concerned, the appropriate procedure is by way of calling to order a member who trespasses into a prohibited area.*

*3. Any matter, whether a Northern Ireland transferred matter or not, can be discussed on a proper motion or a bill.*

*In any case, the ruling of the Chair can be challenged by way of a motion of censure upon him, although this will rarely be resorted to. The Chair in consequence enjoys a wide measure of discretion".*

427  As the summary above suggests, these arrangements developed over time.  In the early days of Stormont "lengthy discussion of transferred matters sometime took place, though there was considerable uncertainty as to the proper bounds".  No definitive ruling was give until 1923 - but this too left considerable discretion in the hands of the Speaker.  Similar guidelines to those summarised above will be required for the handling of Scottish business at Westminster after devolution.  It would clearly help if those guidelines were promulgated at the same time as the establishment of the Scottish Parliament.

428  That said, there will still be a strong and legitimate interest on the part of Scottish MPs in all aspects of the operation of the devolution settlement, particularly in the early years, since it will crucially affect the interests of their constituents.  It might be open to any one of them obliquely to raise questions about devolved policies either as specific examples of strain in the constitutional machinery, or as flowing from the financial settlement for which Westminster will remain responsible.  Rather than waiting for such concerns to arise on the floor of the House in the course of debate or parliamentary questions, it would be wise - and useful - to provide a specific forum where they might be aired and followed up in some detail.  This suggests the establishment of a Select Committee with responsibility for 'devolution affairs' which could conduct enquiries and produce reports on the operation of aspects of the devolution legislation, and generally monitor the devolution settlement in Scotland and other devolved territories and regions.  If devolution to Scotland happens in advance of other changes, the Committee might well start life as a Select Committee for Scottish Affairs.  Its membership should be predominantly Scottish, but open to other MPs as well.

## Whitehall: the Civil Service

429  When Northern Ireland gained its own Assembly it also established a separate Northern Ireland Civil Service.  There were thus two civil services active in Northern Ireland, an indigenous one serving the devolved functions and the other Home (or 'Imperial') Civil Service dealing with reserved matters in the Province such as Revenue, Customs and Defence.  There was virtually no transferability between the two.

430  The Royal Commission concluded that a separate civil service should be established for Scotland "on the grounds that a devolved administration would wish to choose its own senior officials, might not be content for general personnel matters to be handled by a Government Department, and would want to be able to rely on the undivided loyalty of their officials dealing with the Government, for example on the block grant".[115]

431 The Government had reservations about this conclusion and did not provide for a separate civil service in the 1978 Act. They noted that a separate service would be more expensive, reproducing many of the central administrative functions in Edinburgh, and that it could not be assumed that all serving officials in the Scottish Office would wish to transfer to it. They thought that civil servants would be able to cope with the problem of 'divided loyalty' since they were used to giving "wholehearted service to whichever Ministers are in charge of their Departments". They saw advantages in maintaining a unified civil service in allowing the Scottish Executive "to draw its officials more easily from a wide pool of talent and experience" and fostering the co-operative relationships with other Ministries which were required to make devolution work. They were content to consider a separate service in the future if that was what the Scottish administration, in consultation with staff representatives, concluded was necessary, but thought that in any event it would take 'some years' to establish.

432 Where does the balance of argument lie today? The practical argument is still strong: it seems wise to establish the Parliament with a tried and tested civil service machine. There might also be problems in trying anything different, given that recruitment to a *new* service would have to be provisional subject to Scottish Parliamentary decisions about terms of employment - not a promising start.

433 As for the principle, if anything developments in the civil service since the 1970s have brought the two positions closer together. The Government's White Paper of July 1994, *The Civil Service: Continuity and Change* (Cm 2627) proposed a number of changes designed to devolve greater autonomy to individual departments to manage their staff and resources while "the defining principles and standards of the Civil Service will continue to be centrally prescribed and mandatory for all departments and agencies". In addition the Government have accepted a recommendation from the Treasury and Civil Service Select Committee, backed by the Council of Civil Service Unions, that there should be a new Civil Service Code "to set out...the constitutional framework within which all civil servants work and the values which they are expected to uphold".[116] This is now in force.

434 These changes have created a potentially more encouraging framework in which to maintain a unified civil service. The Civil Service Code will underpin the feeling in the 1970s that the political impartiality and integrity of the civil service could be relied upon to deal with any conflict of loyalties. It might be noted too that the experience of working closely with officials in other member states of the European Union may already have sensitised a portion of the civil service to this form of intergovernmental co-operation in a way which was not true in the 1970s. The greater delegation of authority for pay, staff structures, management to departments from 1 April this year will also give a Scottish administration flexibility within a unified civil service. And more open recruitment practices for the senior civil service, including from outside government, will emphasise the benefits of the 'wide pool of talent' identified in the 1970s.

435 In view of this environment, this report comes down in favour of following the 1978 Act and maintaining the link with the Home Civil Service. That should not rule out establishing a separate service in the future, especially as devolution becomes the norm and relations between the regions and territories of the UK become progressively more important compared with the relationship with the centre. The devolution legislation should make it clear that a separate Scottish Civil Service could be established without primary legislation, subject only to suitable notice to and consultation with the UK Government and existing civil servants in Scotland.

436 Even if the balance of argument appears to favour maintaining the status quo, there would still need to be some changes in practice to reflect the new circumstances of civil servants working for the Scottish Executive. The convention that promotions within the senior grades need central approval, and that promotions to the top rank require the approval of the Prime Minister, for example, would need to be modified. Final responsibility for senior promotions should lie within the Scottish Civil Service itself, and for the most senior officials approval of the head of the Scottish Executive should replace that of the Prime Minister. No legislative act would be required to effect these changes: they would simply require a change in practice.

437 Alternatively, even within a unified civil service, a practice might develop over time in which some officials might see it as their mission to work in and for Scotland, while others might continue to aspire to positions in the wider administration of the UK. Those in the latter category would still need approval in the normal way to serve in senior posts, or to be promoted into senior posts, in the civil service outside Scotland. If people who had demonstrated a loyalty to the Scottish Executive either in opting to serve only in Scotland or in working there temporarily appeared to be encountering problems in the wider civil service network, then the case for maintaining a unified service would have to be reviewed.

438 Finally, given the special circumstances of civil servants working for the Scottish Executive within a continuing UK framework, it might be sensible to earmark one of the Civil Service Commissioners as having special responsibility for Scotland, in particular for the purpose of receiving representations about conflicts of loyalty and the preservation of the civil service's impartiality.

## Interlocking Machinery

439 Under devolution Scotland will remain part of the UK. Relations with Westminster and Whitehall will be conducted not just as between neighbours but between members of the same household. Whatever the formal division of competences, there will be overlap between Scottish and UK interests across the board. Policies pursued in London will have an impact in Scotland and *vice versa*. Two areas of particular mutual concern have already been covered in separate chapters: Europe and finance. But the need for cooperation, and possibly for institutional machinery to bolster it, goes far wider.

440 As an indication of the sorts of contact that will have to be maintained, both for the exchange of information and for the resolution of disputes, look at the German system. There are three levels of intergovernmental relationships. At the level of the 'whole state' (*Gesamtstaat*) there is, for example, a Conference of Heads of Governments of the Federation and the Länder which meets roughly quarterly, whole state level co-ordination within the political parties and co-ordination between the Federal and Länder Parliaments. At the level of the 'federal state' (*Bundesstaat*) the Bundesrat plays the central role in linking the Länder with the Federation, assisted by the network of Land Missions in Bonn. At the 'third level' there is a network of horizontal cooperation between the Länder themselves, for example through the regular Conference of Minister-Presidents, which is itself prepared by meetings between Heads of the Länder Cabinet Offices.[117] The Royal Commission noted that six Ministries of North Rhine Westphalia, for example, were involved in about four hundred federal/Land committees.

441 Whilst it is not suggested that the machinery associated with devolution to Scotland should be as comprehensive as for Federal Germany, it too will need intergovernmental arrangements. These might include:

- the intergovernmental arrangements already proposed (chapter 6) for co-ordination of European policy.
- presence of Members of the Scottish Parliament in a reformed House of Lords by analogy with the Bundesrat. This was advocated in the Memorandum of Dissent to the Royal Commission (see especially paragraphs 298 and 302), and is also discussed in the Constitution Unit's report, *Reform of the House of Lords*.[118]
- maintenance of the existing range of contacts between Scottish Office officials and their opposite numbers in Whitehall. These need be no more formal than they are at present. The important thing will be that the contacts are maintained.
- the establishment of a new range of contacts with other devolved administrations. This part of the machinery will assume greater importance over time as the number of analogues grows.
- In a statement in July 1977 the Lord President (Michael Foot) announced that the Government would set up Joint Councils for Scotland and Wales "on which representatives of the Government and the new administrations could consult as necessary on matters of common concern".[119] Some such intergovernmental forum would be a useful part of the settlement today.

442 Cooperation is essential in European matters, as discussed in the previous chapter. But for the most part these arrangements need not be formalised and can be left to evolve over time, (as they did in Northern Ireland: see paragraph 394 above). But three positive things can be done to make sure that they do develop smoothly:

- the Secretary of State for Scotland should see it as part of the role to facilitate the development of these co-operative relationships. It may take some clout to establish a pattern of cooperation and information sharing. It would be best to make this effort before the Government that launched the devolution Act leaves office.
- the Scottish Executive will in any event require a London office. The success of the office in establishing links with Whitehall and Westminster in the early years of devolution could have a significant impact, not only on the success or failure of the venture, but more directly on the case for maintaining a Secretary of State beyond the transition.
- a Joint Council of the two governments, supported by a small permanent secretariat, could be a useful feature of the early years of devolution. This would be a forum in which concerns on either side about the 'fair and effective operation' (to quote from the Joint Framework Document for Northern Ireland) of the devolution legislation could be raised (including the financial provisions), and information exchanged for example about legislative intentions which might have consequences for the other party. The Council could meet at both official and Ministerial level, and remain in being for as long as it continued to play a useful role.

# Chapter 8

## Relations with Local Government

# Introduction

443  It is expected that responsibility for local government in Scotland will be devolved to the Scottish Parliament. This was broadly the case in the 1978 Act, which transferred responsibility for: "Constitution, area and general powers and duties of local authorities and similar bodies. Investigation of maladministration. Revenue and expenditure of local authorities and similar bodies. Rating and valuation for rating. Rate support grants and grants for specific purposes".[120] But the Act also listed a number of 'scheduled functions' which local government would continue to perform on behalf of the UK Government. That list included such diverse functions as police, electoral registration, rodent control and the protection of birds. Responsibility for the electoral system was not devolved.

444  The SCC proposals match this earlier settlement, and if anything - by remaining silent about the sorts of qualification noted above - go beyond it: "The Scottish Parliament will be responsible for the system of local government in Scotland, its role, functions, structure and financing". In essence it is envisaged that the present relationship between Scottish local government and UK central government will be replaced in all significant respects by a relationship with the Scottish Executive and Parliament.

445  There is inevitably some apprehension that in a nation of only 5 million people, and in the wake of the abolition of regional Councils, a Parliament may encroach on powers and responsibilities previously the preserve of local government. The Parliament will also take over responsibility for both the quantum and the distribution formula for local government finance, both highly contentious issues. At the least, the establishment of a Scottish Parliament will provide an opportunity for an assessment of the appropriate roles in the Scottish political system of the Parliament, local government and quangos.[121] The Labour Party have proposed that an independent review should conduct such an assessment, with a broad remit.[122]

446  This chapter looks not so much at how local government's role will change, as at the formal framework - within the devolution legislation or outside it - which might be put in place to govern the process. As such it concentrates on the possible contents of the devolution Act with special relevance to local government, and on measures which might be taken to encourage a co-operative relationship to develop between the two levels of government in Scotland. It does not attempt to consider wider questions of the role of local government in the UK political system. There is a limit to how far an Act establishing a Scottish Parliament can also be used as the vehicle to restore the position of local government and give it a more robust role in the UK constitution. That is a question which needs to be tackled on a UK-wide basis.

447  Even so, the SCC have proposed a number of measures which might find a place in the devolution legislation, or in the new Parliament's overall approach, which aim to bolster the work of local government *in Scotland*: an obligation to maintain a strong and effective system of local government, for example, or a commitment to operate in accordance with the principle of subsidiarity. This chapter aims to draw out the implications of the Convention's recommendations and to consider to what extent there might be other desirable formal safeguards for the role and functions of local government which are worth exploring. It concludes that this is an area where local government itself will wish to make a large input, and that the less constraining the devolution legislation the more likely it is to be effective in practice.

## Context

448 The present Secretary of State for Scotland, Michael Forsyth, has taken a great interest in local government in Scotland. Soon after his appointment he established a Task Force to report on standards within local government. Following the problems many councils faced in setting budgets for 1996-97 he ordered a study of local government spending, calling for an "objective needs-based assessment".[123] He has also initiated a dialogue with the Convention of Scottish Local Authorities (COSLA) on how to enhance the powers of local government.[124]

449 These proposals have all arisen out of a dialogue with COSLA, but have not gone nearly as far as local government in Scotland would like. COSLA have set out three essential principles to govern a new relationship with central government:
- agreement about the allocation of responsibilities between central and local government: reserving to central government the role of setting the framework and, where appropriate, national standards within which local government should operate; but allowing local authorities autonomy within that framework to determine service delivery arrangements and their own internal structures and management.
- stability about the functions of local government: a period of stability in which to let the new unitary authorities bed down without further encroachment on their powers or responsibilities from central government.
- a local government finance system which secures local accountability: measures to increase substantially the amount of income local government raises itself from the present 15%, to be initiated by an independent commission to review the financing of local government in Scotland.

450 It is tempting to assume that it will fall to a Scottish Parliament and its Scottish Executive to respond to these desiderata. Yet even on the most optimistic scenarios it is unrealistic to expect a Scottish Parliament to be up and running much before, say, summer 1999. What will the landscape look like by then?

451 First, there will have been up to three years experience operating under a system of unitary authorities. The present preoccupations relating to the delivery and planning of services in the absence of a regional tier will have moved from discussion of structures to criticism of any obvious practical failings in the patchwork which will by then have developed. Ad hoc arrangements for joint committees, joint working, inter-authority agreements and other forms of co-ordination will have evolved. They will not be uniform by any means, either in terms of geographical coverage, or in terms of function. Some arrangements will be working better than others.

452 Second, given that the establishment of a Scottish Parliament (a premise for this discussion) implies a change of Government, a significant proportion of the time between now and the Parliament's arrival will have been spent under a different administration in St Andrew's House. Some of the issues of concern now will already have been addressed with that administration. The Scottish Labour Party is committed to 'the return of water to local democratic control', for example, and the new administration in Westminster may well have instigated action on quangos - appointments, role, democratic scrutiny etc. The independent review mentioned in paragraph 445 above will be well under way, if not completed. Some significant parts of the present landscape may already have changed.

453 Third, before the Parliament is established there will have been elections to determine its membership. These will have been preceded by a large and public exercise in the selection of candidates and by an election campaign. It will be possible then to get a sense of the nature of the future chamber. In particular it will become apparent whether the Parliament will recruit its membership largely from the present ranks of local government or whether it has successfully tapped new sources of political talent and commitment. This could be significant: it may be more difficult for ex-local councillors to restrain themselves from getting involved in the detail of local government which they know so well.

## The Scottish Parliament/Local Government Relationship

454 What is desired, whatever the circumstances in which the Parliament is born, is a co-operative relationship between the two levels of government. The establishment of a Scottish Parliament should promote a dialogue with local government, about its role in the democratic system and about the delivery and standard of services which has a longer term perspective than at present. Joint committee arrangements may well have developed in some areas to cover the loss of the regional authorities. That might be far from ideal, not least in terms of accountability, and the Parliament may want to consider how to remedy any deficiencies. Changes will be made in the light of experience: they cannot be prescribed now. Hence the most important factor will be the establishment of a continuing dialogue with local government so that decisions are clearly taken in the public interest and in the interests of the local communities which local authorities represent. How can this co-operative relationship be encouraged?

455 The SCC's proposals suggest that the relationship between local government and a Scottish Parliament should be structured within a framework containing three elements:
- a commitment in the devolution legislation that the Parliament will "secure and maintain a strong and effective system of local government".
- the Act to "embody the principle of subsidiarity to guarantee the important role of local government in service delivery".
- the Parliament to embody the principles contained in the European Charter of Local Self Government, in particular the 'power of general competence' (not the Convention's term) for local government contained in Article 4 of the Charter.

Each of these elements is examined in detail below.

## Securing and Maintaining Local Government: a Constitutional Guarantee?

456 The problem of giving local government a clear statutory basis for its role and functions in the state is not confined to Scotland. Local government in England and Wales is in the same predicament. Indeed an erosion of the autonomy of local government has been a Europe-wide phenomenon in the post war years. The Council of European Municipalities pressed the need for a constitutional guarantee of the principles of local autonomy in response to these trends. It was out of such pressures that during the early 1980s the Standing Conference of Local and Regional Authorities of Europe drafted a European Charter of Local Self-Government. This was eventually adopted by the Council of Europe, opened for signature in 1985, and came into force

on 1 September 1988. The Charter sets out a democratic standard with which all pluralist democracies in Europe should ideally comply. Article 2 states that "the principle of local self government shall be recognised in domestic legislation, and where practicable in the constitution".

457  Eleven member states of the EU have signed and ratified the Charter. Two (France and Belgium) signed the Charter in 1985 but have still to ratify it. Ireland and the United Kingdom have done neither (although Ireland introduced a power of general competence for local government in 1990). The United Kingdom provides no constitutional entrenchment of the role or functions of local government. This is widely seen as a defect in the political system. The Commission for Local Democracy's report issued earlier this year,[125] for example, urged the UK Government to sign the Charter and to enact appropriate declaratory provisions in UK legislation to define the role and status of local government in UK law.

458  If this were to happen at the UK level, the need to protect and entrench the position of local government in the Scottish devolution legislation would be less pressing. However, in the absence of UK action, the SCC effectively recommend some constitutional entrenchment of local government, in accordance with the principles of the Charter, in the devolution Act itself. Such a clause might read simply:

> *The Scottish Parliament shall secure and maintain a strong and effective system of local government.*

This is a simple declaratory provision, and it is difficult to imagine a case arising under it in the courts. Nevertheless, it might have a salutary and desirable political effect in extreme circumstances and might therefore, though not strictly necessary, be worth including in the Act.

## Power of General Competence?

459  Article 4.2 of the European Charter states the principle that "local authorities shall, within the limits of the law, have full discretion to exercise their initiative with regard to any matter which is not excluded from their competence nor assigned to any other authority". The SCC suggest that the Parliament will need to 'embody' this principle in its relationship with local government. What might that mean in practice?

460  This too is an issue which concerns local government throughout the UK. It is notable that, unlike many European countries where local government has a special legal status and the right to act for the general well being of their areas, in the UK the powers and duties of local authorities are founded in statute and any activity outside the statutory framework is deemed *ultra vires* and therefore unlawful. Both the Redcliffe Maud report on Local Government Reform and the Wheatley Royal Commission on Local Government in Scotland, published in 1969, recommended that local authorities should be given a power of general competence to act in the interest of their areas. The recommendation was not implemented, and the debate has continued.

461 Today Labour's 1995 policy paper *Renewing Democracy. Rebuilding Communities* proposes a power of community initiative so long as any action resulting is legal and does not duplicate the duties of other statutory bodies. There were reports too that the Department of the Environment were considering allowing an experimental group of local authorities the chance to operate a power of general competence in 1994, but the idea was dropped in anticipation of Treasury opposition.[126]

462 The problem about a power of general competence is that "there is no consensus on what such a power would mean within the British legal, financial, and democratic structures".[127] The Commission for Local Democracy's report (paragraph 6.8) expressed some of the difficulties in putting the principle into effect:

> "the argument for a power of general competence is compelling but we recognise that it must be subject to some general and overriding principles. For example, local authorities will be subject to the rule of law; they will have to work within the legislation establishing and regulating services; there should be limitations in their capacity to engage in solely commercial enterprises; they should not encroach on the powers or duties of other public bodies; they should not be able to discriminate, speculate, or expropriate; they should not be able to borrow without any central override at all".

463 It is true in all countries which embody a power of general competence for local government that it is subject to qualification and conditions. CLD nevertheless thought it worth striving to attain the concept if only for its 'symbolic' value:

> "it emphasises the importance of local government's responsibility for and to its community..A local authority exercising a power of general competence should generate debate and controversy. Support for its actions will have to be found from the electorate and this in itself will contribute to democratic accountability".

464 Perhaps the best approach, as advocated in CLD's later research paper by Hilary Kitchin, is to learn from the experience of other European countries and allow local authorities to participate in experimenting with wider powers (e.g. involving exemption from national legislation or regulation) with the consent and support of central government. For example, selected local authorities or groups of authorities might be given responsibility for primary healthcare, or the establishment of joint provision of social services and primary care. Financial controls might be relaxed to allow selected authorities a more active role in local economic development. Kitchin concludes: "A period of experiment in local government, with positive support from the Government of the day, set up with a view to identifying areas of permanent change, could be an alternative to, or an enhancement of, a reform programme based upon untested, and possibly over-cautious, ideas".

465 This looks like an attractive model for Scotland following devolution. The Parliament will have the powers to experiment with local government initiatives in the way suggested, and might then consider entrenching successful practice. As a practical way of 'embodying the principle' of general competence this option has much to commend it, especially while the debate at the UK level about the wisdom of embodying the concept in legislation remains unresolved.

## Subsidiarity

466 The SCC have proposed that "the Act...will embody the principle of subsidiarity so as to guarantee the important role of local government in service delivery". It is not clear in what terms the principle should be so embodied. The best example of a statutory commitment to the principle is in the Maastricht Treaty. This might provide some pointers as to how the principle can be embodied in law and subsequently applied, even though relations between two levels of government *within* the state cannot be seen as directly analogous to relations *between* states in the European Union.

467 Subsidiarity is enshrined explicitly in three new clauses in the Maastricht Treaty, and in its (non-justiciable) preamble. The preamble talks of a Union "in which decisions are taken as closely as possible to the citizen in accordance with the principle of subsidiarity". Article A welcomes a new stage in European unification "in which decisions are taken as closely as possible to the citizen". Article B says that the Treaty's objectives shall be achieved "while respecting the principle of subsidiarity as defined in Article 3b". Article 3b says:

> "The community shall act within the limits of the powers conferred upon it by this treaty and of the objectives assigned to it therein.
> In areas which do not fall within its exclusive competence, the community shall take action, in accordance with the principle of subsidiarity, only if and in so far as the objectives of the proposed action cannot be sufficiently achieved by the member states and can therefore, by reason of the scale or effects of the proposed action, be better achieved by the community.
> Any action by the community shall not go beyond what is necessary to achieve the objectives of this treaty".

468 The Edinburgh European Council in December 1992 adopted a lengthy text annexed to its conclusions giving guidance on how this Article of the treaty should be applied in practice. The Edinburgh Annex broke down the principle of subsidiarity into three 'distinct legal concepts': the principle that the community can only act where given the power to do so; the principle that the community should only take action where an objective can be better attained at the level of the community than at the level of the individual member states; and the principle that the means to be employed by the community should be proportional to the objective pursued. It makes very clear that "the principle of subsidiarity does not relate to and cannot call into question the powers conferred on the European Community by the treaty as interpreted by the court".[128] Thus the principle of subsidiarity in the European context only applies to the exercise of powers, not to the conferment of them.

469 The Edinburgh Annex suggests guidelines for applying the subsidiarity test in practice: does the issue under consideration have transnational aspects, for example, will member state or community action conflict with other requirements of the treaty, are there economies of scale to be had from community action, are there qualitative or quantitative indicators demonstrating that community action will be more effective than member state action? These guidelines are an attempt to make more rational and objective a decision that in the end must be a matter of judgement. There is no objectively 'correct' choice, for example, about how educational responsibilities should be divided between national, regional or local tiers of government. Ultimately opinions about the 'best level' for deciding and implementing any given policy necessarily reflect political preferences

470 This is how the application of subsidiarity within the European Community is working out in practice. No case has yet been brought before the ECJ on subsidiarity grounds. If that were to happen, the judges involved could do no better than look to the Edinburgh Annex itself for guidance on how the principle ought to be applied in practice. Yet the very point of writing down those guidelines, and concluding an interinstitutional agreement between the Council, the Commission and the European Parliament in October 1993 committing all three to honouring the principle in practice, was to prevent such a case ever arising. The aim has been to embody the principle in the political process itself, in the process of formulating and negotiating community legislation at every stage. These subsequent texts, agreed since the Maastricht provisions, aim to put some flesh on the bones of the principle, to make it bite *in practice,* rather than in theory through ultimate recourse to the courts.[129]

471 In its relationship with local government, the Scottish Parliament should follow a similar approach. The principle of subsidiarity should be embodied in the processes for formulating and negotiating legislation and in the relationship between central and local government. If necessary, that principle might be embodied in the equivalent of an inter-institutional agreement between central and local government setting out the broad principles governing the relationship and decisions about the respective roles of local and Scottish government. This agreement might formally establish a practice whereby central government sets framework law while leaving service delivery and choices about how to fulfil national standards to the local level. Such an approach will allow a co-operative relationship to develop.

472 By analogy, the operation of subsidiarity in the assignment of *powers* between Westminster and Edinburgh will be clear from the content of the list of reserved powers and from the debates in Parliament which determine its content. The principle of subsidiarity will thus be 'embodied' in the Act without any specific reference to it by name.

473 The alternative approach, making explicit reference to respect for the "principle of subsidiarity" in the devolution legislation, carries some drawbacks. First, the option of applying to the courts for a ruling on the division between central government and local government action in a specific case may tend to undermine the necessary search for consensus through the political process that is required to make these judgements. It will give an individual aggrieved partner who has lost the argument the opportunity to continue it by other means through judicial challenge. This may undermine the chances for consensus operation in general.

474 Even if the principle of subsidiarity is referred to in the Act, there will surely be a need for some clarifying document (as was adopted at the Edinburgh summit) explaining how that principle is to be interpreted in practice. It is no surprise that there are suggestions the Edinburgh Annex should be incorporated into the Treaty and given the force of law at this year's Intergovernmental Conference.[130] For making the decisions that matter, it will be a detailed document of this kind which is important, not a bald reference to the principle alone. And if such a document is agreed and implemented in practice there should be no need to invoke the principle in the courts in any case.

475 Though it is tempting to include the principle in legislation in order to give local government something concrete to point to in insisting on the development of a co-operative relationship, it would be unwise to assume that the principle would then never be invoked in the courts. There is likely to be some resistance to allowing this novel concept into UK law without greater clarity

about how it is to be applied, even if only as a guide to interpretation. The House of Lords can be expected to subject the idea to intense scrutiny if it appears in the devolution bill.  They will be reluctant to place judges in a position where they would be expected to make decisions which normally fall to the process of representative politics. It should be instructive that a 1994 report to the Council of Europe Steering Committee on Local and Regional Government found that the principle of subsidiarity as defined in the European Charter of Local Self-Government was "explicitly referred to in very few legislations (sic), essentially Germany and Austria".[131]

## A Central/Local Concordat?

476 The argument above suggested that the principle of subsidiarity might be better embodied in a document agreed between local government and a Scottish Parliament, rather than in the devolution legislation.  If that idea were adopted, it could prove a useful means for formalising other guidelines for the conduct of the Edinburgh/local government relationship.  Such an agreement, or Concordat, between the two levels of government could be negotiated early in the Parliament's first term between the Scottish Executive on the one hand and COSLA, as the representative of local government, on the other. The final text would then need to be endorsed by the Parliament - and local authorities - as a whole.

477 The Concordat could enshrine general principles for the conduct of the relationship, and in particular could provide for:
  - consultation with local government on all legislative proposals, or at least on all those which impinge on them (including, for example, redrawing the boundaries or changes in the electoral system).
  - consultation with local government and a right to submit evidence in the annual allocation of the budget.
  - the practical criteria to be evaluated by the Scottish Parliament  in making decisions about the appropriate level of government for a specific function i.e. the subsidiarity test.
  - the establishment of a practice whereby the Parliament may co-opt representatives from local government on to relevant Committees for the purpose of monitoring the relationship, scrutinising legislation, conducting enquiries.  The local authority members should have speaking but no voting rights.

478 The SCC's assertion that a Scottish Parliament will "embody the principles contained in the European Charter of  Local Self-Government" in its relations with local government could be realised in practice in such a Concordat.  But too much emphasis should not be placed on the Charter.  A report delivered to the Copenhagen Conference on the Tenth Anniversary of the Charter's agreement noted "insufficient awareness of the provisions of the Charter even in those countries which had ratified it".[132] Although some states have made significant changes to their legislation since ratifying the Charter, many have not.  Overall the report concluded that signature and ratification would be "highly symbolic acts" to impress newly democratising States, and that the Charter "has acquired a value of its own and has become an emblem which it is in the interest of the Council of Europe to strengthen".

## Dual Mandates

479   According to the SCC's proposals, the devolution Act should explicitly rule out dual mandates for the Parliament and any other elected body:

> "*Membership of Scotland's Parliament will be considered a full-time appointment.  It will therefore not be possible for MSPs to hold a dual mandate, for example simultaneously to be members of the UK or European Parliaments or of local authorities.  The only exception will arise in the first Parliament.  Any Members of the first Parliament who are elected to, or are already, members of another Parliament or of a local authority will be allowed to serve out their original terms*".

480   This is an important point.  The Government reached a different conclusion in the 1970s, as this commentary on the relevant provision (section 8) of the 1978 Act shows:

> "*Members of local authorities, the Welsh Assembly, the House of Commons and the Assembly of the European Communities are not precluded from membership of the Assembly.  [Section 9 of the Act makes clear that peers and members of the clergy would not be disqualified either].  The Government accepted the view of the Kilbrandon Report, para 1142, that dual membership of the Assembly and the UK Parliament should be permissible, and might even be desirable as a means of providing cross-fertilisation between one body and the other; it was also felt that to preclude dual membership by statute would be inconsistent with the stated desire to maintain the political unity of the UK...Given the extremely heavy workload involved in dual membership, however, it is not anticipated that it will become a common phenomenon*".[133]

481   There is no reason to dissent from this judgement today.  In addition there are other arguments which bolster the case for permitting dual mandates beyond the first session:

- it is far from clear that the Scottish Parliament *will* be a full time job in the sense that the activities of, say, a local councillor could not be combined with it.  Many state legislatures in federal systems sit for only a portion of the year and only a fraction of the time Westminster is in session.  The Australian state parliaments sit for only 50 to 60 days a year, the largest Canadian ones (Quebec and Ontario) for only 100 days.  Membership of most of these state legislatures is not a full-time occupation.

- some Members of the Scottish Parliament may well hold positions on other bodies at the same time - on the European Committee of the Regions, for example (see chapter 6), or perhaps in a reformed House of Lords (chapter 7).  This weakens the case for exclusivity.

- in the context of cementing a co-operative relationship with local government, some 'double hatting' would surely be desirable between the two tiers.  In Wales, Plaid Cymru are advocating a second chamber comprising local government representatives in order to achieve the same purpose.

- ultimately it should be for the electorate to decide who they want to represent them at either level.  If they feel the burden is too onerous, or too powerful, for one person they can reject him or her at the ballot box.  At most all that is required is a limitation to two simultaneous mandates.

482   It would be a positive advantage, including for the maintenance of a close relationship between the Parliament and local government, to omit any prohibition on dual mandates from the devolution Act.

## Conclusion

483   The paragraphs above have suggested how a co-operative relationship between the new Scottish Parliament and local government might be encouraged through the devolution legislation itself, through a Concordat between the two tiers, and through practical steps like the availability of a dual mandate.

484   But they also suggest that the time between now and the establishment of a Parliament can be usefully used by local government to prepare the way.  It will fall to local government to make the new unitary authorities work, for example, and to implement the joint arrangements necessary in a way which minimises the scope for criticism and change when the Parliament is established.  Likewise with reference to a power of general competence, COSLA will doubtless continue to pursue the main points of its agenda (capping, CCT, finance, quangos) with the Westminster Government, whatever its persuasion, between now and the arrival of the Parliament.  But it is open to individual local authorities to begin thinking about the sorts of experimental schemes they might ask a Scottish Parliament committed in principle to a power of general competence to sanction (see paragraphs 459 to 465 above).

485   The Act establishing the Parliament can do little more, as this chapter suggests, than create the climate for a productive relationship.  The principal element in the legal framework will be the devolution of substantial powers in relation to the local government system.  But there will be limits to what a Scottish Parliament can do in a constitutional sense, even given its relative autonomy in one part of the UK.  Without some support and encouragement from central government for its objectives in relation to strengthening the role of local government and in particular the system of local government finance, its impact must remain constrained.

# Chapter 9

## Economic and Industrial Policy

## Introduction

486　One of the hopes for devolution in the 1970s was that it would bring increased prosperity to Scotland. "Support for devolution...appears to be associated with an assumption...that it would bring an improvement in the material welfare of the people", the Royal Commission noted.[134] Hence the proposed Assembly's economic and industrial powers came under close scrutiny. Yet equally the commitment to maintain, after devolution, the 'economic and political unity' of the UK meant that in practice this was a field in which the room for devolving powers and responsibilities proved to be very constrained.

487　This chapter considers the room for devolution of economic and industrial powers today. The first section looks back at the debate in the 1970s and suggests what has changed in the interim. The second looks in some detail at the scope for devolution today, in particular in the field of regional policy. The final section considers the extent to which the establishment of a Parliament with broad powers might influence economic development by other means and the conditions necessary for such benefits to materialise.

## Devolution and Economic Development

488　The devolution debates in the 1970s took place against a background of perceived failure in national economic policies. In Scotland, as to a lesser extent in the rest of the UK, these were policies with a deliberate regional bias. Macmillan's Government had converted to regional planning in the early 1960s. The Toothill report on the Scottish economy, set up following the Conservatives' poor showing in Scotland in the 1959 election, advocated stimulating a new industrial structure to replace the old decaying heavy industries. The return of a Labour Government in 1964 set the seal on this new direction in policy. Regional Economic Planning boards were established throughout Britain advised by Regional Economic Planning Councils. The Welsh Office and Secretary of State were created. The Highlands and Islands Development Board (HIDB) was established in 1965. The National Plan of October 1965 was followed by a Plan for Scotland a few months later. "The Scottish Office led the way in promoting [the] notion of a Scottish national economic interest, no matter that it was part of the UK Government and therefore nominally subordinate to the British national interest".[135]

489　The process of increased regional autonomy in economic matters took a major step forward under the 1974 Labour administation: the Scottish Development Agency (SDA) was set up in 1975, and at the same time the Scottish Office took over the DTI's office in Glasgow together with responsibility for administering regional selective financial assistance in Scotland. "The Scottish Office regulated the Scottish economy in a system [that can be] described as a negotiated order...It was not independent: because it relied on regional policy, ultimately it depended on resources and legislation from the UK state. But it was more autonomous than an English region, notably because of the dense interconnectedness of all policy networks".[136]

490　Thus, as the demand for devolution grew through the 1960s it was partly fuelled by a sense that there was a distinct Scottish economy which was being inadequately managed from the centre. Unemployment in Scotland was significantly above the UK average (sometimes as much as twice the average), there was continuing net emigration, and GDP per head was below the UK average (in the range of 88 to 93 per cent). Although regional policy in Scotland was in fact more effective than in England, due in part to the existence of the Scottish Office and the presence of the Secretary of State to chair the Scottish Economic Planning Council, these figures lent substance to the view that Scotland was not getting a fair deal.

491 The development of North Sea oil added to the feeling of inequity. There was a strong, and justified, sense that the Westminster Government was mismanaging an important Scottish resource which might have been used to regenerate the Scottish economy. Instead the Heath Government was slow to realise the potential revenue importance of the discovery and arrangements for its effective taxation to secure benefits for the UK and for Scotland were not in place by the February 1974 election. At that time the Government were still saying that they estimated the annual income from tax and royalties would amount to some £50 million. In fact revenues at their peak in the early 1980s reached nine percent of total UK tax revenue, with major implications for the Westminster Government's finances and for the exchange rate. This too inevitably changed the terms of the devolution debate. The feeling grew that devolution would allow a change of course: the pursuit of a Scottish economic policy, in Scotland's interests, and with Scottish resources. The hope of increased prosperity was an important factor in most Scots' support for devolution, although the Royal Commission's report's survey found that a sixth of those in favour would still support it even if it left them worse off.[137]

492 The devolution legislation, however, did little to increase Scotland's economic autonomy. The 1975 White Paper stressed that devolution would not be pursued "at the expense of the benefits which flow from the political and economic unity of the United Kingdom". Economic unity meant that the UK Government needed to continue to manage the macroeconomy. It also meant that regional development policy had to be retained at the centre: "It would not be practicable even to leave particular areas to draw up their own schemes of economic support and assistance within an overall allocation, since divergences could easily distort competition in ways incompatible with a unified economy".[138] So in fact the 'economic' powers in relation to agriculture, fisheries and industrial support, particularly Regional Selective Assistance, were an important part of the proposed continuing responsibilities of the Secretary of State.

493 The 1978 Scotland Act failed to devolve full responsibility for the SDA and the HIDB. In three areas it permitted only executive devolution, subject to guidelines to be laid down by the Secretary of State: the industrial development functions of the SDA, the economic development functions of the HIDB (including in industry, fishing and agriculture), and the disposal of land or premises for industrial purposes (section 42). The split was fought hard from the Scottish Office who suggested it made no sense at all in terms of effectively managing Scotland's industrial and economic policy.

494 The concerns expressed in the 1970s about economic unity, and in particular the dangers of introducing competition between regions for industrial investment - 'a price war' as the 1975 White Paper put it - are still expressed today. If anything the scope for Scotland to pursue its own regional development policy has reduced in the meantime. The influence of the European Union in determining the framework for member states' regional policies has increased. Enthusiasm in the UK for such policies has over the same period decreased from its zenith in the 1960s and 1970s The 1972 Industry Act set UK limits for industrial assistance at the maximum levels then permitted by the EC. But UK limits are now effectively set below the maximum (the criteria are not exactly the same).

495 The decreasing emphasis on regional economic development policies on the part of the UK Government is matched by a lower profile for the economic case for devolution in the present debate, compared with the 1970s. Part of the explanation is the fact that the Scottish economy is performing better relative to the UK overall than it was then (see paragraph 490). Since 1992 Scottish unemployment rates have been below the UK average, GDP per head is at most one percentage point below the average and Scotland is not substantially poorer than other parts of the UK (with the exception of the South East), although net emigration continues. The economic motivation for devolution has in consequence faded. Seventeen years of Conservative administration have put other concerns higher on the agenda, especially the 'democratic deficit' in Scotland (see chapter 1).

## The Scope for Autonomy Today

496 The paragraphs above aim to establish the context in which the devolution of economic and industrial powers is contemplated today. This section considers in detail the scope for devolution in a number of key policy areas, against the background of the SCC's proposals in this field.

### The Scottish Constitutional Convention's Proposals

497 The SCC make clear, in *Scotland's Parliament. Scotland's Right,* that Westminster will retain 'central economic and fiscal responsibilities', but within that framework suggest a number of areas in which the Scottish Parliament might have an influential role:

> "it will be the Scottish Parliament's responsibility to channel the energies and the knowledge of the people of Scotland into creating an economy of efficient, competitive companies providing worthwhile jobs..."
>
> "[the Parliament] will have powers to ensure high quality provision of services like... electricity and gas...to organise training and retraining... to generate industrial development...to promote investment in Scotland by both indigenous and overseas companies , to support research and development, and to develop industries like agriculture, fisheries, forestry and tourism..."
>
> "the Secretary of State's existing powers in respect of public control and ownership [in Scottish Enterprise and Highlands and Islands Enterprise legislation] will be transferred in full to the Scottish Parliament.."
>
> "The Parliament will want to create a vibrant partnership with industry and commerce, and...the UK level playing field in respect of financial regulation and supervision will be preserved....The way in which Scotland's Parliament exercises its economic powers will play a major part, along with the UK Government and the EU, in determining the health of Scotland's economy . The Parliament will for example have a positive role in relation to European Union grants and regional assistance..."
>
> "Taken together these powers and obligations will create a powerful psychology of economic responsibility. It is the belief of the Convention partners that they would be used to stimulate a Scottish economic renaissance".

498 The recognition in these paragraphs that the Scottish Parliament will need to act with the UK Government and with the EU in the fields of economic and industrial policy is clearly sensible. The following paragraphs explore how the balance of responsibility between these three jurisdictions might be set in specific areas.

## Scottish Policies To Match Scottish Needs

499    There are two aspects of importance in any effective regional economic policy: institutional arrangements that work and are cost effective, and the level of preferential assitance that can be offered. A devolved Scotland would find it difficult to achieve any greater level of overall assistance than at present: constraints would still be imposed by the EU, and by the need to avoid disastrous competitive bidding between the territories and regions of the UK. But a Scottish Parliament would have considerable scope to tailor the institutional arrangements for delivering and applying that assistance to whatever structure was thought best.

500    Governments in the past have adopted this approach in Scotland: it was initiatives from past Secretaries of State which led both to the HIDB and the SDA. Both required a Secretary of State with considerable clout to gain Cabinet acquiescence in these Scottish institutions. A Scottish Executive in the future would also need to consult their counterparts elsewhere in the UK if they wished to make major changes of this kind, but a devolved Government would have more discretion than a Secretary of State.

501    Developing the effectiveness with which assistance is used would leave considerable scope for policy initiatives which would not affect the big picture of the financial allocation mechanisms: advice and consultancy help for small firms, equity participation schemes, publicly owned nest factories etc. There might be scope too for some reorganisation of the existing web of machinery - Scottish Enterprise and Highlands and Islands Enterprise, the Local Enterprise Companies etc. The aim would be to reinvigorate the partnerships and networks which already operate in developing the Scottish economy. The ability of a Scottish Parliament to implement EC directives in Scotland would also allow a more sensitive approach to local needs than is possible from Westminster, especially given the concerns about 'gold-plating' (regulating beyond what the directive strictly requires).

502    The co-operative networks which a Scottish Parliament could encourage are already well-developed in Scotland, and admired elsewhere. Alan Harding's recent research on regional economic development for the Rowntree Foundation concludes that having the right institutional machinery can make a significant difference to the effectiveness and innovation with which development funds can be used:

> "In Scotland, many of the main economic development partnerships tend to develop at the local level...but added value is gained from networking at the Scottish level too. A Scottish Enterprise scheme for capping business loans and guaranteeing a stable financial environment for firms...aroused Treasury suspicion but SE, backed by the Scottish Office and helped by Cabinet-level intervention from the Secretary of State, was able to argue, successfully, that the scheme represented a Scottish answer to a Scottish problem, that there was no necessary implication for the rest of the UK but that if the scheme worked well it could be tried elsewhere".[139]

503    Scotland is used to operating under these circumstances, carefully pushing its autonomy only to the point where the UK as a whole is not affected. As one distinguished observer has put it: "The main ingredient of our success is perhaps that we exploit to the full our privileged position as a small obstreperous minority within the UK framework. Provided we do not go too far, we can extract concessions out of central government which mean a lot to us but are not large enough to upset the balance of government expenditure".[140] The Scottish Parliament should not find it unfamiliar therefore developing innovative policy, in partnership with others, under the eye of a constraining macroeconomy.

## Parliament More Responsive to Business?

504 The SCC's proposals point out the benefits of proximity for business in having a Parliament in Edinburgh rather than London. These advantages are difficult to quantify. More tangible would be the presence in the Parliament itself of a number of business people and industrialists who are unable to participate directly in the process of government as politicians at Westminster. As presently proposed, the SCC's scheme would appear to rule out this potential benefit since they insist that 'Membership of Scotland's Parliament will be considered a full-time appointment'.

505 As argued elsewhere in relation to dual mandates for local councillors (see chapter 8, paragraph 481), the Parliament is unlikely to sit for more than a 100 days a year - probably significantly fewer - and will be close enough to many businesses to allow active participation by representatives from that sector. This might involve a more active participation in pre-legislative scrutiny, giving evidence on proposed bills to the relevant committees, or it might involve election to the Parliament itself. Clearly strong provision for the declaration of interests (following Nolan) would then be appropriate. In any event, the presence of a Parliament in Edinburgh promises a greater degree of access to the legislators - and potentially responsiveness from them - for Scottish business than the present arrangements.

## Financial Assistance for Regional Development

506 There are a number of sources of regional development funds - at the European level, at the UK Government level and at a local level. In practice the European Commission places limits on the totality of all such assistance. The following paragraphs examine the present arrangements and suggest how they might change under devolution.

### Regional Selective Assistance

507 The key instrument of UK regional development policy is Regional Selective Assistance (RSA). RSA takes the form of grants from central government to stimulate or attract new industrial development in designated areas of the UK. The Treasury sets overall limits on the amount of grant for any one project in terms of Cost per Job (cpj). The departments concerned (Scottish Office, Welsh Office and DTI) work within these limits, which as mentioned above are substantially below the limits set by the European Commission and therefore below the amounts payable by competition elsewhere in the EU. The cpj limit can be raised for individual cases, but this requires Treasury Ministers' consent which is very rarely given. It is also agreed that within the UK no one territory or region can top an offer to any company made by another territory or region. RSA can only be paid for developments within areas defined by an Assisted Areas map.

508 Existing practice also provides for consultation amongst UK territories and regions on sectoral issues i.e. RSA is not paid to increase capacity in one region at the expense of costing jobs elsewhere in the Assisted Areas, or to increase capacity in an industry which is already suffering from over-capacity. EC rules also prohibit or restrict support to some sectors where over-capacity exists EC-wide: for example steel, shipbuilding, and textiles. Nor is RSA paid in the UK for retail developments - which generally result in substantial local displacement e.g. when a super or hyper market creates jobs on its site at the expense of the closure of many small retail outlets.

509 All changes in the RSA scheme (as well as to the Assisted Areas map: see below) need European Commission approval, in order to ensure fairness throughout the EU. This is sought via UKRep, the UK Government's office in Brussels, following agreement among all the domestic departments concerned. The total provision in Scotland for RSA for both indigenous and inward investment now varies between £80-£100m per year depending on the expected demands on it. Hitherto it has always been a demand led scheme, but it was incorporated in the Scottish block in 1993 together with other industrial support activities such as funding for Scottish Enterprise and is now cash limited. Between 1984 and 1994 about £450m was paid out in Scotland in support of around 140,000 new jobs and jobs safeguarded, as compared with £350m in Wales and £770m in England.

510 The Whitehall arrangements described above serve to minimise dispute and competitive bidding for inward investment between the territories and regions of the UK, and keep UK regional assistance within the agreed EU limits. The key question for the future is how these twin aims might be achieved under devolution?

511 Retaining something like the present framework - working within common guidelines and cpj limits - would undoubtedly exacerbate inter-regional tensions which are already incipient. The political repercussions are easy to imagine if, for example, the UK Treasury refused an application from the Scottish Executive to exceed the cpj limits for a particularly desirable scheme - whether or not it was one which would otherwise go elsewhere in the UK. Similarly there would be tension if a Whitehall department opposed the payment of a grant to a firm in Scotland on grounds of adverse impact elsewhere in the sector in another part of the UK.

512 An alternative would be to allow free competition between Scotland, Wales and the English regions, relying only on the European level limits to impose constraints. Because EC rules limit the maximum proportion of capital spend which can be paid in grant rather than being tied to the number of jobs being created, this could result in substantial increases in grant to capital intensive projects - which are the most sought after and politically sensitive. Given the size of the Scottish block (around £14 billion) in relation to current levels of RSA (less than £100m a year), Scotland would not be significantly constrained in increasing RSA for high profile projects. There could then be substantial increases in RSA expenditure throughout the UK, on the assumption that England and Wales would retaliate if Scotland stepped up grant levels.

513 On balance, and despite the risks of exacerbating tensions which are never far from the surface, it would probably be best in the general UK interest to avoid such financial competition ('smokestack chasing' as it is known in the US, where this is a severe problem between states). Thoughts on how this might be achieved are in paragraph 525 below.

## The Assisted Areas Map

514 One of the pillars of regional policy is the Assisted Areas map which defines the areas in which RSA and certain other forms of grant aid can be paid - and which is closely allied, if not completely coterminous, with the areas in which European Structural Funds can be used to support economic development. The map is prepared by DTI in consultation with the Scottish and Welsh Offices and its final form has to be approved by the Commission who set out broad guidelines across the EC.

515 A Scottish Parliament will need to recognise that settling the map is an area where ultimate responsibility lies with the UK Government and the Commission. This is not necessarily a bad thing. Scotland does pretty well out of the present arrangements. Also, the Commission will always take a close interest in the map (as will the EU Committee of the Regions) and the criteria which underlie it (related to unemployment trends, population structure, household income etc) - so the UK Government will not be able to change the Assisted Area at will. Even so, there will have to be arrangements to ensure that Scotland's interests in setting the map are taken into account.

## State Aids Generally

516 Under the EC competition and state aids rules all publicly funded schemes for industrial support, including that from local authorities and Local Enterprise Companies (LECs), need to be notified to the Commission and cannot be implemented without approval. If the Scottish Parliament is to introduce support schemes, for example, for small businesses and encouraging innovation or exports, they will need Commission approval. The absence of opposition from the UK Government in seeking that approval might be an important condition for gaining it.

517 The definition of 'state aids' is drawn widely. For example, changes in training arrangements introduced by the Scottish Executive, if dependent on the use of public funds to support the private sector, would almost certainly fall into this category. Commitment of public funds to employers to support retraining of employees (as distinct from the unemployed) would also need approval under the 'state aids' regime. However, if the UK Government adopted EC objective 4 programmes under the European Social Fund, which the Conservative Government have resolutely opposed, there might be direct support for such a programme from Brussels (see below).

## European Funds

518 The structural funds are the Commission's own funds and the ground rules for their disbursement are set by the Commission with the approval of the Council. There are four structural funds (the European Regional Development Fund - ERDF, European Social Fund - ESF, the Guidance Section of the European Agricultural Guidance and Guarantee Fund - EAGGF, and the Financial Instrument for Fisheries Guidance - FIFG), all with the aim of encouraging convergence and reducing regional disparities. They do this in support of five defined objectives - to encourage underdeveloped areas (Objective 1), to regenerate areas of industrial decline (2), to reduce long term unemployment and facilitate entry into the labour market (3), to facilitate retraining (4) (which the UK has not accepted for application within the UK), and to speed up agricultural and fisheries reorganisation and promote rural development (5b). A sixth objective relating to especially sparsely populated areas was introduced with the admission of Finland, Sweden and Austria in 1995. The Highlands and Islands falls just outside the population density required to qualify.

519 Scotland has been the major UK beneficiary and has received more than £1.5billion from these funds since 1979. The Highlands and Islands region qualifies as an objective 1 area (GDP per capita under 75% of the EU average), and much of the rest of the country falls within objective 2 or 5b (rural areas). Once again, this coverage is the result not only of need but of persuasive advocacy by officials and Ministers, both within the UK and as part of the UK team in negotiation with the Commission. As with the Assisted Areas map, the Commission is heavily policed by the other member states not to stretch the objective criteria (set out in regulations) too far in any individual case. The Scottish interest will be best served by influencing the UK line in the negotiation of the underlying regulations.

## Mechanisms for UK Co-ordination

520 What should be clear from the descriptions of the present regimes above is that the oversight functions of the European Commission are paramount in this area. The first conclusion for any scheme of devolution therefore must be that arrangements which allow for consultation and cooperation with the Scottish Executive on *all* these issues (negotiating the structural funds regulations, the Assisted Areas map, state aids approval, etc.) should be a central feature of the intergovernmental agreement on European issues proposed in chapter 6.

521 The involvement of the EU in this area inevitably reduces the scope for Scotland to operate entirely independently of the UK Government. But the significance of that should not be exaggerated, for two reasons.

522 Enlargement of the EU is likely significantly to reduce the amounts of structural funds spending in Scotland in the future. Since the current regulations expire in 1999, it could well be that they have changed considerably - in anticipation of enlargement - before the Scottish Parliament is even established. It is estimated, for example, that if Poland, Hungary and the Czech and Slovak Republics join the Union then around 30 areas currently in receipt of objective 1 funds will become ineligible. That would include the Highlands and Islands region. The nature of EU regional policy could change markedly in preparation for such enlargement.[141]

523 Even under existing arrangements the Scottish Office have been moderately successful in influencing Commission decisions at the margins. It is possible, for example, to obtain small grants from the Commission direct for 'Community Initiatives' which are intended as pilot schemes for possible development across the EC in due course. It is also in the UK's interests to maximise the overall take from the funds: any additional pressure or expertise the Scottish Parliament will be able to bear should be welcomed (as it is now: the Highlands and Islands' objective 1 status was very much on the border line).

524 The more difficult problem is the risk of competition between the UK regions for RSA. Here there is no alternative to the UK Government holding the ring, just as the Commission does at the European level. The Commission's task is made easier by the existence of objective criteria agreed by all the member states and diligently policed by them, so the UK Government's task would be far more straightforward were it genuinely holding the ring between representatives from all the territories and regions of the UK. In time, with the establishment of Regional Chambers in the English regions (on which see the Constitution Unit's report, *Regional Government in England*), it may be possible to preserve the 'economic unity of the UK' in the same way - through a genuinely intergovernmental process agreeing the criteria for RSA and applying them in practice.

525 But until analogues for the Scottish and Welsh representatives in such a negotiation can be identified, there is probably no alternative but to seek to preserve the existing, admittedly friable, arrangements for consultation and cooperation with the Welsh Office/ Scottish Executive and the DTI. These might be formalised in a separate agreement between all three parties providing for:
- close contacts at official level (a standing working group?).
- guidelines on competitive bidding.
- consultation on cost per job limits for RSA.
- the possibility of exceeding cost per job limits with the consent of UK Ministers, following discussion with all parties.

- even-handed treatment of all parties by the instruments of central government deployed to assist in the attraction of inward investment to the UK (UK Ministerial visits, FCO lobbying by posts abroad, work of the Invest in Britain Bureau in DTI etc).
- an annual ceiling on RSA expenditure in each country.

526  If this were not felt to be tough enough to prevent damaging competition between regions (some degree of competition should be welcomed) then the provisions of the 1978 Act allowing for the Secretary of State (it could equally well be the President of the Board of Trade) to establish guidelines by order under section 42 could be adapted for inclusion in the devolution legislation itself.  These should impose as few restrictions as possible, and should be introduced only after consultation with the Scottish Parliament and preferably with their agreement (see paragraph 106 above - Chapter 3 - for an example of such a clause).  The guidelines - if introduced - should be subject to automatic review after, say, three years in order that they might lapse when the conditions exist for a genuinely UK-wide intergovernmental forum for negotiation, as described in paragraph 524.

527  A third possibility might be to treat industrial assistance for inward investors through  RSA as being subject to executive devolution - i.e. the Scottish Executive would administer the UK scheme in Scotland and be responsible, as Locate In Scotland is at present, for marketing and promoting Scotland overseas, but would administer in Scotland a UK budget (the Scottish share of which would be outside the budget assigned by formula) and a UK scheme, the details of which would of course have been the subject of negotiation between the UK and Scottish Governments.

528  Finally a word of caution about the significance of these arrangements is appropriate too.  The sums involved in RSA are very small indeed compared with the transfers which occur between regions naturally in the PES round in the pursuit of equalisation according to need.  These run into billions of pounds for Scotland, Wales and some of the English regions, while RSA in all these cases is less than £100 million.[142]  It is very much in Scotland's interests to avoid financial battles with Wales and the English regions over these small sums, which could poison the atmosphere for the wider question of Scotland's overall financial settlement.  The same logic will apply to Wales post-devolution.

## Privatised Utilities

529  The SCC list among the "principal areas which will fall within the powers of Scotland's Parliament", "energy, including electricity generation and supply...**transportation including public passenger and freight services**, and payment of subsidies to operators of [transport] services", and also suggest powers for the Parliament to "ensure high quality provision of services like...**electricity and gas**".  It is not clear what the role of the Scottish Parliament would be in practice.  Both the electricity and gas industries are subject to a UK regulator (telecommunications is not mentioned in the SCC report).  As for electricity generation and supply, the industries have been largely privatised (with nuclear to be privatised in 1996) and Scottish Power and Hydro Electric are significant operators south of the border in what is a genuinely UK market.

530  It would make sense if these services continued to be regulated on a UK basis - although it would be desirable to provide that the consumer committees appointed by the regulators in Scotland should be chosen following consultation with the Scottish Executive.

531 Similar arguments will apply to **British Rail** following privatisation. If, as the SCC suggest, the Scottish Executive were to assume responsibility for subsidising passenger transport across the board, then a substantial addition to the Scottish Block would be necessary for rail services. It is difficult to say at this stage just how large a call on Scottish resources that would be, although that will become transparent on completion of rail privatisation. Difficult questions would have to be resolved on respective responsibilities for support for cross border traffic such as the Anglo Scottish sleepers and indeed the main East and West Coast day services. There would also need to be some provision for the operations in Scotland of Opraf (the rail franchiser) which will be responsible for entering into franchising agreements with the operators and agreeing the level of subsidies within an overall limit of sums allocated for that purpose by the Department of Transport and perhaps the Scottish Executive.

532 Given the importance to Scotland of rail links to and from the south, future arrangements for the regulation of Railtrack and the train operating companies, if and when privatised, will be very relevant to the Scottish Executive. But it is likely to be preferable (subject to any changes in policy introduced by a new Government in Westminster) to maintain responsibility for the overall regulation and management of the railways and other passenger services (e.g. bus services) at national level, with a strong role for the Scottish and other regional administrations in the decision-making processes and continuing scope for financial support by local authorities as at present for local essential services.

## Agriculture And Fisheries

533 This chapter does not consider in any detail the issues arising from the SCC's suggestion that the Scottish Parliament should have powers to "develop industries like agriculture [and] fisheries". The SCC is silent as to whether this area of activity will contain any reservations. The 1978 Act did not devolve "general agricultural policy including subsidies, grants, price support...".

534 The reservations in 1978 were inserted for similar considerations as those relating to other grants discussed above. But the EC has an even more dominant role, because agriculture is one of the policy areas where the EC has exclusive competence. The Council (in which all major agricultural decisions are negotiated and decided by qualified majority) and the Commission have very tight control over policy, including support to individual producers or for structural change. Broadly similar considerations apply to fishing issues.

535 Agricultural support prices are manipulated on an EC wide basis, by means of variable levies on EC food imports, subsidies on EC exports and various forms of intervention buying. In the UK these are carried out by the Intervention Board on behalf of all the Agriculture Ministers. This might include representatives of the Scottish Executive after devolution: they would have a strong interest even if only in implementation of the policy (this point too could be covered in the intergovernmental agreement on European issues suggested in Chapter 6).

536 In Scotland in 1995 about £500m was spent (outside the formal Scottish block mechanism) in support of agriculture and fisheries (which employ some 70,000 people in Scotland) and some 70% of that came from EC Funds. The support schemes for producers of livestock and arable, expected to amount to £400m in 1995 (up from around £50m in 1989), were wholly funded

from the EC. While the 1992 reforms to the Common Agricultural Policy (CAP) brought more local room for manoeuvre, the details of the schemes and their administration are prescribed from Brussels - because of the need to level the playing field so far as practicable in what is a genuinely EC wide market. Similar considerations apply in the various agricultural structural funds, although there is a little more room for local discretion, subject to Brussels approval.

537 In agriculture and fisheries therefore close working between the devolved and UK administrations will be essential. The Scottish Executive may have responsibility for administering the EC schemes, but the UK Government will be answerable to the Commission for the effectiveness of such administration. Even the German Federal Government is so responsible, although under the German constitution the Länder are the competent body. The central importance of agriculture to the EC and the desire of the UK Government (and other net contributors) to contain and reduce expenditure on it suggest that this is an area for which the UK Government will wish to retain ultimate responsibility.

538 That conclusion need not be greeted in Scotland with too much dismay. Given the lack of local discretion, it would seem sensible to maintain present arrangements in which expenditure in support of EC programmes on agriculture is outside the block and the formula arrangement i.e. the EC funds would pass direct to the Scottish administration earmarked for agricultural purposes. The alternative is the prospect of finding funds from within the block for what amounts to mandatory expenditure in support of policies in agriculture over which the Scottish Executive will have very little control.

## Economic Policy and Other Aspects of the Settlement

539 The impact of the Scottish Parliament on the Scottish economy will not be confined to the exercise of 'economic' powers. Other elements in the package will also have a significant effect: education policy, transport, roads, housing, land use planning. But perhaps the biggest factor in the settlement which will determine its impact on the Scottish economy is the coherence of the whole package:

> "The consequences of devolution for [the business, financial and commercial sectors] would depend on the nature of the devolved structure and powers devolved, the perceived stability of that structure and the political context within which devolution took place...If the devolved structure was perceived as unstable, the uncertainties associated with independence would come into play".[143]

540 Thus this chapter finishes by reinforcing messages already derived in earlier chapters: that the devolution legislation should be comprehensible and principled, that the financial provisions should allow a reasonable expectation of long term stability, that co-operative machinery will need to be put in place to ensure that devolution works in practice, and that the whole exercise should be pursued in a generous spirit and as part of a programme bringing benefits to all areas of the UK. This must be a confident measure if it is to win the confidence of the Scottish people, Scottish business and the markets.

# Chapter 10

# The Transition: from Royal Assent to Establishment

## Introduction

541 The bulk of this report has dealt with the technical issues involved in establishing a Parliament and making it work - the provisions of the devolution legislation, financing, machinery of government and the need for a variety of intergovernmental arrangements. But there are other issues of a more practical nature which also need to be covered, such as the need for premises and staff for the Parliament, the first elections, the smooth transfer of responsibilities from Westminster and central government to new Scottish institutions. These issues are briefly dealt with in this chapter.

542 **Table 8** summarises the tasks that will need to be performed and a suggested schedule (these are tasks not associated with the legislation itself e.g. policy-making, White Papers, etc). It divides the period between the election of a Government committed to legislative devolution and the establishment of a Parliament into three phases: between election and Royal Assent to the devolution legislation; between that moment and the first elections; and between the establishment of a Scottish Executive at the first meeting of the Parliament and the establishment of the Parliament with full powers. Most of the tasks fall to the Government in the first two phases, thereafter the Scottish Parliament and Executive will have to begin taking decisions.

543 Both the range of tasks, and the timetable are speculative. The first will depend on how much detail, for example relating to the Parliament's Standing Orders, is put in the devolution Act itself. The second will depend on when the Bill is introduced and how long it takes to get through its parliamentary stages.

544 The rest of this chapter fleshes out the tabular outline in more detail.

### Table 8: Suggested Schedule for the Establishment of the Scottish Parliament

| TIMING | TASK |
| --- | --- |
| **Pre-Royal Assent** | • Prepare the Parliament building for operation, and consider staffing requirements and costs.<br>• Plan necessary changes in staffing and organisation of the Scottish Office in Edinburgh and London.<br>• Draw up draft proposals for a Concordat between the Scottish executive and local government (COSLA's task too).<br>• Draw up draft intergovernmental arrangements for the conduct of EU business.<br>• Consider forward planning for needs assessment exercise. |
| **Post-Royal Assent** | • Plan for first elections - date, registration, selection of candidates (for political parties), arrangements for regional list system, public information campaign.<br>• Hold elections.<br>• Prepare draft standing orders. |

| After Elections: First Meeting | • Election of Presiding officers.<br>• Election of the First Minister.<br>• First formal consideration of draft Standing Orders.<br>• Recruit permanent staff for the Parliament.<br>• Make necessary changes in Scottish Office.<br>• Implement provisions of the Scotland Act as necessary to discharge these tasks (eg early calls on Scottish Parliament's budget).<br>• Period of 'running in', establishing committees, testing the machinery with the Scottish Office, etc. |
|---|---|
| Establishment | • State Opening.<br>• Adoption of Standing Orders.<br>• Full powers under the Scotland Act. |

## Pre-Royal Assent

### Intergovernmental Machinery

545 This report has advocated in a number of places the establishment of special arrangements for the operation of the devolution settlement which need not necessarily be embodied in legislation. Although they would come into effect only following the establishment of the Parliament, there is no need to wait for the Act to gain Royal Assent in order to begin planning for them. It will also be easier to defend the Bill in Parliament if the Government is able to point to concrete proposals in these areas during its passage. Otherwise there will be a temptation to amend the legislation as if they did not exist.

546 The Government would be wise therefore to begin work early in its term of office on the substance of two intergovernmental agreements which this report has suggested: a Concordat with local government covering powers, subsidiarity, consultation, information, etc; and arrangements with the Scottish Executive and its officials for the conduct of EU business post-devolution. The first of these tasks will fall to COSLA too, and might be wrapped up in the work of the independent review of the future relationship between local government and a Scottish Parliament already proposed by the Labour Party (see chapter 8).

547 Neither set of arrangements may be finalised until there is a Scottish Parliament and Executive to act as the second party to them. They may be amended in negotiation once the Parliament is established and is able to express its own view. But these are important elements in the infrastructure which will allow devolution to function, and therefore a legitimate concern for central government in advance of the Parliament's establishment.

### Preparing the Chamber

548 Preparing the Parliament building for operation will take some time. Planning should begin as soon as possible. Actual work on conversion could commence once the Bill had secured a

second reading. Preparation of the Royal High School building, for example, began well before Royal Assent to the 1978 Act - indeed a great deal was done on the strength of the 1976 Bill having secured a second reading.

549 The bigger problem will be the recruitment and appointment of parliamentary staff, many of whom will have to be specialists able to draw on previous experience of parliamentary work elsewhere. The obvious source of such personnel are the specialist staff serving in both Houses at Westminster. The new Parliament will have to recruit or second such staff at least on a temporary basis in order to guide it through the process of establishment and its early operation.

550 The principal task should be to identify a core specialist staff, including a Parliamentary Clerk, for the Parliament as early as possible and to discuss with them the terms on which secondment or temporary transfer might be effected. Those negotiations will inevitably have to take place between the UK Government (rather than the Scottish Parliament) and the individuals involved. It can be anticipated that they will be concerned to obtain some guarantee about future permanent employment, and about the terms and conditions of that employment given the prospect potentially of a very different set of operating conditions for a Parliament in Scotland compared with Westminster. This is one area then where the dictates of the market may force the Government initially to offer, and the Scottish Parliament subsequently to confirm, rough equality of treatment with similar specialist staff at Westminster (including the right to return?) if they are to obtain the calibre of personnel necessary. It will be a sound investment.

## The Scottish Office

551 The establishment of the Parliament, as discussed in chapter 7, will have an effect on the structure and organisation of the Scottish Office - both that part of it which becomes responsible to the Scottish Executive and that which remains responsible to the Secretary of State. Plans for operating in these new circumstances should be developed from the start of the devolution process.

552 The Financial and Explanatory Memorandum to the 1977 Bill estimated an increase of 750 in the numbers of civil servants in the Scottish Office following devolution. The figure was based on the following assumptions:

- 25-30% of the increase would be involved with new functions, such as the negotiation of the block grant and serving a newly created Scottish Executive.
- about 40% of them would be needed because of the loss of economies of scale (finance, information services, personnel matters, etc) and because in some cases the new Scottish administration would need to duplicate expertise still required by the Secretary of State e.g. in agriculture and fisheries, regional policy.
- about 25% of them would be needed to cope with the increase in activity that an Assembly would generate - debates, questions, evidence to committees, MSPs' correspondence. etc.

553 Staff will certainly be needed to cope with new tasks in all three categories. Two more factors might be added as well. The increased importance of the European dimension argues for strengthening the Scottish Office's expertise and resources in that area too; and the Scottish Executive will need its own staff (and offices) in Brussels and in London. Both of these factors fall under the first category above.

554 Even so, it is unlikely that the increase in overall staffing levels would match that suggested in 1977. Increased delegation to departments has reduced the areas where economies of scale can be said to exist, and an overall reduction in the size of the civil service by nearly 30% since 1979 means the Government machine generally is far leaner than it was. The Scottish Office, for example, has just undergone a Fundamental Expenditure Review, the result of which is a planned loss of some 15-20% of core staff over the next two years in line with reductions in running costs. Devolution might require at least the restoration of some of those posts.

### Needs Assessment

555 Chapter 5 on the financial provisions for the Parliament advocated a periodic needs assessment to establish relative levels of need in Scotland, Wales, Northern Ireland and the English Regions. It suggested that the assessment should be conducted by an independent body appointed partly by the UK Government and partly by the Governments of the devolved territories and regions. The establishment of this Commission cannot take place in advance of the establishment of the Parliament. But there might still be useful steps that a forward-looking Government could take to facilitate the smooth conduct of that difficult exercise when it occurs. For example:

- consider what changes, if any, need to be made in the systems of Government accounting to accommodate devolution, including the potential impact of Resource Budgeting.
- consider how to meet the requirement for accurate and reliable statistical data on spending, and perhaps revenue, disaggregated for the territories and regions of the UK. Some change in present practices might need to be initiated to facilitate the needs assessment exercise in due course.
- identify personnel for appointment to the Commission. A proportion of the membership will be appointed by the UK Government. It would be helpful for the initial assessment if the UK appointees included a Commission Chair who could be involved informally in any preparatory planning that occurs within the UK Government. All Commissioners should be independent of Government, and nothing should be done to compromise this position even during these informal exchanges.

## Post-Royal Assent

### The First Elections

556 The major item during this phase will be arranging the first elections. The 1978 Act specified that the timing of the first elections would be laid down by Order of the Secretary of State. There is a good case for specifying the date for the initial elections in the Act itself, not least to simplify the legislation and reduce the scope for dispute as it goes through parliament. But on balance it seems right that the new devolution legislation should follow the same procedure - in order to provide flexibility to cater for unforeseen circumstances. Even so, the drafting might be tightened to introduce a greater degree of certainty about the date of the first elections: the Act could specify a date from which departure would have to be justified by Order of the Secretary of State, and a time limit for the elections under any circumstances, say of one year from the date of Royal Assent.

557 It would be helpful to all concerned if the date for the first elections could be decided as early as possible. The determining factors will be the time the political parties need to organise for the elections, including the selection of candidates, and any technical work which needs to be done to bring the electoral register up to date. Arrangements will need to be made too for postal voting (the political parties can be expected to use their overseas networks to alert potential voters), and for the introduction of the regional list system for electing additional members (separate ballot boxes, separate counts, regional returning officers?).

558 This last point is critical. There will need to be an extensive public information campaign in Scotland in advance of the first election to explain the mechanics of the additional member system and the use of two votes in a single election. Even if the other details above can be ironed out relatively quickly, it would be advisable to allow several months for the information campaign to have its effect in preparing Scottish voters for change. A target for the first elections nine months after Royal Assent might be sensible. The fact that an up-to-date electoral register is published in February each year might be factored into the calculation.

## First Meeting of the Parliament

559 Once the elections have been held, there will need to be a pre-planned period of time before the Parliament meets for the first time. It might be several weeks (the European Parliament meets five weeks after the election). Time will be needed to recover from the election campaign, to allow alliances and groupings to form, to reach initial agreement on the number and remits of committees, and to prepare the ground for the election at the Parliament's first meeting of Presiding Officers and a First Minister.

560 Aside from the ceremonial, the first meeting of the Parliament will need to conduct the following business - and in the following order:
- agreement to procedures for the election of Presiding Officers (Speaker and two deputies) and for the election of the First Minister.
- election of Presiding Officers.
- election of a First Minister: candidates for the election will presumably be chosen by their political parties. The appointment of the rest of the Scottish Executive will follow.
- consideration of draft Standing Orders and appointment of a committee (respecting party balance) to revise the draft as appropriate.
- agreement on an initial Committee structure for the Parliament.
- (possibly) agreement on staffing structure and salaries for the Parliament to permit permanent recruitment and appointment to commence. This point is dealt with in more detail below.

### Standing Orders

561 The Parliament's Standing Orders should be adopted by the Parliament itself. But some rules for the conduct of business will be needed from the start. The 1978 Act included a provision allowing the Secretary of State to "give directions for regulating [the Assembly's] procedure pending the making of standing orders" (section 7). It also set out a number of procedural provisions which any standing orders would have to respect e.g. three stages in the legislative process - section 26. The balance will need to be considered afresh for the new devolution

legislation. Westminster might still wish to constrain the standing orders in some ways e.g. to insist on a requirement to seek the Queen's consent before introducing legislation touching on the Royal prerogative - see 1978 Act, section 24. But if it can be demonstrated during the passage of legislation that there is widespread cross-party support for example for the main features of the Bernard Crick and David Millar's standing orders[144] already on the table, then the constraints might be reduced. The legislation might remain silent on detailed parliamentary procedures but simply include a fallback provision which would allow the UK Government to fill the void if the Scottish Parliament could not reach agreement in a reasonable time - to remain in force until they did so.

562 The first business of the Parliament might either be conducted under rules laid down at the direction of the Secretary of State (or in the legislation itself - as the SCC have proposed), or under rules agreed at the first meeting. As far as the management of the Parliament is concerned (as opposed to more fundamental rules for example on qualification for membership, existence of a Speaker and of a Scottish Executive), the latter course is suggested above - on the assumption that there will be none in this first meeting who see it as their role disrupt proceedings from the start. If business is disrupted, it should be open to the Chair to suspend proceedings, or adjourn until the following day. These initial rules would also need to cover the election of Presiding Officers and of the First Minister, if these points were not specified in the legislation.

563 Ideally the Parliament should have before it at the first meeting a set of draft standing orders incorporating the provisions for these elections. But it will not be possible for the Parliament to adopt them immediately, even given a period of weeks between the elections and the first meeting. Hence the suggestion that a committee be appointed to consider the draft.

564 The draft might be drawn up by the core specialist staff already identified for secondment to the Parliament following its establishment. Drafting should commence as soon as possible: a good deal of work will need to be done in any event in determining how far the Bill should specify procedures. A priority following Royal Assent will be to attempt to refine a draft in informal cross-party talks invoving the parties which did not participate in the work of the SCC. The prospect of standing orders imposed from Westminster should concentrate minds and promote agreement at this stage. But the standing orders would still need to be adopted - and possibly adapted - following the elections by the Scottish Parliament itself.

## The Chair

565 The SCC propose that the Secretary of State should take the chair for the first meeting of the Parliament. That is unnecessary and undesirable. The only business that will have to be conducted in the absence of the permanent Presiding Officer of the Parliament is the election of somebody into that position and of two deputies. Erskine May specifically rules out Ministers presiding at the election of the Speaker in the House of Commons, in order to take the politics out of the process as far as possible. Erskine May suggests that the Member "who has served for the longest period continuously as a Member of the House" can take the chair in those circumstances. That could not apply at the first meeting of the Parliament. Alternatively, putting the oldest Member in the Chair for the election of the President of the Parliament is a rule in the European Parliament, which Crick and Millar have suggested be the rule in the Scottish Parliament too. That seems far preferable to what the SCC propose. The oldest Member would preside at the first meeting only until the Presiding Officer had been elected.

## Running In Operations

566 Following the first meeting of the Parliament, the appointment of the Executive, and ideally the establishment of an initial committee structure, there should follow a period of 'running in'. That will allow the members of the Executive to become familiar with the administration they are about to inherit, committees of the Parliament to be formed, a testing of the mechanisms for the operation of Parliamentary government, and an opportunity for the new Executive to consider policy, and in particular legislation, for the first session of the Parliament. The Parliament would for the most part not meet at all during this period - except to agree as a whole provisional arrangements adopted by the Executive (e.g. the appointment of Ministers), or by the Clerk (staffing, committee structure and membership etc).

### Commencement Orders

567 The Parliament will not be ready to take on the full range of its responsibilities on day one after the election. But it will need to have some statutory powers sooner than others - for example all those relating to the first meeting of the Parliament and the formation of an Executive. It will also need the capacity to spend from an early stage - and therefore the related audit and scrutiny for maladministration functions which go with it.

568 These are highly technical matters. The effect would be obtained in practice by incorporating 'common form' provisions on commencement into the devolution Act. These would specify that:

> *(1) The preceding provisions of this Act (and the Schedules relating to them) shall not come into operation until such day as the Secretary of State may by order appoint.*
> *(2) Different days may be appointed under this section for different provisions of this Act and for different purposes of the same provision.*[145]

### Running Costs?

569 Establishing the Parliament will cost money. Costs will fall into two categories: initial start-up costs and subsequent running costs. The first element is easier to estimate than the second, although both will be dependent on a number of variables. Start-up costs will comprise the following:
- cost of running the first election, including public information campaign.
- cost of equipping the Parliament building for operation.
- cost of obtaining any further office accommodation.
- cost of initial staff recruitment exercise.

Running costs associated with the Parliament might comprise:
- cost of any additional staff in the Scottish Office.
- cost of leasing or purchasing and servicing the Parliament building and any other offices associated with its establishment.
- cost of Parliamentary staff and Members.

All of these elements are difficult to estimate with any degree of certainty until the Parliament is established and has settled into a working pattern.

*1977 Estimates*

570    The 1977 Financial Memorandum accompanying the Scotland Bill estimated total start-up costs at about £5.25 million. This comprised £4.25 million for the purchase of the Royal High School buildings for the Assembly, the conversion of the buildings and the provision of office space for Assembly staff and additional Scottish Office civil servants; and £1 million for the conduct of the initial elections and associated publicity (being just over half of the £1.5 million estimated for Scotland and Wales combined in the memorandum for the 1976 Bill). It was envisaged that all these initial start-up costs should fall to the UK exchequer. The start-up sums envisaged in 1977 would amount to about £20 million at today's prices.

571    The annual running costs were estimated in 1977 as £13 million, comprising £6.75 million for staff and Members' salaries (at Westminster levels) and services for the Parliament; and £6.25 million for salaries and accommodation services for extra civil servants. These sums would amount to around £44 million at today's prices.

572    This last estimate is similar to the £41.5 million figure used by the Secretary of State, Michael Forsyth, as an estimate of the proposed Parliament's running costs today.[146] That too is a projection of the estimates and assumptions from the 1970s into today's prices. Yet those assumptions are questionable today, and it is not clear they had any grounding in reality when they were first included in the Financial Memorandum to the Scotland and Wales Bill in November 1976 (they were not amended for the 1977 Bill).

*Members' and Parliamentary Staff Remuneration*

573    The length of the Parliamentary session and the Parliament's sitting hours will have an effect on the numbers of staff the Parliament might need, their remuneration and the remuneration of the Members themselves. The point was made during the passage of the 1978 Act, which allowed the Secretary of State to determine initial levels of remuneration, but granted the Assembly the power to depart from them once established. Some - in the Lords Committee and Report stages - argued that determining the levels of remuneration should remain the Secretary of State's responsibility for good. The Government argued against on the grounds that rates of remuneration would depend on the working hours of the Assembly and the workload of Members. Since both factors would be under the control of the Assembly, so should remuneration.[147] The Commons accepted this argument and the Lords gave way.

574    The same arguments apply today. It will be for the Parliament to determine its working hours, its workload, and appropriate staffing levels and remuneration to match. However, it will not be the best start for the Parliament if it has to spend its first sessions dwelling on detailed terms and conditions of employment for its staff, and its first major vote is on the level of remuneration for its own Members. Thus there is a lot to be said for the solution adopted in the 1978 Act, at least to get the Parliament up and running. Adjustments might be made in the future - at least for MSPs' pay - probably in a downward direction. The presentational advantages of this sequence are obvious.

*1977 Assumptions*

575    As noted, the estimated expenditure on the Assembly in the 1970s was based on a number of assumptions which are of questionable validity today. The figures for extra Scottish Office staff seem exaggerated (see paragraph 554). Those for parliamentary staff and the parliamentarians themselves are also likely to be out of line: the 1977 estimates were based on a larger Parliament

(144 members), and Westminster levels of remuneration for MSPs are certainly not assumed today, at least not once the Parliament has established its working pattern.

576 On balance therefore, it would appear that the figure of £41.5 million for annual running costs is at the top end of any possible scale. Even so, it represents only about 0.3% of the present Scottish budget. Officials in the 1970s tended to argue that the cost would not exceed half of one per cent of the budget.

## State Opening

577 Eventually the Parliament and the Executive will be ready to commence full operation. All powers will by then have been transferred. The Scottish Executive will be ready to present its first legislative programme. This should be announced to the Parliament by the First Minister, rather than in a 'Queen's Speech' since the Scottish Executive - although holding office at Her Majesty's pleasure - will have no direct access to the Queen and will not be 'her Government' in the same way that the UK Government is.[148]

578 The SCC's suggestion that the Parliament should be opened by the Head of State at the start of each term is a nice one, but also seems out of place in the context of a rolling programme of devolution across the UK. The symbolic presence of the Head of State at the opening of each term will come to be both less practical and less relevant. It would be better not to start on that road at all, if only to avoid the mischief that would be made when the function, a purely ceremonial one, is inevitably delegated into other hands.

# Chapter 11

## Concluding Observations

## Introduction

579 The preceding chapters have dealt in some detail with specific aspects of the devolution settlement in Scotland: how to frame the legislation, how to operate under it, what machinery will need to be established to finance the Parliament's operations and to manage the relationship with the UK Government. The approach has been for the most part technical and institutional. The report has only hinted at broader ideas which will be just as important: the need for a new political maturity and tolerance at the centre to make devolution work, the consequential changes in the political system as a whole which Scottish devolution on the lines described might prompt in its wake, the need for a fresh perception of the nature of the British state. This final chapter, by way of concluding observations, briefly identifies and explores some of these wider, less tangible themes.

## Reclaiming The Legacy of the 1970s

580 There is an assumption that any incoming Government will base itself on the twin pillars of the 1978 Scotland Act and the report of the Scottish Constitutional Convention. The presence of the Act in the statute book bolsters confidence that the Convention's scheme can be delivered. This report has drawn heavily on the 1978 provisions for guidance and illumination. For all the reservations expressed in Chapter 3 about the method it used to allocate legislative competences, there is still a great deal in the Act that would need to be in any devolution bill today. It will give future legislators a flying start, if the structural building blocks it contains are used with discernment and discretion.

581 The same can be said of the 1973 Royal Commission report. There has been a tendency in the current debates to write this off too as a dead letter: the Commission failed to reach a consensus, and no successful change in the government of the United Kingdom resulted from all its years of effort. Yet, as the frequent references to the report in the preceding pages demonstrate, it remains a highly relevant and competent quarry of detailed analysis and research of just the same issues as face the would-be devolver today. The Labour Government in 1974 chose selectively from its menu of analysis and recommendations: there is a good deal of wisdom in its pages which deserves to be studied afresh.

582 There will be those who question this approach, who argue that the world has changed dramatically in the intervening twenty years and that a radical new approach to devolution is surely called for today. There is some force in this point. But one need only compare accounts of the arcane parliamentary battles over devolution with those associated with the passage of the Maastricht Bill in 1992-93 to see just how little the landscape that matters - Whitehall and Westminster - has changed in the meantime. This report has chosen to work with the grain of the system we might expect to deliver legislative devolution following a general election, and has therefore unashamedly drawn as much as possible from the experience of the 1970s.

## The Visible State

583   The point is made elsewhere in this report that the nature of the Barnett formula will change when it is transformed from a formula governing an internal allocation of resources *within* Government to an external transfer of resources *between* separate administrations.  This is a particular example of what will be a general phenomenon under devolution: the exposure of a good deal of what Peter Hennessy calls the 'hidden wiring' of the British state.

584   There are other examples noted in the text.  Not only the distribution of resources will become common knowledge, so will the attitude of Whitehall Ministers and departments to Scottish issues become more obvious.  The introduction of a system of proportional representation in one part of the state will throw into sharper focus the distortions of 'first past the post' voting elsewhere.  A proliferation of 'British' executive actors in the European Union, and of Parliamentary scrutiny mechanisms, will make the management of information about Union policies and British responses more difficult.  Competition between nations and regions for resources, for inward investment and for influence might induce a greater temptation for 'whistle-blowing' when rules are bent in one region's favour.

585   In short, the environment in which the political debate is conducted will change, will become much more open and informed, less easy to control, less susceptible to 'spin'.  It will require a change in approach from politicians at all levels, and might encourage a more active, critical and participative engagement from the British people.

## The Break Up of Britain?

586   As  noted in Chapter 2, the Westminster debates in the 1970s resolved themselves around a single, fundamental question: is legislative devolution possible within a unitary state?  This report has sought to show that it is, and has outlined the structures and machinery which might be put in place to make it so.  But the English have always distrusted theoretical constructs or institutional solutions to political problems, and the ideas outlined in this report may not therefore convince.[149]

587   Perhaps rightly so.  The system, the machinery, however well devised, still has to be operated by people, and in a potentially difficult political atmosphere.  The Royal Commission noted (paragraph 520) that even with the benefit of a perfect written constitution a certain degree of common sense and political accommodation is required to make the system work:

> *"It is widely accepted that even at its best federalism is an awkward system to operate.  It depends a great deal on co-operation between governments.  Our impression is that even in countries where it has worked satisfactorily this is not because of its intrinsic merits but because those concerned with government have been successful in overcoming its drawbacks.  It is almost as if they have agreed among themselves that the sensible thing to do is to work round the system".*

588   The same may well be said of devolution.  There is no system which can succeed without the political will on all sides to make it do so.  However well-designed the devolution legislation, it cannot signal the last word on the process.  There will need to be a constant negotiation

between Edinburgh and the centre to make it work, a new degree of trust and tolerance, a willingness at the centre to accommodate difference and in Edinburgh to respond to that accommodation in a constructive fashion.

589 In some ways the absence of a 'system', a written constitution, in the United Kingdom is a handicap in this respect. The backstop of a written constitution has made devolution in other European countries - Spain, France, Belgium etc. - relatively straightforward. Within such a framework, for example, it has been possible for Spain to establish a rolling programme of differential devolution throughout the state. The bulwark of the constitution provides a stability and a durability to that programme which is simply unachievable under the doctrine of parliamentary sovereignty and the constraint of constitutional convention.

590 Yet in a way the absence of a written constitution means there is less of a system in the United Kingdom to 'work round' (in Kilbrandon's words). That introduces a flexibility which should be exploited. James Cornford expresses the point well in the recent IPPR publication on devolution:
> *"the parliamentary constitution not only provides an effective instrument for majoritarian government; it is also a capacious umbrella under which all sorts of exceptions and differences can be accommodated with relative ease, provided always that no other institution has legitimate independence to challenge the supremacy of Parliament".*[150]

591 Here is an answer to those who claim legislative devolution is not possible within a unitary state. If it fulfils only this one condition - respect for the ultimate supremacy of Parliament - then anything is possible within the British system. But ingenuity and political will are essential ingredients in realising this potential, and perhaps even, in Cornford's words describing efforts to accommodate membership of the European Union within this framework, 'some agility and sleight of hand'.

## The Union State

592 There is a second answer. It involves a reappraisal of the nature of the British state, a move from a 'unitary' state mentality to a 'union' state. The terms are drawn from Stein Rokkan and Derek Urwin's work on state formation.[151] They are summarised thus:
> *"The **unitary** state, built up around one unambiguous political centre which enjoys economic dominance and pursues a more or less undeviating policy of administrative standardisation. All areas of the state are treated alike, and all institutions are directly under the control of the centre. The **union** state [is] not the result of straightforward dynastic conquest. Incorporation of at least parts of its territory... [is] through personal dynastic union, for example by treaty, marriage or inheritance. Integration is less than perfect. While administrative standardisation prevails over most of the territory, the consequences of personal union entail survival of pre-union rights and institutional infrastructures which preserve some degree of regional autonomy and serve as agencies of indigenous elite recruitment".*[152]

593 Perhaps the most significant part of the infrastructure of the British state that devolution will help to expose is the extent to which we are already living in this second type of state, a union state, and always have done. The existing asymmetrical devolution of executive power as

between Scotland, Wales and the English regions is a manifestation of that. So is the special treatment which has been accorded over the years to Northern Ireland: the Framework Documents drawn up by the British and Irish Governments are shot through with the language of the union state.

594 The programme of asymmetrical, non-uniform, rolling devolution now proposed for Scotland, Wales and the English regions will make this perception of the British state more explicit, and the traditionalists' view of the United Kingdom as a unitary state increasingly untenable. The adjustment will be gradual, will force new issues on to the political agenda, and may be painful for the political parties themselves. But there may be benefits to be gained too in a more honest and wholehearted accommodation with the existing diversity within the British state. Our relationship with the European Union, for example, might become less problematic, more constructive, and potentially more influential once we are able to engage with partners who see Europe not as the 'superstate' the British fear but, if as a state at all, as a union state.

595 The Constitution Unit intends to return to this theme - the changing nature of the British state under devolution and the wider implications of the rolling programme of constitutional reform now proposed - in a further publication later in the year.

## The Next Steps?

596 This report has attempted to consider, in some detail, the fundamental outlines of a devolution settlement in Scotland. But it is not comprehensive, and does not claim to be. There are still questions to answer, details to be sketched in, options to be sifted before a comprehensive bill could be drafted.

597 It will have succeeded in its purpose if it moves the debate in Scotland on from the point represented by the St Andrew's day report of the Constitutional Convention, and if in addition it succeeds in stimulating a wider debate south of the border. It has suggested a number of areas where public and private discussion might usefully now focus: on what needs to be retained at Westminster rather than what can be devolved to Scotland; on the means of securing stability in the financial settlement rather than the mechanism for varying it potentially at the margins (tax raising powers); on the implications for central government on which the Convention remains silent, and in particular the practical implications of the overlap in Brussels and Edinburgh competences; and the wider implications of a rolling programme of devolution for the way in which the Scotland/UK political relationship is to be managed.

598 In all of these areas the report has suggested possible solutions and responses, a range of possible options. It is not intended to be in any way prescriptive, or exclusive of other ideas. It is offered not as a blueprint but as a contribution to the debate. Above all, it recognises that devolution - if it occurs - should not be considered as a gift graciously offered by the centre, but as a response to a demand from part or parts of the state which has to be met.

599 There is now a growing recognition that systemic reform is necessary to reinvigorate the political process in the UK. The pressure for such reform comes from the people in the regions, localities and territories of the United Kingdom who are on the receiving end of government

which does not adequately reflect their concerns, their desires or their priorities. Devolution, and any wider reform of the political system, will grow out of these concerns and demands of participants, and perhaps more importantly non-participants, in the political process. It is bound to fail unless it is seen as an attempt to harness these strong political forces to a constructive purpose. Any attempt to impose a solution in Scotland which does not accord with what Scots themselves want risks failure, and would arguably be a negation of the idea of genuine devolution from the start. This report is offered in that spirit.

# A Chronology
# of Devolution
# 1885-1979

1885 Secretaryship for Scotland and Scottish Office established with responsibility for education, health, poor law, local government, fisheries, police, prisons, roads and public works (Secretary for Scotland Act).

1886 Establishment of Scottish Home Rule Association.

1897 Scottish Trades Union Congress founded.

1912 Scottish Board of Agriculture founded.

1919 Scottish Board of Health founded, with Parliamentary Under-Secretary.

1926 Scottish Secretary becomes full Secretary of State.

1934 Scottish National Party formed.

1936 Edinburgh office of the Secretary of State for Scotland opened.

1937 Gilmour Committee report on Scottish Central Administration (Cmd. 5563).

1939 Scottish departments (Agriculture, Education, Fisheries, Health, Prisons) vested directly in Secretary of State.

St Andrew's House, Edinburgh, opened.

1941 Secretary of State for Scotland, Tom Johnston, sets up Council of State comprising all living former Scottish Secretaries. Allows for meetings of the Scottish Grand Committee in Scotland.

1942 John MacCormick founds Scottish Convention.

1945 Motherwell won by SNP (Robert McIntyre) in April by - election, defeating Labour. Lost in General Election.

Scottish Office takes over forestry, loses National Insurance.

1946 Scottish Council (Development & Industry) formed.

1948 White paper on Scottish Affairs (Cmd 7308) proposes changes in Parliamentary procedures and an enquiry into Anglo-Scottish financial relations.

1954 Balfour Commission report on Scottish Affairs (Cmd. 9212). Electricity transferred to Scottish Office.

1955 Food, animal health, appointment of JPs transferred.

1956 Roads and bridges transferred.

1961 Bridgeton by-election, 16th Nov. SNP wins 18.7% of votes.

1962　West Lothian by-election, 14th June. SNP wins 23.3% of votes.

　　　Scottish departments reorganised. Scottish Development Department formed.

1964　General election, 15th October.  SNP contests 15 seats and wins 2.4% of the vote.

1965　Highlands and Islands Development Board founded.

1966　General election, 31st March.  SNP contests 23 seats and wins 5% of the vote.

　　　Carmarthen by-election, 14th July. Plaid Cymru wins with 39% of the vote.

1967　Pollok by-election, 9th March.  SNP wins 28.2% of vote.

　　　Hamilton by-election, 2nd Nov.  SNP (Winifred Ewing) wins seat with 46.1% of vote.

1968　May. Major SNP gains in local elections. They win 37.2% of vote in Glasgow.

　　　May. 'Declaration of Perth' - Edward Heath announces establishment of Douglas-Home Committee.

　　　Passenger road transport and sea transport transferred: Scottish Transport Group founded.

　　　December. Crowther Royal Commission on Constitution appointed.

1969　September. Wheatley Commission reports on local government reorganisation (Cmnd 4150).

1970　Ayrshire South by-election, 19th March. SNP wins 20.4% of vote.

　　　General election, 18th June. SNP contests 65 seats out of 71 and wins 11.4% of vote. Loses Hamilton but gains Western Isles.

　　　Douglas-Home Committee reports, recommending elected "Scottish Convention".

1971　February. White Paper: 'The Reform of Local Government in Scotland' (Cmnd. 4503).

　　　Stirling and Falkirk by-election, 16th September.  SNP wins 34.6% of vote.

1973　Scottish Economic Planning Department formed.

　　　Dundee East by-election, 1st March. SNP wins 30.2% of vote, close second to Labour.

　　　October. Report of Royal Commission on Constitution (now chaired by Kilbrandon) published, with Memorandum of Dissent by Crowther-Hunt and Peacock (Cmnd 5460).

　　　Govan by-election, 8th November. SNP (Margo MacDonald) wins with 41.9% of vote.

**1974** General election, February 28th. SNP contests 70 seats, wins 21.9% of vote, loses Govan but gains Argyll, Banff, Aberdeenshire East, Dundee East, Moray and Nairn, Stirlingshire East and Clackmannan.

March 12th. Queen's Speech: Government "will initiate discussions in Scotland and Wales on the report of the Royal Commission on the Constitution and will bring forward proposals for consideration". Lord Crowther-Hunt appointed Minister of State, Privy Council Office with responsibility for devolution.

May. First elections to Scottish regions and districts.

June 3rd. Green Paper 'Devolution within the UK: some alternatives for discussion' published.

June 22nd. Scottish Executive of Labour Party rejects devolution proposals.

August 17th. Special Scottish Labour Conference overturns Executive decision.

September 7th. White Paper 'Democracy and Devolution: Proposals for Scotland and Wales' (Cmnd 5732) published.

October 10th. General election. SNP wins 30.4% of vote, gains Angus South, Dunbartonshire East, Galloway, Perth and East Perthshire.

**1975** Industry powers transferred to Scottish Office.

Scottish Development Agency founded.

November 22nd. Devolution White Paper 'Our Changing Democracy' (Cmnd. 6348) published.

**1976** August 1st. 'Devolution to Scotland and Wales: Supplementary Statement' (Cmnd 6585) published.

Main changes: at least two Assembly seats for all constituencies; Assembly alone to nominate Chief Executive; UK Government to be able to object to Assembly Bills only if causing "unacceptable repercussions" on non-devolved matters, and unable to take back devolved powers; judicial review of Assembly legislation to be allowed; Assembly power to surcharge rates dropped; SDA operations, administration of the courts, private law, regulation of teaching and legal professions to be devolved.

November 28th. Scotland and Wales Bill published.

December 8th. 'Devolution - the English dimension' published.

December 16th. Bill given second reading by 292-247 after Government concedes referendums once Bill is enacted.

**1977** January 13th - February 15th. Committee stage of Bill on floor of the House: three clauses and referendum clause approved. Only amendment agreed: Orkney and Shetland each to have one Assembly member.

February 22nd. Motion to guillotine proceedings defeated by 312-283.

April. Manpower services transferred to Scottish Office.

July 26th. Lord President's statement in Commons: separate bills for Scotland and Wales in next session; head of executive retitled 'First Secretary'; premature dissolution of Assembly to be possible on vote of two-thirds of members; legislation on maladministration, teachers' pay and rent regulation to be devolved; block grant to be fixed for "a number of years" by percentage formula; "independent advisory board" on devolution financing; 'Joint Council' between Government and Executive proposed.

'Devolution - Financing the Devolved Services' (Cmnd 6890) published.

November 4th. Scotland Bill published.

November 14th. Bill given second reading by 307 - 263. Wales Bill passes second reading by 295 to 264 votes.

November 16th. Guillotine motion carried by 313-287.

November 22nd. Committee stage begins. Clause I (declaration on unity of UK) removed by 199-184.

December 7th. Clause 40 (national pay policy) removed by 290-107.

**1978** January 25th. Cunningham amendment that "if it appears to the Secretary of State that less than 40% of the persons entitled to vote in the referendum have voted 'Yes'...he shall lay before Parliament the draft of an Order in Council for the repeal of this Act" carried 168-142.

Grimond amendment that if Orkney or Shetland vote 'No' in referendum "the Secretary of State shall lay before Parliament the draft of an Order in Council providing that...the Act shall not apply to them, and providing also for the establishment of a commission to recommend such changes in the government of that area or those areas as may be desirable" carried 204 -118.

February 14th. During report stage, Dalyell's new clause stipulating that if Parliament is dissolved before the referendum is held, it must be deferred until three months after polling, approved 242-223.

Canavan amendment to remove '40% rule' defeated 298-248.

February 22nd. Bill given third reading by 297-257.

March 15th. Bill given unopposed second reading in Lords.

April 4th. During committee stage, Lords vote 155-64 for Additional Member voting system.

May 17th. Lords' committee stage ends, after Lords vote to withdraw from Assembly responsibility abortion, aerodromes, forestry and afforestation, inland waterways and road passenger service licensing.

7 June. Lords Report Stage of Scotland Bill begins. Main amendments inserted: Assembly committees required to reflect party balance; purchase grants for libraries, museums and art galleries reserved; requirement for fourteen days interval followed by second vote if Bill not affecting Scotland carried by Commons only because of votes of Scottish MPs; new Government clause on Orkney and Shetland to replace 'Grimond amendment'.

20 June. Report Stage concluded.

29 June. Unopposed third reading.

4 July. Commons timetable motion for consideration of Lords amendments.

6 July. Consideration begins. Alternative Member voting system defeated.

26 July. Consideration concluded. Government defeated on committee balance, second vote in Commons and reservation of forestry.

27 July. Lords accepted Commons amendments.

31 July. Royal Assent.

1 Nov. Referendum date announced.

1979   1 March. Referendum held. Of those who voted, 51.6% voted 'Yes' and 48.4% voted 'No'. Of the total electorate, 32.9% voted 'Yes', 30.8% voted 'No' and 36.3% did not vote. Wales votes heavily against devolution proposals by 79.7% to 20.3%.

22 March. Statement to Commons by Prime Minister Callaghan declining to set date for vote on order to repeal Scotland Act and calling for all-party consultations. Motion of no-confidence put down by SNP.

28 March. Government defeated on Conservative motion of no-confidence.

3 May. General election. SNP lose nine seats, leaving them with only two, and 17.2% of the vote.

20 June. Commons passes repeal order for Scotland Act by 301 votes to 206. Of the Scottish MPs, forty-three voted against repeal, nineteen in favour and nine were absent. Mr George Younger, Secretary of State, offered all-party talks to consider "the scope for improving the handling of Scottish business in Parliament".

Sources: *The Scottish Government Yearbook*, 1979 and 1980. James Mitchell, *Strategies for Self-Government*, 1996.

# Appendix B

Comparison of the proposed functions of the Scotland Act 1978, Scotland Bill 1987 and Scotland's Parliament. Scotland's Right

| SCOTLAND ACT 1978 | SCOTLAND BILL 1987 | CONSTITUTIONAL CONVENTION 1995 (Appendix I) |
|---|---|---|
| HEALTH – The National Health Service, family planning, ethical questions but NOT abortion, control of food and drugs, health and safety at work. | HEALTH – Prevention, treatment and alleviation of disease or illness, including injury, disability and mental disorder. Family planning. Abortion. The structure, organisation and operation of the Health Service. Private health care. Investigation of maladministration. | HEALTH – The structure, organisation and administration of the National Health Service. Prevention, treatment and alleviation of disease or illness including injury, disability, and mental illness. Community Care. Family planning. Private health care. |
| SOCIAL WELFARE – the care of children and adoption, the handicapped and the elderly but NOT social security or the employment of the disabled. | SOCIAL WELFARE – Social welfare, including children and adoption. | SOCIAL WELFARE – Social welfare including children and adoption. Care of the elderly. Strategic planning of welfare services. |
| EDUCATION AND LEISURE – the education service including the teaching profession, the arts, sport, museums and libraries but NOT the universities, research councils or careers guidance service. | EDUCATION, ETC. – Education, the Arts, social, cultural and recreational activities. Higher Education including responsibility for Scottish Universities. The teaching profession. Private schools in Scotland. Libraries, museums and art galleries. Parks and open spaces. Markets and fairs. Allotments. | EDUCATION AND LEISURE – Education at all levels, including nursery, primary, secondary, tertiary and higher provision. The teaching profession. Private schools in Scotland. Arts and culture, including libraries, museums and art galleries. Recreation, including sports provision, parks, open spaces, markets and fairs, allotments. Broadcasting. |
| HOUSING – public sector housing, rent control and allowances, mobile homes and caravans, building standards but NOT private housing finance. | HOUSING – Housing. Regulation of rents. Rent allowances and rebates. Mobile homes and caravans. | HOUSING – Housing. Regulation of rents,. Rent allowances and rebates. Mobile homes and caravans. |
| LOCAL GOVERNMENT – the structure of local government, allocation of rate support grant but NOT voting systems of local government, the frequency of elections nor the principle of rating. | LOCAL GOVERNMENT AND LOCAL FINANCE – Constitution, area and general powers and duties of local authorities and similar bodies. Investigation of maladministration. Revenue and expenditure of local authorities and similar bodies. Rating and valuation for rating. Rate support grants and grants for specific purposes. Revenue raising powers of local authorities, including the power to impose, alter or abolish any local government tax. | LOCAL GOVERNMENT – areas, powers and duties of local authorities and similar bodies. Revenue and expenditure of local authorities. Investigation of maladministration. Rating and valuation. Rate support grants and grants. Local government taxation. |
| TRANSPORT – the provision of public passenger and freight transport services within Scotland, payment of subsidies to operators, inland waterways, harbours and boatslips, the provision of roads, including motorways and bridges but NOT vehicle standards, British Rail, major ports, air services and freight services (except through the Scottish Transport Group), motoring offences, and traffic wardens. | TRANSPORT – Provision of public passenger and freight transport services. Payment of subsidies to operators of such services within Scotland. Insulation of nearby buildings from noise and vibration attributable to the use of aerodromes. Aerodromes, but without prejudice to the regulatory powers of the Civil Aviation Authority. Provision, improvement and maintenance of streets, roads and bridges. Provision, improvement and maintenance of harbours and boatslips principally used or required for the fishing or agricultural industries or for the maintenance of communications between places in Scotland. Provision of financial assistance for the execution of works, in connection with any other harbours, for the benefit of the fishing industry. | TRANSPORT – Transportation, including public passenger and freight services. Payment of subsidies to operators of services. Roads, including provision, improvement and maintenance of streets, roads and bridges. Harbours and boatslips. Inland waterways. |

| | | |
|---|---|---|
| ENVIRONMENT - Town and Country Planning, the environmental powers of the Scottish Development Agency, new towns, protection of countryside amenity, water supply, river management, sewerage, erosion and flooding, pollution (with some exceptions), ancient monuments and miscellaneous land use powers but NOT aspects of the Community Land Act and compulsory purchase procedures. | ENVIRONMENT - Town and country planning. New towns. Industrial sites. Improvement of derelict land. Mitigation of the injurious effects of public works. Powers of the Scottish Development Agency and the Highlands and Islands Development Board. Control of pollution, other than as respects motor vehicles, aircraft, hovercraft, dumping at sea and vessels outside inland waters. Protection of the coast against erosion and encroachment from the sea. Prevention or mitigation of flooding of land. Development of the countryside for public enjoyment and the conservation and enhancement of its natural beauty and amenity. Supply of water and safety of reservoirs, inland waterways. Ancient monuments and historic buildings. | ENVIRONMENT - Town and country planning and land use. Building control. New towns. Industrial sites. Land improvement. Water and sewage, including water supply and reservoirs. Environment and sustainability, including pollution control, regulation of emissions and of dumping. Coastal protection. Flood prevention and mitigation. Countryside development and conservation. Historic buildings and monuments. |
| AGRICULTURE AND FISHERIES - fresh water fishing, tenure and management of agricultural land, crofting but NOT seawater fisheries, general agricultural policy including subsidies, grants, price support, plant health or the control of animal disease. NOT forestry. | AGRICULTURE AND FISHERIES - Tenure and management of agricultural land. Grants, loans and subsidies payable in relation to landholders in respect of their landholding. Crofting, including grants, loans and subsidies payable primarily to crofters, cotters and persons of substantially the same economic status. Protection, improvement and maintenance of salmon, migratory trout and fresh water fisheries in any waters, including any part of the sea (in territorial water adjacent to any part of the coast of Scotland) or, where an esturial limit fixed under the Salmon Fisheries (Scotland) Acts 1828 to 1868 extends beyond that distance, up to that esturial limit. Protection, improvement and maintenance of all other fishing. All forestry matters. | AGRICULTURE AND FISHERIES - Agriculture including land tenure and management. Crofting. Fisheries, both marine and fresh-water, including protection, improvement and maintenance. Forestry. |
| TOURISM - the development of tourism in Scotland, the Scottish Tourist Board. | TOURISM - Development of tourism. | TOURISM - tourism promotion and development, including the Scottish Tourist Board. |

LEGAL SYSTEM - civil and criminal law, the legal profession, legal aid, courts, criminal procedure, tribunals in devolved areas, the treatment of offenders but NOT the law affecting non-devolved areas such as motoring offences and employment law, the police, the prerogative of mercy, appointment of judges and sheriffs, continued existence and jurisdictions of the High Court and Court of Session.

LEGAL SYSTEM - Jurisdiction and procedure of courts, including juries. Contempt of court. Vexetious litigation. Number of judges of the High Court of Justiciary and Court of Session. Numbers of territorial jurisdiction of sheriffs. Numbers of members of the Scottish Land Court. Justices of the Peace. Legal profession. Legal aid, advice and assistance. Tribunals and inquiries related to matters included within the legislative competence of Assembly and within the powers of the Scottish Executive. The Land Tribunal for Scotland. Natural and juristic persons and unincorporated bodies. Corporate public bodies dealing with matters included within the legislative competence of Assembly and within the powers of the Scottish Executive. Obligations, including voluntary and conventional obligations, obligations of restitution and obligations of reparation, but excluding insurance, banking, intellectual property and safety standards for goods, trade unions and employer associations, trade disputes and labour relations. Heritable and moveable property. Conveyancing. Trusts. Bankruptcy. Succession. Remedies. Evidence. Diligence. Arbitration. Prescription and limitation of actions. Private international law. The organisation and structure within which the police operate. The role of Chief Constables. Terms and conditions of service. Principles of criminal liability. Offences against the person. Sexual offences. Offences against property. Offences of dishonesty. Offences against public order, decency and religion. Offences against the administration of justice. Offences related to matters included within the legislative competence of Assembly and within the powers of the Scottish Executive. Criminal penalties. Treatment of offenders (including children and young persons, and mental health patients, involved in crime). Compensation out of public funds for victims of crime. Criminal evidence. Criminal procedure, including arrest, search, custody and time limits for prosecutions. Recognition and enforcement of court orders. Criminal research. BUT NOT to include legal tender, monopoly and restrictive trade pacts, regulation of interest rates and credit, regulation of charges and prices of terms and conditions of employment other than those charged by or concerning persons employed by a Scottish Secretary or by a person operating under an enactment concerned with matters included within the legislative competence of Assembly and within the powers of the Scottish Executive. AND NOT deportation and extradition, and any provision for criminal penalties, evidence or procedure specifically related to matters not included within the legislative competence of Assembly and within the powers of the Scottish Executive.

LEGAL SYSTEM - Courts and legal system. Court jurisdiction and procedure. Juries. Contempt. Vexatious litigation. Judges, sheriffs, Justices of the Peace, members of the Scottish land court. Legal profession. Legal aid. Tribunals and inquiries, including the Lands Tribunal for Scotland. Police, including organisation and structure, terms and conditions of service, role of chief constables. Civil law, including property, conveyancing, trusts, bankruptcy, succession, remedies, evidence, diligence, arbitration, prescription and limitation of actions, private international law, recognition and enforcement of court orders. Prison service. Law and order, including principles of criminal liability.

| | | |
|---|---|---|
| MISCELLANEOUS - the fire service, public holidays, lotteries and charities, registration including population statistics, local licensing, shop hours but NOT betting and gaming or taking of censuses. | MISCELLANEOUS - Fire services and fire precautions. Registration of births, deaths and adoptions. Population statistics but NOT the taking of the census. Records of the Scottish Assembly, the Scottish Executive and the courts and of any body created by or under any Scottish Assembly Act or whose functions are matters which are wholly within the legislative competence of the Assembly. Private records. Any records in the custody of the Keeper of the records of Scotland on the coming into force within the legislative competence of Assembly and within the powers of the Scottish Executive. Charities, including collections for charities. Public holidays. Deer and sale of venison. Local regulation of trades. Provision or control by local authorities of facilities and local activities. Lotteries. Liquor licensing. Local licensing. Shop hours. Burial and cremation. Licensing of dogs and keepers of dogs. Control of stray dogs. | MISCELLANEOUS - Fire services. Fire precautions. Public records, including records of the Scottish Parliament, the Scottish Executive, the courts, and any other body for which the Parliament is responsible. Private records. Records held by the Keeper of the Records in Scotland. Registration of births, deaths, marriages and adoption. Population statistics. Equal opportunities. Charities. Public holidays. Deer. Local regulation of trades. Provision or control by local authorities of facilities and local activities. Lotteries. Liquor licensing. Local licensing. Shop hours. Burial and cremation. Licensing of and control of dogs. |
| | ELECTRICITY - Management and control of the Electricity Supply Industry and of electricity generation in Scotland. | ELECTRICITY - Energy, including electricity generation and supply. |
| | | INDUSTRIAL DEVELOPMENT - Industrial development, including the Enterprise networks. |
| | MANPOWER AND TRAINING - Responsibility for training and re-training. Responsibility for youth and for training programmes. | VOCATIONAL TRAINING AND RE-TRAINING - Training provision, including youth and adult training and re-training, and special needs training. |

Note: This is an updated version of a table first prepared by James Mitchell, Territorial Politics Research Centre, Strathclyde University. I am grateful to him for permission to reproduce it here. The description of the 1978 Act includes the exceptions in each area (as the Act did). The description of the SCC's proposals is taken from Appendix I of *Scotland's Parliament*. *Scotland's Right* which describes only "some of the principal areas which will fall within the powers of Scotland's Parliament".

# Notes

1   The Scottish National Party have proposed a written constitution for an independent Scotland based firmly on the popular sovereignty of the Scottish people, to include *inter alia* a Bill of Rights, a single chamber Parliament of 200 members elected by the Additional Member System, the Queen as head of state to be represented in Scotland by the Chancellor of Scotland (the presiding officer of the Parliament), EU membership with 16 MEPs and a Commissioner, membership of the UN and other international organisations, and the promotion of an Association of States of the British Isles. See SNP, *Citizens not Subjects: The Parliament and Constitution of an Independent Scotland,* 1995.

2   Lindsay Paterson, *The Autonomy of Modern Scotland,* 1994.

3   Lindsay Paterson, *The Autonomy of Modern Scotland,* 1994.

4   *Report of the Gilmour Committee on Scottish Central Administration,* Cmd 5563, October 1937.

5   James Kellas, *The Scottish Political System,* fourth edition 1988.

6   Lindsay Paterson, *The Autonomy of Modern Scotland,* 1994.

7   Tom Nairn, 'Upper and Lower Cases' (a review of Paterson's book), *London Review of Books,* 24 August 1995.

8   A view expressed succinctly in the debate with Stephen Maxwell in Henry Drucker ed., *John P Mackintosh on Scotland,* 1982.

9   Alice Brown, David McCrone and Lindsay Paterson, *Politics and Society in Scotland,* 1996.

10  James Mitchell, *Strategies for Self-Government,* 1996.

11  The figures also serve to demonstrate that Labour's dominance in Scotland has only been a feature since the 1950s and directly reflects the decline in Conservative support. In 1987 Labour's 50 seats was a modern record for any party in Scotland, obtained with only 42.2% of the vote. The image of Scotland as a Labour stronghold is therefore a comparatively recent one, and one which rests on the mechanics of the 'first past the post' system. Wales and the North of England have in fact averaged a higher percentage of Left seats than Scotland in the period since the war; and Wales returned Liberal or Labour candidates for 70% of seats fought between 1868 and 1983, while the figure for Scotland was 58% (figures from David McCrone, *Understanding Scotland,* 1992).

12  David McCrone, 'Politics in a Cold Country', in *Understanding Scotland,* 1992.

13  Peter Jones, 'Politics', in Magnus Linklater and Robin Denniston eds., *Chambers Anatomy of Scotland,* 1992.

14  *The Scotsman,* 24 February 1992.

15  *Scotland in the Union: a partnership for good,* Cm 2225, March 1993.

16  House of Commons, *Official Report,* 9 March 1993, col 787-8.

17  29 November 1995, HC Deb Vol 267 Col 1230.

18  Rt Hon Michael Forsyth MP, *Richard Stewart Memorial Lecture,* 30 November 1995.

19  Scottish Constitutional Convention, *Towards Scotland's Parliament,* 1990.

20  Scottish Constitutional Commission, *Further Steps: Towards a Scheme for Scotland's Parliament,* 1994.

21  Royal Commission on the Constitution 1969 - 1973, *Report,* Cmnd 5460 and *Memorandum of Dissent,* Cmnd 5460-1, October 1973.

22  Sir Reginald Coupland, *Welsh and Scottish Nationalism,* 1954; Richard Finlay, *Independent and Free: Scottish Politics and the Origins of the Scottish National Party, 1918-1945,* 1994; Jack Brand, *The National Movement in Scotland,* 1978; Christopher Harvie, *Scotland and Nationalism: Scottish Society and Politics 1707-1994,* 1994; James Mitchell, *Strategies for Self-government,* 1996.

23  David McCrone, *Understanding Scotland: the Sociology of a Stateless Nation,* 1992.

24  Christopher Harvie, *Scotland and Nationalism,* 1994.

25  Royal Commission on the Constitution 1969 - 1973, *Report,* Cmnd 5460 and *Memorandum of Dissent,* Cmnd 5460-1, October 1973.

26  *Devolution Within the United Kingdom: Some Alternatives for Discussion,* June 1974.

27  *Democracy and Devolution: Proposals for Scotland and Wales,* Cmnd 5732, September 1974.

28  *Our Changing Democracy: Devolution to Scotland and Wales,* Cmnd 6348, November 1975.

29  The government's majority of three from the October 1974 election was wiped out shortly after Jim Callaghan's election with the decision of John Stonehouse to stand as an independent and the defection of two Scottish members disenchanted by the slow progress on devolution.

30  *Devolution to Scotland and Wales: Supplementary Statement,* Cmnd 6585, August 1976.

31  For a full discussion of this distinction and the implications of Kilbrandon's recommendation see chapter 3.

32  *Devolution: The English Dimension,* December 1976.

33  Quoted in James Mitchell, *Conservatives and the Union,* 1990.

34  Patrick Cosgrave, *The Lives of Enoch Powell,* 1990.

35  John Kerr, 'The Failure of the Scotland and Wales Bill', in *Scottish Government Yearbook,* 1978.

36  James Callaghan, *Time and Chance,* 1988.

37  James Naughtie, 'The Scotland Bill in the House of Commons', in *Scottish Government Yearbook,* 1979.

38  P D Lindley, *The Scotland Act in Parliament: A Chronological Summary,* Civil Service College Working Paper No 4, December 1978.

39  House of Commons, *Official Report,* 31 January 1978, col 299.

40  Henry Drucker and Gordon Brown, *The Politics of Nationalsim and Devolution,* 1980.

41  Changes in parliamentary procedures to ease the passage of a constitutional reform programme are considered in detail in The Constitution Unit, *Delivering Constitutional Reform,* April 1996.

42  Henry Drucker and Gordon Brown, *The Politics of Nationalsim and Devolution,* 1980.

43  Prepared on a voluntary basis by the one time Head of the Scottish Office Devolution Division.

44  Vernon Bogdanor, *Devolution,* 1979.

45  Neil MacCormick, 'Constitutional Points', in Donald Mackay ed., *Scotland: The Framework for Change,* 1979.

46  Harry Calvert, *Constitutional Law in Northern Ireland,* 1968.

47  Royal Commission on the Constitution 1969 - 1973, *Report* Cmnd 5460, October 1973 (paragraphs 737-745).

48  *Memorandum by the Scottish Law Commission to the Lord Advocate on Devolution, Scots Law and the Role of the Commission,* 27 May 1975, paragraphs 11-12.

49  Scottish Law Commission, *Memorandum No 32: Comments on White Paper 'Our Changing Democracy: Devolution to Scotland and Wales',* 18 June 1976.

50  As noted in paragraph 76 the detail of the powers to be transferred to the Assembly under the 1978 legislation was actually very little debated in the House of Commons.

51  A clause to this effect in the Scotland and Wales Bill (clause 1) was struck out in debate on the grounds that having to state the principle in a specific Act might call its general validity into question.

52  Vernon Bogdanor, *Devolution,* 1979.

53  *Memorandum by the Scottish Law Commission to the Lord Advocate on Devolution, Scots Law and the Role of the Commission,* 27 May 1975.

54  Colin Munro, 'The Union of 1707 and the British Constitution', in *Scotland and the Union,* Hume Papers on Public Policy Vol 2 No 2, summer 1994.

55  James McCormick and Wendy Alexander, 'Firm Foundations: Securing the Scottish Parliament', in Stephen Tindale ed., *The State and the Nations,* 1996.

56  The conduct of referendums - the framing of the question, whether there needs to be an independent Commission to advise and assist the integrity of the process, whether there should be special majorities and different ways of counting votes etc - are all questions under consideration by the Commission on the Conduct of Referendums whose report will be published by the Constitution Unit in autumn 1996.

57  Bernard Crick and David Millar, *To Make the Parliament of Scotland a Model for Democracy,* 1995.

58  Perry Anderson, 'The Light of Europe', in *English Questions,* 1992.

59  Hansard Society, Commission on Electoral Campaigns, *Agenda for Change,* September 1991.

60  In the SCC's earlier report of November 1990 the list of devolved functions included: 'Civil law, with the possible exception of some areas of commercial and contract law'.

61  *Scotland Act 1978,* Schedule 10, Part II, para 20.

62  Scottish Office, *Government Expenditure and Revenue in Scotland 1993-1994,* October 1995.

63  'The population rounding inherent in 10:5:85 (Barnett)...has a non-trivial effect. Taking 1976 populations Scotland's share of GB population was 9.57% (10 was a rounding up); Wales's was 5.12% (5 was a rounding down); and England's was 85.31% (85 was a rounding down).... The smaller the population proportion, the greater the potential rounding error.': David Heald, *Formula-Based Territorial Public Expenditure in the United Kingdom,* 1992.

64  David Heald, *Formula-Based Territorial Public Expenditure in the United Kingdom,* 1992

65  Central Statistical Office, *Annual Abstract of Statistics,* 1992: quoted in David Heald, *Formula-Based Territorial Public Expenditure in the United Kingdom,* 1992.

66  Scottish Office, *Government Expenditure and Revenue in Scotland 1993-1994,* October 1995.

67  Laura Blow, John Haull & Stephen Smith, *Financing Regional Government in Britain,* 1996 (table 4.2)

68  All figures taken from Scottish Office, *Government Expenditure and Revenue in Scotland 1993-1994,* October 1995, tables 3 and 4.

69  George Goschen as Chancellor introduced a formula in the 1880s which allocated changes in certain elements of public spending in the ratio Scotland 11%, Ireland 9%, England and Wales 80%. But it was not systematically applied and fell into disuse in the late 1950s.

70  Laura Blow, John Hall & Steven Smith, *Financing Regional Government in Britain,* 1996

71  Arthur Midwinter and Murray McVicar, 'Uncharted Waters? Problems of Financing Labour's Scottish Parliament', *Public Money and Management,* April-June 1996.

72  H M Treasury, *Needs Assessment Study - Report,* December 1979.

73  This is the subject of a separate Constitution Unit report, *Regional Government in England,* June 1996.

74  H M Treasury, *Needs Assessment Study - Report,* December 1979.

75  David Heald and Neal Geaughan, 'Financing a Scottish Parliament', in Stephen Tindale ed., *The State and the Nations,* 1996.

76  House of Lords, *Official Report,* 14 March 1978, col 1218.

77  David Heald and Neal Geaughan, 'Financing a Scottish Parliament', in Stephen Tindale ed., *The State and the Nations,* 1996.

78  David Heald, *Financing a Scottish Parliament: Options for Debate,* 1990.

79  Scottish Constitutional Convention, *Towards Scotland's Parliament,* 1990.

80  Debates of the EP, *Annex to Official Journal no 2-367,* 6 July 1988, p140.

81  The term 'Community' is used here deliberately rather than the wider concept of 'Union'. The Union embraces three 'pillars': two dealing on an intergovernmental basis with foreign and security policy and justice and home affairs; and the 'European Community' which acts in policy areas derived from the original Treaty of Rome as amended by the Single European Act and the Maastricht Treaty. It is only the Community pillar which may adopt Community law.

82  R v Secretary of State for Transport; ex parte Factortame Ltd [1989].

83  Article 169 of the EC Treaty empowers the Commission to take any member state which has failed to fulfil an obligation under the Treaty to the ECJ. It is the state which must answer for the failure. The Belgian government, for example, has on many occasions had to account to the Commission for failures by the Belgian Community governments to enforce EC law.

84  For example Barry Jones and Michael Keating eds., *The European Union and the Regions,* 1995.

85  K H Goetz, 'National Governance and European Integration', *Journal of Common Market Studies,* Vol 33 No 1, March 1995.

86  K Stolz, 'The Committee of the Regions and Scottish Self-government: a German Perspective', *Scottish Affairs,* Autumn 1994.

87  Bernard Crick and David Millar, *To Make the Parliament of Scotland a Model for Democracy,* 1995.

88  James Mitchell, 'Lobbying Brussels: the Case of Scotland Europa', *European Urban and Regional Studies,* 1995 2(4). This article gives a good summary of the policy debates surrounding the establishment of the Office, including the study of other regional offices in Brussels. A Scottish Parliament would be well advised to consult these earlier papers before making its own decision.

89  This will be easier if such officials remain part of a UK-wide civil service, as advocated in Chapter 7.

90  William Nicoll, 'Representing the States' in Andrew Duff, John Pinder, Roy Pryce eds., *Maastricht and Beyond,* 1994.

91  Liesbet Hooghe, 'Belgian Federalism and the European Community', in Barry Jones and Michael Keating eds., *The European Union and the Regions,* 1995.

92  Hans-Georg Gerstenlauer, 'German Länder and the European Community', in Barry Jones and Michael Keating eds., *The European Union and the Regions,* 1995.

93  Scottish Labour, *A Parliament for Scotland: Labour's Plan,* 1995.

94  Scottish Liberal Democrats, *The Final Steps,* April 1995.

95  *Democracy and Devolution: Proposals for Scotland and Wales,* Cmnd 5732, September 1974.

96  Quoted in John Gibson, *The Thistle and the Crown: A History of the Scottish Office,* 1985.

97  Quoted in Arthur Midwinter, Michael Keating and James Mitchell, *Politics and Public Policy in Scotland,* 1991.

98  John P Mackintosh, 'The Power of the Secretary of State', *New Edinburgh Review,* No 31, February 1976.

99  It is possible that the Parliament might decide in the future to hold its elections on a day other than Thursday, for example at the weekend. This eventuality might be covered by the Parliament passing an Act effectively amending this provision in UK electoral law (assuming it is a devolved subject: see the discussion in chapter 4) and reinterpreting the devolution legislation on this point (with the UK Government's blessing). Otherwise the devolution legislation would have to include a power to vary the date by five days either way, which is a complication best avoided.

100 Bernard Crick and David Millar suggest such a procedure - election by single transferable vote with up to three ballots - in Order 9 of their draft Standing orders for a Scottish Parliament, *To Make the Parliament of Scotland a Model for Democracy,* 1995.

101 See for example David Butler, *Governing Without a Majority*, 1983, Vernon Bogdanor, *Multi-party Politics and the Constitution*, 1983, and Peter Hennessy, *The Hidden Wiring*, 1995

102 House of Commons (Northern Ireland), *Official Report*, vol 47, col 231-232.

103 James Kellas, 'The Policy Process', in Donald Mackay ed., *Scotland: The Framework for Change*, 1979.

104 House of Commons, *Official Report*, 31 January 1978, col 296. The speech contains an elegant refutation of all four 'answers' to the West Lothian question.

105 *The Scotsman*, 23 January 1995.

106 Source: OPCS Electoral Statistics, 1994.

107 Scottish Liberal Democrats, *The Final Steps*, April 1995.

108 Hansard Society, Commission on Electoral Campaigns, *Agenda for Change*, September 1991.

109 *Second Report from the Home Affairs Committee, Session 1986-87*, HC 97

110 House of Commons, *Official Report*, 31 January 1978, col 301.

111 As described by the Vivian Committee which recommended the establishment of permanent boundary commissions in 1942

112 This reference and much of the material in the previous paragraphs is drawn from the survey of the history of Scottish and Welsh representation contained in Iain McLean, 'Are Scotland and Wales Over-represented in the House of Commons?', *Political Quarterly*, Oct-Dec 1995.

113 David Butler, 'Modifying Electoral Arrangements', in David Butler and A M Halsey eds., *Policy and Politics*, 1978.

114 Harry Calvert, *Constitutional Law in Northern Ireland*, 1968

115 Kilbrandon Report's position as summarised in *Our Changing Democracy: Devolution to Scotland and Wales*, Cmnd 6348, November 1975 (paragraph 81).

116 *The Civil Service: Taking Forward Continuity and Change*, Cm 2748, January 1995.

117 Uwe Leonardy, 'The German Model of Federalism', conference paper delivered at University of Melbourne, 14/15 July 1994.

118 Constitution Unit, *Reform of the House of Lords*, April 1996.

119 House of Commons, *Official Report*, 26 July 1977, col 315.

120 *Scotland Act 1978*, Schedule 10, Part I, Group 5.

121 The Constitution Unit's reports on devolution to Wales and the English regions, *An Assembly for Wales* and *Regional Government in England*, both contain substantial chapters on the relationship between quangos and regional government. The issue is not therefore addressed in detail in this report.

122 Scottish Labour Party , *Partners in Scotland's Future*, 1996.

123 'Inquiry into Scottish council spending launched', *Financial Times*, 8 March 1996.

124 The Rt. Hon. Michael Forsyth MP, *Richard Stewart Memorial Lecture*, 30 November 1995.

125 Commission for Local Democracy, *Taking Charge: The Rebirth of Local Democracy*, 1995.

126 Reported in Hilary Kitchin, *A Power of General Competence for Local Authorities in Britain in the Context of European Experiments*, CLD research report No 16, November 1995.

127 Hilary Kitchin, *A Power of General Competence for Local Authorities in Britain in the Context of European Experiments*, CLD research report No 16, November 1995.

128 The Edinburgh Annex is included as an appendix to Andrew Duff ed., *Subsidiarity Within the European Community*, Federal Trust Report, 1993, on which this section draws.

129 Counsel to the Speaker, in giving legal advice on the justiciability of subsidiarity to the House of Commons Select Committee on European Legislation, concluded that "actually mounting a challenge on a subsidiarity issue may involve considerable difficulty": Ninth Report, Session 1992-93, HC 79-ix.

130 Reflection Group's Report, Brussels 5 December 1995, SN 520/95 (REFLEX 21), page 22.

131  Alain Delcamp, *Monitoring the implementation of the European Charter of Local Self-Government in the Member States which have ratified it: The experience of Western European countries'*, April 1996

132  Alain Delcamp, *Monitoring the implementation of the European Charter of Local Self-Government in the Member States which have ratified it: The experience of Western European countries'*, April 1996.

133  A W Bradley and D J Christie, *The Scotland Act 1978*, 1979.

134  Royal Commission on the Constitution 1969 - 1973, *Report*, Cmnd 5460, October 1973 (paragraph 372).

135  Lindsay Paterson, *The Autonomy of Modern Scotland*, 1994.

136  Lindsay Paterson, *The Autonomy of Modern Scotland*, 1994.

137  Royal Commission on the Constitution 1969 - 1973, *Report*, Cmnd 5460, October 1973.

138  *Our Changing Democracy: Devolution to Scotland and Wales*, Cmnd 6348, November 1975.

139  Alan Harding, Richard Evans, Michael Parkinson and Peter Garside, *Regionalisation, Regional Economic Competitiveness and the Case for Regional Government in the United Kingdom*, June 1996.

140  Gerald Elliot, 'Separation: for richer or for poorer?', in *Scotland and the* Union, Hume Papers on Public Policy Vol 2 No 2, summer 1994.

141  'European Regional Policy and Enlargement Eastwards', conference paper delivered by Charlie Woods, Chief Executive, Scotland Europa at John Wheatley Centre conference 'Making the new Europe Work', East Kilbride, 29 February 1996.

142  See chapter 5, 'Financial Provisions', for a fuller discussion of the regional transfers associated with equalisation.

143  Andrew Bain, 'Constitutional Change and the Scottish financial sector', in *Scotland and the Union*, Hume Papers on Public Policy Vol 2 No 2, summer 1994.

144  Bernard Crick and David Millar, *To Make the Parliament of Scotland a Model for Democracy*, 1995.

145  These are taken from the *Scotland Act 1978*, section 83(1) and (2).

146  Rt Hon Michael Forsyth MP, *Richard Stewart Memorial Lecture*, 30 November 1995.

147  See A W Bradley and D J Christie, *The Scotland Act 1978*, 1979, commentary on Section 34.

148  For a fuller discussion of the role of the Queen see chapter 7 paragraphs 378 to 385.

149  For an excellent historical analysis of this tendency see David Simpson, *Romanticism, Nationalism and the Revolt Against Theory*, 1993.

150  James Cornford, 'Constitutional Reform in the UK', in Stephen Tindale ed., *The State and the Nations*, 1996.

151  The terms have been helpfully introduced into the Scottish debate by James Mitchell of Strathclyde University.

152  Stein Rokkan and Derek Urwin, 'Introduction: Centres and Peripheries in Western Europe', in Rokkan and Urwin eds., *The Politics of Territorial Identity: Studies in European Regionalism*.